THE
MEDIEVAL IDEA
OF
MARRIAGE

Christopher N. L. Brooke

CLARENDON PRESS · OXFORD

Oxford University Press, Walton Street, Oxford OX2 6DP

Oxford New York

*Athens Auckland Bangkok Bombay
Calcutta Cape Town Dar es Salaam Delhi
Florence Hong Kong Istanbul Karachi
Kuala Lumpur Madras Madrid Melbourne
Mexico City Nairobi Paris Singapore
Taipei Tokyo Toronto*

*and associated companies in
Berlin Ibadan*

Oxford is a trade mark of Oxford University Press

*Published in the United States
by Oxford University Press Inc., New York*

*First published 1989
First issued as an Oxford University Press paperback 1991
Reissued as a Clarendon Paperback 1994*

*British Library Cataloguing in Publication Data
Data available*

*Library of Congress Cataloging in Publication Data
Brooke, Christopher Nugent Lawrence.
The medieval idea of marriage/Christopher N. L. Brooke
p. cm.
Reprinted. Originally published: 1989.
ISBN 0–19–820504–X*

3 5 7 9 10 8 6 4

*Printed in Malta
on acid-free paper by
Interprint Ltd.*

CONTENTS

Contents

Contents

For Rosalind

PREFACE

I first had the notion of writing a history of medieval marriage in 1962, and I now offer the public some footprints of a great idea. The first conception rapidly grew into an ambitious scheme—perhaps to be realized in my old age; but as I contemplated it I gradually became aware that a historical theme which used to be remarkably neglected had become the centre of fashion; since 1962 the history of marriage has been a major growth area in historical studies, and medieval marriage has had its share. So numerous and profound are the books and articles and research projects which have flourished since 1962 that my ambitious idea has grown very modest again.

A general history of medieval marriage would still be immensely ambitious, for the literature is vast, and the disciplines to be traversed numerous and intensely diverse. I have neither the learning nor the inclination to gather an encyclopaedia of the subject. But it seems to me that there is something still to say. Marriage has been studied by social historians, theologians, legal historians, students of literature in many languages, and experts on art and architecture. But they have not always fully understood each other's tongues. My aim is ecumenical: to draw together experts in these various disciplines, to try to bring them into a single room, to see their contributions discussed in a common language. I have made the period 1100–1500 the centre of my discourse—though there is indeed much more on the twelfth and early thirteenth centuries than on the rest; I have looked back to the Bible and the fathers; I have looked forward to Shakespeare. But my chief aim has been to show through a series of vignettes and case-studies the means by which a historian may explore the kaleidoscope of sources: I study approaches rather than look for large general statements.

For above all it is insight that I seek. It is a theme which touches many regions of human experience; it plays delicate chords; to understand we must be very receptive listeners. Yet what can be more rewarding than to gain insight into human experience in this field—in which the most intimate, rich, and rare, and yet most common—of human emotions, of love and hate, domestic comfort and discomfort, adventure and routine are mingled? This is a reflective book, to open windows, to view perspectives and horizons.

Two questions recur throughout it like themes in an opera. What is marriage—what sets it apart from other human relations? Is it the product of chance, of social forces merely; or does it in some forms and under some aspects answer to a really profound, unique demand in the depths of human nature for a special kind of relation between a man and a woman? And again, is Christian marriage something different in its nature from other relationships? One of my favourite examples is the brilliant and terrifying epic *Willehalm* by Wolfram von Eschenbach, written perhaps in the late 1210s: its central character is a convert heathen, Arabel-Giburc. She has been married twice, once in heathendom, once in Christianity, and a central question in the poem is precisely this: what difference does it make?[1]

The history of Christian marriage is most curiously compounded of human experience, social custom, theological speculation, the sturdy common sense and the

[1] See pp. 202–10.

uncommon chicanery of lawyers—and much else.[2] A clear and lucid basis was not to be found in the Bible. The vision of domestic felicity in Ecclesiasticus and the great sayings of Jesus and the author of Ephesians are indeed among the most inspiring elements in the story. Yet it is noticeable that the image of Christ and the Church in Ephesians[3] does not make husband and wife partners as we understand the term—they are not equals; and the point of the marriage at Cana lies in the wine rather than the marriage, as was emphasized in innumerable medieval portrayals of the scene from the wooden doors of Santa Sabina at Rome to the enchanting fresco in the Kariye Çamie at Istanbul. It is no doubt the case that the inwardness and depth of Christian marriage—the very possibility of which Paul fought so strenuously, and ambiguously, to defend in 1 Corinthians[4]—owes much to the Jewish marriage customs of the day. Yet the Old Testament was largely written about or for polygamous people, and the churchmen of the Middle Ages who taught that king-making should be modelled on the story of David and Solomon had frequently to remind their hearers also of the story of David and Bathsheba. The author of the narrative in the Second Book of Samuel condemned David so roundly for his part in this affair that it cannot escape notice that Bathsheba had been the cause of her first husband's destruction before she became a legitimate queen. Nor did this escape Thomas Hardy when he gave her name to the heroine of *Far from the Madding Crowd*.

Let us for a moment consider the case of Rembrandt.[5] Studying Rembrandt the man is like studying Shakespeare: few can contemplate his works without receiving the

---

[2] What follows resumes Brooke 1978, pp. 9–12.
[3] See p. 51.   [4] See p. 48–9.
[5] What follows is based on Rembrandt's *Bathsheba* in the Louvre: see esp. Gerson, 1968, p. 499 (no. 272); Clark 1966, figs. 75–6 and pp. 82–4; and references in Brooke 1978, p. 35, for which I was much indebted to David Freedberg.

impression of a deep and powerful mind of extraordinary range and penetration; yet those who try to delineate his personality have found only what they want to find. The legal documents, sadly describing the activities of Rembrandt's creditors and mistresses, none the less may hint at a strange mixture of easygoing kindness, ruthlessness, shrewdness, obstinacy, integrity, self-will, and sheer incompetence. After the death of his legitimate wife Saskia he came increasingly to depend on her marriage settlement to keep himself and his household from starving. The settlement would have been forfeit if he had made a second marriage; and this was one reason—or so it is generally supposed—why he never married his housekeeper, the faithful Hendrickje. She bore him children, and was several times summoned before the elders of the local church and condemned for the immorality of her life. Rembrandt's most famous painting of her, as Bathsheba, owed some of its elements to seventeenth-century engravings of Roman reliefs and the like, based ultimately on Greek models.[6] It owes much to all manner of other themes in Rembrandt's study and inspiration. Most obviously, its interpreter needs to know that essential textbook of the history of art (as an eminent art historian has called it), the Bible. But when all is said and done it is a deeply moving tribute to his concubine and a comment on her situation (Pl. 1).

'And it came to pass, in an eveningtide, that David . . . walked upon the roof of the king's house: and from the roof he saw a woman washing herself; and the woman was very beautiful to look upon. And David sent and enquired after the woman. And one said, "Is not this Bathsheba, the daughter of Eliam, the wife of Uriah the Hittite?" And David sent messengers'[7]—and so Rembrandt has portrayed her, with a letter in her hand,

[6] Clark 1966, pp. 82–4.
[7] 2 Samuel (2 Kgs) 11: 2–4 (AV).

and an expression in which pleasure, melancholy, and thoughtfulness are nicely mingled; but the irony of the picture is deepened by the knowledge which we have, and Bathsheba did not, that for all the suffering which will follow and for all the punishment David will receive for it, she will be queen of Israel and mother of the greatest of its kings.

In a brief discussion we have encountered the Old Testament and the New, law, theology, and the history of art—and a striking piece of social history. These are a few of the elements in the book. An example from a later century seems to me to grasp most poignantly some of the questions which swirl and eddy in this book.

For the rest, let the book speak for itself. It is modest in claim, but ambitious in scope; and I have been particularly indebted to those who have helped me to explore some of its distant regions—Nicholas Brooke, Diana Greenway, David Luscombe, Carolyn Moule May, Richard Smith, Marianne Wynn in particular—and many other colleagues and friends who have helped and guided me over the years. I make particular mention of Charles Brink, David Freedberg, David Howlett, Erik Kooper, Virginia Murphy, Richard Sharpe, and Rodney Thomson. I have had invaluable help in typing from Edna Pilmer, Ann Kemp, and Lorna Hofton. I am grateful to Andrew McLennan of Longman for readily agreeing to the arrangement whereby chapter 20 of my 2nd edition of *Europe in the Central Middle Ages* (1987) should appear here in a more extended version as Chapters 5 and 6. For permission to quote copyright material we are indebted to Professor Domenico Maffei, Dr Carolyn Moule May, Dr Virginia Murphy, Dr W. Shiels, and the Ecclesiastical History Society, the Syndics of the Cambridge University Press, Sidgwick and Jackson Ltd., Penguin Books Ltd.; and for the illustrations, the Trustees of the National Gallery, the Louvre, the Metropolitan Museum, New York, the Uffizi, Florence, the

National Monuments Record. Many chapters have served their apprenticeship as lectures, and I am grateful to many colloquia and societies for the help and stimulus their invitations provided. I owe a particular debt of gratitude to the Delegates and staff of the Oxford University Press, and especially Robert Faber, Sophie MacCallum, Gill Metcalfe, Benita Stoney, Leofranc Holford-Strevens and Christine Hauch.

St Bernard of Clairvaux once asked what the Apostles had taught us—not the art of tent-making surely, he said—they taught us how to *live*. If there is any truth in this book, Christian marriage is a very large slice of human life and human experience, and if I have lived any part of it, I owe it to one who promised to share this experience with me in 1951; and if there is any value in the book I offer it to her, as a small return, in 1988.

1988   C.N.L.B.

The opportunity of the reprint as a Clarendon Paperback has been taken to incorporate a small number of corrections and additions: see especially p. 312.

1993   C.N.L.B.

ILLUSTRATIONS

1

APPROACHES

A Catena of Disciplines

In 1957 I ended a lecture on *The Dullness of the Past* with a
quotation from Jacob Burckhardt.

> An artist must be a master or nothing. . . . In learning,
> on the other hand, a man can only be a master in one
> particular field, namely as a specialist, and in some field
> he *should* be a specialist. But if he is not to forfeit his
> capacity for taking general views or even his respect for
> general views, he should be an amateur at as many
> points as possible. . . . Otherwise he will remain
> ignorant in any field outside his own speciality and
> perhaps, as a man, a barbarian.[1]

I have always felt a difficulty in Burckhardt's use of the
word amateur; for what the historian needs is precisely a
professional approach to the other disciplines along his
frontiers. There is still plenty of room for old-fashioned
history—biographies, narratives, economic and social
history, what-have-you. All of these flourish and open
new vistas year by year. But if we wish to keep history
alive, to refresh it with the nourishment which can only
come from a wider view of human knowledge, to enrich it
with a knowledge which can only come from a deeper
understanding of human nature, the historian must
struggle with other disciplines—strive to understand and

---

[1] Reprinted in Brooke 1971, p. 38, from Burckhardt's *Reflections*, introd.,
quoted by A. Dru, *The Letters of Jacob Burckhardt* (London, 1955), p. 20.

practise them. Yet how can this be? Must he not be an incurable amateur, a dabbler, in such activities? There is indeed a graver danger. In human enquiry advance depends on two quite different principles. The first is that knowledge is useless unless it is interesting, coherent, intellectually challenging; it is this which opens the mind, the imagination, lifts the horizon. The second is that a scholar's prime responsibility, his or her only true function, is the pursuit of truth. The two are often not in perfect harmony. Many a time I have heard the pursuit of mere facts decried—I have heard it denounced as antiquarian research rather than true history. This is a false perspective. Every scholar must engage in fact-grubbing or he can have no conception what scholarship is. The most ethereal argument pursued in this book is the defence of the authenticity of Heloise—not only of her letters but of her personality; and one crucial limb of the argument derives (oddly enough) from a purely antiquarian attempt to collect the canons of St Paul's in her lifetime.[2] But the argument in reverse is equally telling. Some reviewers have sought to assess the value of the researches of Georges Duby or Emmanuel le Roy Ladurie by counting the errors in their footnotes.[3] This is a useful task, but it has little bearing on their value to historical science: for they and the whole school of *Annalistes* have lifted social history, as an intellectual discipline, on to a higher plane of intellectual and imaginative enquiry. It is very important for us to realize that they have issued some imaginative literature in the

---

[2] See p. 84–7; Brooke, 1951. My study of the prebendal catalogue of St Paul's has been related to a lifelong attempt to catalogue the clergy of twelfth-century England, inspired by my father—with many historical interests in mind, as the event has shown; but in itself a search for facts of a purely 'antiquarian' character.

[3] e.g. *Times Literary Supplement*, 7 Sept. 1962, p. 676. Boyle 1981, on Ladurie's *Montaillou*, is of quite a different character, for it strikes at the basic methods used: see pp. 157–8. For Duby, see esp. pp. 119–20.

process. But we must also acknowledge ourselves dwarfs on their shoulders when we do so.

There are no rights in these arguments, only some wrongs. Just as the greatest advances in applied science have been made possible, time and again, by theoretical speculations regarded as entirely abstract or wild even by the theorists, so history must be a theoretical as well as a scholarly subject; and it behoves the scholar to remember in humility that he cannot do without either.

A proper respect for both fact-grubbing and theory, for the antiquarian and the speculative approach, should not nowadays be too difficult—though historians are now so much divided into specialisms themselves that we still often hear old-fashioned denunciations uttered by scholars who believe them to be the latest discovery. But it is a much more difficult matter to approach other disciplines with a professional eye. The demographers have established, by subtle statistical methods, the mean ages of marriage of different segments of society between the sixteenth and the twentieth centuries in many different parts of the world. They have naturally been indignant with lovers of Shakespeare or Jane Austen, who say 'But Juliet was thirteen or Lydia Bennet sixteen; so much for your statistics.'[4] Mean ages are intensely interesting, and have been used to throw floods of light on population growth, for example, in the eighteenth and nineteenth centuries. But if we wish to understand their inner meaning—the reasons why women married earlier in some societies and some walks of life than in others; what marriage meant to them—we have to investigate a very wide range of topics with insight, precision, and subtlety; and one of these is the motives which lead women to marry. Of this Jane Austen was outstandingly

[4] See p. 174 and Laslett 1976, 1983, chap. 4. For the techniques involved and the results achieved, esp. for the eighteenth and nineteenth centuries, see Wrigley and Schofield 1981.

3

the most subtle and penetrating observer of her generation whose works have survived. But her works are imaginative literature, not treatises or sermons; they have to be interpreted as literature—with all the analytic and interpretative skills of the critic.

Here is Jane Bennet asking her sister about her love for Mr Darcy.

' "Will you tell me how long you have loved him?"

"It has been coming on so gradually, that I hardly know when it began. But I believe I must date it from my first seeing his beautiful grounds at Pemberley." '[5]

Many readers have been shocked by this jest; others have thought it was not a jest at all. But the imaginative reader who recalls Elizabeth's first visit to Pemberley observes that there is sufficient grain of truth in it to make clear that, in characteristic fashion, Jane Austen is laughing at Elizabeth, at herself, and at her readers, and that a careful reading of *Pride and Prejudice* unfolds an astonishingly wide variety of reasons for entering marriage. It may be that the analysis is loaded by Miss Austen's point of view; but that is not to the point. It is certain that she tells us nothing of the economic and social pressures on factory girls. But she tells us a great deal of the range of motives which affected choice and opportunity in her day. The historian can feed ages into a computer; he cannot feed motives. They remain incurably qualitative; and to refuse to listen to Jane Austen would be wilful deafness.

The core of this book is an enquiry into marriage—into some aspects of what can be known about marriage—in the mid and late Middle Ages. There are very few statistics available for most of it, so that demography as properly understood plays a small role. For that reason I shall be supposed indifferent to them, and to all

---

[5] *Pride and Prejudice*, chap. 59.

quantitative study. This is not so; it is simply that where numbers cannot be counted, I am averse to inventing them.[6] For demography properly conducted I have the deepest respect; and I shall presently expound some of what late medieval demographers have taught us. But first, a rather wider view is needed.

I gave a lecture in 1962 addressed to some of the general problems of a church historian, and I used the history of marriage as a specific example.[7]

State the case that a historian has it in mind to write a history of Christian marriage. He would find that he had many predecessors in the field, and that much important work had been done on many aspects of it; yet he would also find that he had started a project of profound interest and relevance, and of almost insurmountable difficulty. The interest and the relevance need no underlining. In no age has the ideal of Christian marriage been so widely studied, or—within countries once Christian—so widely attacked. The Churches have asserted their views with much firmness, diversity, and heat; and sometimes with charity too. There can be no doubt, to my mind, that charity is what is needed above all—charity towards one another's differences, and towards the non-Christian point of view. Nor can the study of the history of Christian marriage fail to arouse in the theologian or the lawyer a sense of humility, a realization of the Church's failings and inadequacies. We need not take this too seriously: the Churches are young. Two thousand years may seem a long time in relation to recorded human history, but as a slice of the world's history, and of human experience, it is extremely short. None the less it is

---

[6] A false obscurantism can easily be read into phrases of this kind: that is not my intention, as I hope is clear from what follows.
[7] Reprinted in Brooke 1971, pp. 48–9, from Brooke 1964, pp. 10–12.

sufficiently long for us to learn many lessons from it, and not least the difficulty, the prevarication, the constant ambiguity of the Church's attitude to marriage. And if this teaches our theologians that the problems are not so easy as some of them think, it will have done good.

Study of the history of marriage is exceedingly difficult. It can never be divorced from current prejudice; it cannot, it should not, be written without love or hate; it is no task for the Laodicean. Yet it is a task of extreme delicacy. The sacrament is performed by the parties themselves; in what it consists has never been clearly defined—and a theologian who tries to do so is guilty of interfering in matters which are not his concern. 'Those whom God hath joined together let no man put asunder'[8] is a proposition to which most Christians would say heartily, Amen; but no Church has ever claimed to know, when man had witnessed a ceremony of marriage, whether in every case God had joined the couple. This may seem at first sight mere casuistry, but a little reading in the case-law of the medieval Church (to take no other example) quickly shows that it is not. More important, no Christian has ever been able to evade St Paul's elaborate insistence that the union of husband and wife was the symbol of the union of Christ and his Church; an inspiration and a terror to those for whom the doctrine of Christian marriage lies near the centre of their faith. But that is not all that St Paul said on the subject. In the same passage in Ephesians he gave the husband Christ's role in the union, which has been taken by male commentators to imply male superiority; and in 1 Corinthians 7 he

---

[8] I have quoted the form in the 1662 Book of Common Prayer, which derives from the Gospel passages most commonly read at nuptial mass in the Middle Ages, Matt. 19: 6 and Mark 10: 9, reading 'Who' for 'Quod' (for nuptial masses, see Molin and Mutembe 1974, pp. 213–14). On Ephesians (below) see p. 50 n. 20.

shows a more ambiguous attitude to marriage, twisting and turning between a lofty view and one not so lofty in an attempt (if I have understood recent commentators aright) to save the institution in a chaos of conflicting opinions in the Corinthian Church.

Since those words were written, the subject has blossomed exceedingly. I gave that lecture on the history of Christian marriage in 1962. When I spoke the subject was novel and I had the feeling of being a pioneer. I returned to the field in the mid 1970s; and when I gave some lectures on it at Sewanee in Tennessee in 1977, there were at least two other symposia in the States that spring with the history of marriage at their core. There are institutes and periodicals dedicated to marriage and family history; it is now one of the central themes of the Cambridge Group for the History of Population and Social Structure —and students the world over who study the subject as a feature of social history and demography associate it with Laslett, Wrigley, Schofield, and Richard Smith—now translated to Oxford.

Why has it become so popular? Partly this is sheer fashion; but three elements of a more rational kind help to explain it.

It owes something to the search for relevance in history. The rapid and sensational changes in Western marriage customs in our own age, which carry with them an immense amount of satisfaction and suffering, happiness and sorrow, like every domestic upheaval, have turned us to look at its past. And this is undoubtedly salutary. It helps us to see our own world in perspective. Thus it is generally held that in spite of our rocketing divorce rate, marriage in the mid twentieth century was in one sense a more stable institution than in early modern times, or in the Middle Ages. Divorce as we use the term was forbidden by the law of the Church in the Middle Ages and in most Western countries until the nineteenth century. But I was already able to write in 1962 that 'we should be wrong to assume from the strictness of the law that marriage was a more stable institution in that age than in ours'—a doctrine which has been popularized in a more concrete form by Lawrence Stone's well-known calculation of the expectation of life of married couples in England, entering their first marriages, for which he set the median duration for the eighteenth century never far above 20 for the peasant, a little higher, and rising in the late eighteenth century to 30, for the squire.[9] Even though these figures are based on a narrow range of evidence, it is most unlikely that they will be seriously increased by further research. Allowing the frequency of remarriage, the true expectation must have been set far below this— though how effectively this was realized at the time is another question. But these figures underline how many and profound are the changes of recent generations. Expectation of life has grown, and with it (even more sensationally) the common pattern of divorce and re-marriage; the reduction of child mortality and effective contraception have entirely altered the pattern of family size, family planning, and family relations;[10] partnership has taken a new meaning and Women's Lib has altered the work of the family. While faced with the spectacle of broken marriages, we have come (by a strange paradox which however goes very deep into the roots of our subject) to expect far more from a happy marriage.

The second reason is the fashion for social history. An ever increasing number of historians have come to see social history as the centre of their subject and its health the condition of advance in our science. One has only to

[9] Brooke 1971, p. 52; Stone 1977, pp. 55, 694.

[10] One of the most important findings of Wrigley and Schofield 1981 and other studies, however, is that age of marriage is as important a control on size of family as contraception—a truth which has slowly dawned on those who study population in the contemporary Third World.

read the great Cambridge histories, and especially the old *Cambridge Medieval History*, under whose shadow I was brought up, to see that history was still fundamentally political and constitutional history in the 1900s and the 1920s. Then in the 30s and 40s came the planning and execution of the *Cambridge Economic History*; and I well recall that when I was an undergraduate at Cambridge in the late 1940s two of the most exciting experiences were the lectures in economic history given by the late Sir Michael Postan, and on intellectual history—on political thought—by Michael Oakeshott, happily still very much alive. These subjects are now tried veterans, if I may so describe them. But social history is the newcomer which in the eyes anyway of a very large number of the practitioners of history has overtaken them in the van of historical advance. It is not of course new, but the advent of social sciences of every kind has given it a new look; and even more for some of us, it has come to play the role of master-link between the various elements in what is now a very diverse discipline. We have long been aware of the fascinating parallel studies of marriage by anthropologists—all the more relevant to our theme since much of them concerns societies untouched by Christian influence and showing by likeness or contrast the more starkly some of the peculiar features of marriage which we too readily take for granted.[11] In recent years an eminent anthropologist, Professor Jack Goody, has brought these studies into the historical arena in his

[11] Historians today sometimes speak as if anthropology was a discipline scarcely known to earlier generations of historians; but my father's shelves—like those of every cultivated intellectual of his age—were furnished with Frazer's *Golden Bough*, and H. M. Chadwick's *Heroic Age* (1912) and other works were deeply imbued with anthropology—an influence strongly felt still in my own early years. The truth is that serious collaboration was hampered both by the inadequacy of the tools (which is strongly emphasized in Goody 1983: see below) and by the reluctance of many leading anthropologists in the 1940s and 1950s to set any store by history. This barrier has been swept away long since. [Michael Oakeshott died in 1990.]

fundamental book *The Development of the Family and Marriage in Europe.*[12]

If the question be asked, where do all the various different approaches to history meet?—a common contemporary answer might be, in cultural and social history. My own work has lain primarily in the Middle Ages, and for a medievalist there is an intimate alliance between cultural and social history and the history of the Church, which makes it natural for an ecclesiastical historian to be studying and expounding this sort of subject. This will become clear as we proceed. But a Church historian is not some special kind of animal. We study history as objectively and fair-mindedly as we can; but we do not live in watertight compartments. Whatever my field, I cannot shuffle off my personal beliefs and attitudes simply by walking into my study or the library or the lecture room.[13] I can and do talk a common language with historians of every shade of religious opinion, including, needless to say, agnostics and atheists; just as I can make my theme intelligible to theologians who have little knowledge of history. But if I pretend to my fellow historians that I have no convictions in a region of human experience so vital to our lives as marriage, I should be instantly convicted of cynicism or mendacity; and if I spoke to theologians without expounding my interest in history, I should be absurd. However, in the present setting this is not the first consideration: whatever one's viewpoint the theme demands charity and under-

---

[12] Goody 1983. For a discussion of Goody's distinguished contribution to our theme, see pp. 134–5.

[13] See below, chap. 11. The basic point is put with characteristic subtlety in a passage by Owen Chadwick, quoted in Best 1985, p. 8: 'There is (or was) a view that though the historian is a man he ought not to be'—and this he not only refutes but replaces by the doctrine that 'The man who knows that his personality enters historical study and yet seeks to keep it in control and to broaden his vision will make more contribution to our understanding than the man who believes total detachment possible.'

standing—and this includes historical depth—before dogma.

Demography and Statistics

My intention is to illustrate an immensely rich and exciting field of study; I cannot be comprehensive; I must be ruthlessly selective. Of one field of study especially fruitful today I shall say little, and that is demography. I am a great admirer of modern demography and of the Cambridge Population Group; and I wish there to be no misunderstanding on this point. I shall talk little about statistics and family reconstitution—not for any lack of interest or appreciation; quite the reverse. What is omitted from this book is left aside either because the evidence available to me will not encompass it in the present state of knowledge, or because other scholars have written about it more fully and lucidly than I can. There is an abundant literature on the relation between the inheritance of estates and kingdoms and the history of family and marriage in the Middle Ages, for example. But I shall not say much about it for two reasons: because I have little to add to what others have said, and because too much involvement with inheritance may obscure instead of clarifying marriage, for it is a highly technical subject.[14] I do not talk at length about family structure and about children, for that is the theme for another book— but they will be present in our minds throughout and occasionally peep onto the stage. I say little about statistics because relevant figures scarcely exist in the central Middle Ages.

[14] Deeply studied by many scholars today: Duby 1977 and Holt 1982–5 are admirable examples. For marriage as part of the social structure, see esp. Toubert 1973, i. 736–87. For what follows, see esp. Herlihy 1985, which was not available to me when this chapter was written.

1. Approaches

Modern demographic study depends heavily on biographical data: on the reconstitution from parish registers and the like of innumerable life histories. For many years controversy raged as to why the British population rose in the late eighteenth and early nineteenth centuries, and doctrines were propounded as dogmatic and various as those of the reformers and counter-reformers of the sixteenth century. The brilliant work of the Cambridge Group has now revealed a crucial factor which apparently explains it more than anything else: a lowering in the age of marriage of women, which meant that they started to bear children at an earlier, more fertile age and that the generations turned round faster—to put the matter crudely, so that more grandparents survived the birth of their grandchildren.[15] All this depends on knowing the date of birth of a very large number of folk. Before the sixteenth century we rarely know the date of birth of any but kings and saints and great nobles. In the fifteenth century the nobility sometimes recorded their children's births with great precision in their Calendars: to this we owe our certainty that Margaret of Anjou was 15 when she married King Henry VI of England, and our virtual certainty that Margaret Beaufort was 12 when she married Edmund Tudor.[16] Before the fifteenth century even this information is rare outside royal families; and the only statistics I have been able to gather have related to the frequency of marriage in twelfth-century England—and they relate only to the nobility, who have left some record of their marriages and have been systematically studied. A sample from the more reliable volumes of the *Complete Peerage* produced 63 cases in which husband and wife are only known to have married once; and 55 in which one or

[15] Wrigley and Schofield 1981.
[16] For Margaret Beaufort, see below, n. 67. Margaret of Anjou was born on 23 or 24 Mar. 1430 (not 1429 as commonly stated: see Brooke and Ortenberg 1988) and married Henry on 23 Apr. 1445.

other or both married at least twice. 'In these 55 cases 18 husbands had two wives each, and one three; 31 wives had two husbands, 4 wives had three husbands and one four.'[17] Even in this case the information is not comprehensive and the number of second and third marriages may be much underrated; and it relates only to the nobility. For what it is worth, it strongly suggests that the characteristic occupations of men, especially jousting and war, were more dangerous than child-bearing, which is rather surprising.

Can this barrier ever be broken? Can we hope to find new sources or reinterpret old which will enable us to know about the marriage practices of a wider social group? One's instinct is to say no: it is hard to see how much more light than this can come. But until quite recently we might have said the same of the sixteenth century; and before the recent work of Richard Smith and others on court rolls and taxation records—and before the fundamental work of several American scholars on the Florentine taxation records of the fifteenth century—a like scepticism would have prevailed.[18] Consider an analogy from the history of cities: it was widely and reasonably assumed that the history of early medieval towns could hardly be known; but in the wake of the Winchester project of the 1960s and 1970s, and many like it, a whole dimension has been added to historical knowledge—full of surprises—due to the archaeologist's trowel.[19] Vast quantities of bones have now been lifted from medieval cemeteries and are being scientifically studied; heaven knows what secrets they will reveal—it would be as naïve to predict an Aladdin's cave of discoveries as it would to look for none.

---

[17] Brooke 1971, p. 52 n. 14; cf. Brooke 1987, p. 128.
[18] See below.
[19] See summary in Biddle 1983, and *Winchester Studies*, ed. M. Biddle, in progress.

1. Approaches

Recent enquiries into marriage patterns start from a famous paper by John Hajnal published in 1965, 'European marriage patterns in perspective', in which he showed by statistical methods a common pattern in western Europe in the eighteenth and nineteenth centuries, in which men and women alike marry relatively late (on average 26–7 or more for men; 23–4 or more for women), and a substantial proportion never marry at all. There has been a flurry of effort to discover when this divergence from what is normal in non-European countries, and even in recent centuries in Mediterranean lands, began. The investigation has so far raised more problems than solutions; but that is not yet a ground for despair. For example, Richard Smith has shown how hazardous have been efforts to deduce marriage patterns from the fourteenth-century English poll-tax returns.[20] I own to a built-in prejudice against tax returns: there are few regions of human activity in which stronger motives for evading the precise truth persistently operate; and in falsifying statistics a little lying goes a long way—for modest evasion by a minority may overthrow all the efforts of a conscientious majority, if such ever existed. None the less, the poll-tax returns, like other tax records, offer a mass of detail which the historian is loth to discard as useless; and Smith himself has suggested that more hopeful results may emerge if they can be systematically compared with other evidence.[21] The other evidence so far most studied by social and economic historians has been the court rolls of medieval English manors, and these have been used for family reconstitution in a fashion not entirely different from that of the later parish registers. But not quite the same either: family reconstitution depends on reliable identification, and that

[20] Smith 1979; cf. Razi 1980.
[21] Smith 1979, esp. p. 101. There is now a considerable literature on these problems and possibilities: see Smith 1983; Razi 1980.

14

is hazardous in medieval village records. Thirty years ago I spent many months among the peasants of the villages round Peterborough; and anyone who has had this sort of experience knows how bewildering is the kaleidoscope of common Christian names and variable, not to say chameleon-like, surnames in thirteenth- and fourteenth-century villages.[22] But Smith and the Cambridge Group have performed miracles elsewhere; and his positive results from court rolls are already impressive. More will emerge; but what will happen to the European marriage pattern it is much too early to say.

Meanwhile a remarkable harvest has been garnered by David Herlihy and Christiane Klapisch-Zuber in the vast Tuscan land survey of 1427, and equally fascinating results have been fashioned by the craftsmanship of Julius Kirshner and Anthony Molho out of the Florentine dowry insurance.[23] The *catasto* illustrates every aspect of social and economic life; the dowry insurance, the *Monte delle Doti*, is more restricted, but is an astonishing illustration of the possibilities of such evidence.

In 1425 the city fathers of Florence, scraping about for ways of raising money to finance a war with Milan, devised a brilliant scheme for a dowry insurance. A father could deposit 100 florins against a daughter's marriage, and if it matured after seven and a half years he would get 250 florins, if after fifteen 500; if she died he lost his principal. The plan was well received by the councillors, but failed to attract the fathers of young daughters, and appeared to be stillborn. In due course it was to be savagely attacked by the great ascetic preacher, the Franciscan San Bernardino of Siena, on the ground that

---

[22] Brooke and Postan 1960, esp. pp. xiii–xviii, lxi–lxiii. For studies based on court rolls see the well-known series of books and papers by J. A. Raftis and his pupils, e.g. Raftis 1964; also Razi 1980.

[23] The results of a long series of studies are gathered in Herlihy and Klapisch-Zuber 1978; cf. Smith 1981; for the dowry insurance see Kirshner 1978, Kirshner and Molho 1978.

it was infected with usury, contrary to the Church's teaching.[24] I doubt, however, whether that had much to do with its initial failure, and another eminent friar arose to defend it against the charge and as an instrument of charity and social health. After a few years the city fathers improved the terms and it began to catch on; and suddenly, in 1433, a further improvement was followed by a flood of deposits. The shrewd and anxious fathers who wanted to do the right thing by their daughters reckoned it was now a good investment; fashion evidently took a hold and swept the doubters away, though there were still many good fathers of families who steered clear of it altogether. But the tide came in; and this is very fortunate for us, for it made a unique source of information available to modern research. Some of the new conditions were also advantageous to us, for instance that which allowed the deposit itself to be returned to a father whose daughter died. A later addition of 1437 allowed a daughter who entered a convent to take with her the initial deposit, so that the convent received a modest part of the dowry—as a convent would expect to do, even though it had long been illegal to extract it.[25] These modifications most usefully add to the information we receive. Though we cannot be absolutely sure of the date of marriage of the girls (we only know precisely when the dowry was paid), Kirshner and Molho have calculated all sorts of fascinating figures about life expectancy of young girls, and age of marriage, and so forth. Out of 1,762 cases in which the details can be calculated, 344 girls, or 19.52 per cent of the total, died before they could earn a dowry: the average age at death was nine years ten months. Only 47, or 2.67 per cent, became nuns. The average age of payment in the cases studied was

---

[24] Kirshner 1978, pp. 31–5; Kirshner and Molho 1978, pp. 405–6; for what follows, ibid. pp. 407–9.

[25] Kirshner and Molho 1978, p. 409; for what follows, ibid., pp. 413–14.

eighteen and a quarter which suggests an average age of marriage a little under eighteen.

In modern Europe, as Hajnal showed, there has been a very large percentage of spinsters, much more than in fifteenth-century Florence; and in the modern world (though precise figures are surprisingly difficult to obtain) there have been in the Roman Catholic Church roughly three times the number of women religious to men.[26] We never have figures anything like this for the Middle Ages (anyway in the present state of knowledge) but all the indicators are that the number of male religious many times exceeded that of female between the twelfth and the fifteenth centuries—save that in Germany and the Low Countries there was a sharp rise in the number of female religious in the thirteenth century.[27] The reasons for this are at present very obscure, since we know so little of the detailed structure of the societies from which the nuns came; and it is surprising in itself since there was no respectable alternative for an upper-class or bourgeois girl to marriage or a convent. But even by the normal standards the figures in Florence seem remarkably low, and they are well below what had been assumed by Florentine historians before these details were worked out.

Thus the figures show at once that Hajnal's European pattern does not fit fifteenth-century Florence. They show that quite dramatically by the relatively low age of marriage of the girls; they tell us nothing about age of marriage for men. But as with all such statistics, the interpretation in terms of social structure, family background, ethos, and personal circumstances is full of obscurities. Let me take an example. The investing father

[26] Hajnal 1965. For modern statistics of religious, see Moorhouse 1972, pp. 275–7, who gives figures for the 1960s (1962–7): those for 1967 gave approximately 333,000 for men, 1,073,000 for women. But he notes (p. 277) that the figures 'should be treated with some caution'.

[27] See p. 69.

could choose for himself the size of deposit he thought suitable, and it turns out that fathers of girls who in the event became nuns tended to make higher deposits than those whose daughters married. It has been suggested—and there is some evidence to support it—that this was because the girl was ugly or deformed or otherwise unattractive and would require more inducement to a husband, and because it was this kind of girl who went into a nunnery.[28] But there is another explanation which seems to me equally good, and probably a factor in some of the cases, and that is that the parents had already decided to make the girl a nun and deposited more so as to have a reasonable sum to offer the convent. Earlier historians suggested that entry to a convent had often been decided when the girls were tiny; Kirshner and Molho show that the average age of entry was, by contrast, seventeen.[29] But the statistical evidence throws little light on when decisions were made, and in many cases the destiny may have been largely determined much earlier. Another curious feature of the evidence is that when the girls married they nearly always succeeded in consummating their marriages. This appears because the dowry could not mature until after consummation. The figures show only one failure in 1,370 cases,[30] a figure I view with profound scepticism; I am not sure the young couples always told the truth. Statistics are a wonderful source, but as C. R. Cheney said of records, 'like the little children of long ago, [they] only speak when they are spoken to, and they will not talk to strangers'; and, as Max Beerbohm said of Beatrice and Sidney Webb's statistics, they have been 'most exquisitely cooked'[31]—not by the

---

[28] Kirshner and Molho 1978, pp. 424–5; cf. Origo 1963*a*, p. 64.
[29] Kirshner and Molho 1978, pp. 414, 427.   [30] Ibid. 413–14.
[31] Cheney 1973, p. 8; Behrman 1960, p. 23. There is a view sometimes held that the historian is not interested in individuals, only in thoughts and attitudes and activities of large numbers of folk. Such a view long ago prompted me to the

modern scholars in the case, but by the folk who created them in the fifteenth century.

The dowry insurance has provided us with a splendid source, one full of endless fascination for the historian; I reiterate my admiration for all the recent statistical work that has been done in this field. But what I have just said underlines some vital points very well recognized by its best practitioners. Statistics are hard won and the world of historical literature is full of spurious figures. The famous controversy on the rise in population in eighteenth- and nineteenth-century England well illustrates this.[32] Even now, when we have the beginning of a much clearer understanding of the facts in this case, interpretation is extremely difficult and obscure—and much of the older interpretation, based on wrong facts, or trying to interpret wrong facts, is of little use. A curious lesson for the scholar is that the more precise statistics are the more difficult they often are effectively to interpret, since in the web of historical evidence they are like a piece of new cloth added to an old garment. The little conundrum I propounded about the nuns' dowries shows up in clear perspective how vital it is to know as much as we can about the relation of the statistics to social structure, to the general attitudes, aspirations, ambitions, and vocations of Florentine fathers and daughters. It shows us what we do not know—it is not a substitute for other kinds of evidence but a stimulus to search them out. So the recent growth of statistical evidence does not put the range of other evidence into the shade, but urges us the more to use it.

thought that the only story in the Gospels of interest to such historians is the feeding of the five thousand.

[32] See p. 12 and n. 15.

1. Approaches

My Approach

My own study has mainly been in periods and areas for which virtually no useful statistics exist. I am fascinated by the great variety of approaches, by the search for evidence, by the opportunities to see the human situation within a family and within a marriage which is the ground root from which the more general picture grows. I do not see the individual case and the statistic as in opposition—if they suggest different conclusions that is a stimulus to the historian to work and to think harder: both provide evidence. Only by exploiting a very wide range of evidence can the historian begin to ask—let alone to answer—the kind of questions the statistical evidence stimulates. And let us not be put off by the difficulty of the subject: I have often come back from some frustrating difficulty in the study of medieval marriage to realize how great is the depth and breadth of our ignorance of modern marriage. Few contributions to the history of marriage have been so stimulating and valuable, and yet so deeply flawed, as Lawrence Stone's massive study of the early modern period. Thus he tried to trace 'the growth of affective individualism'—freedom of choice and marriage for love—as something new in the seventeenth and eighteenth centuries; but the dialectic between the arranged marriage and free consent is active in almost every chapter of this present book. Stone's study also contains some extraordinary chapters on the sexual experiences of married men in the seventeenth and eighteenth centuries.[33] I was amazed when I first read the book to find numerous rather sordid details copied out of Pepys's and Boswell's diaries on the apparent assumption that everything they said on the subject must be literally

[33] Stone 1977, chap. 6 and pp. 552–61, 572–99. For another extreme case of credulity, see p. 158.

20

true. But surely there is nothing on which human beings, both men and women, are so commonly and normally mendacious as on their sexual experiences, and in this field the multiplication of examples is often quite simply a multiplication of lies. I do not at all mean that human beings are incapable of telling the truth about their sexual experiences: I only mean that there is possibly no region of human life about which many men and women more readily create, or live in, a world of fantasy. Many, perhaps most, naturally truthful folk are inclined to be reticent. There is an inner core of human experience which remains deeply mysterious to us. There is however a streak of credulity in all of us, and it should be the mark of the true historian that he is sufficiently but not excessively sceptical in handling all his evidence—whether he wishes to believe it or not.

Most of the book explores a series of approaches, through law, theology, literature, and art—each illuminated by examples, vignettes, and case histories. They are not entirely distinct, indeed they constantly overlap; and yet they demand a great variety of approach and discipline if they are to be effectively handled. Even so, they leave vast gaps: our ignorance is always greater than our knowledge.

Yet the evidence is rich, and there are many compensations for its oddity. Thus the central fact about the legal history of marriage in the Middle Ages is that it went out of the secular courts of emperors and kings into the church courts of archdeacons, bishops, and popes: it went to church, so to speak—it became a part of the religious life of Christendom; and this is a massive fact, which it must be a central part of our purpose to grasp.[34] Yet it always had a secular, earthly, earthy element too; it was always in apparent conflict with the celibate

---

[34] See chap. 6.

ideal, immensely powerful and prestigious between the eleventh and the sixteenth centuries—with a long history before and after.[35] The best recorded marriage of the central Middle Ages, that of Heloise and Abelard, was hardly a marriage at all—a cleric and canon, who ought to have been celibate, went through a form of marriage with his mistress which was rapidly dissolved, first because of his castration by some of her uncle's circle, then by both of them entering religious orders. Yet this couple meditated so deeply on the nature of their bond and its meaning— on its relation to human affection and to the love of God— that they told us things no ordinary married folk would have grasped with a like clarity, or could have expounded to us if they had.[36] The experience was eccentric, but the teaching on love and marriage became a central feature of the experience of Christendom. Their letters are works of art, and have sometimes been supposed works of imaginative fiction from a later age than theirs. This I do not believe; but there are remarkable analogies with some of the approaches to marriage in the deeper vernacular literature of the Middle Ages—and with this we must grapple, for it tells us much about attitudes and aspirations we can find nowhere else recorded.[37] But literature has its pitfalls too: fiction can most evidently deceive and there has been much propaganda against it by the searchers after facts. I think this quite misplaced: like all the evidence in this fascinating and treacherous field, it needs delicate handling; and when we are served statistics deliciously cooked we are wise to scatter over them the herbs and spices of imaginative literature very finely ground and sieved.

[35] See chap. 3.
[36] See chaps. 4–5.
[37] See chaps. 7–9—and on art and architecture, chap. 10.

St Catherine of Siena and her Confessor

The approaches in this book are diverse, but they are far from comprehensive. To illustrate this truth I conclude my prologue with four exceptional examples of approaches hardly touched elsewhere. Most families practise a certain reticence: the public revelations of family life are hardly a random sample, and they are exceedingly rare in medieval sources. But wives and mothers, sons and daughters, were much readier to talk to their confessors, and the *Life of St Catherine of Siena* is a rare biography based on the confessional, written by a man who had heard the most private revelations of Catherine and her mother. It is also rare for a sermon by a great preacher to be recorded in vernacular dress in the form in which it was delivered; this lends a special piquancy to the Sermons of San Bernardino of Siena. Rarest of all are the private letters between husband and wife, and the correspondence of the early fifteenth-century Merchant of Prato comprises a uniquely revealing source. Different in character, but poignant and illuminating too, are the entries in the personal calendar of a celebrated queen mother, the Lady Margaret Beaufort, mother of Henry VII of England, and the light they throw on a strange personal experience.

Catherine or Caterina of Siena lived for a little over thirty years in the mid and late fourteenth century, and Raymond of Capua's *Life* of St Caterina provides a relatively brief, but fascinating insight into the childhood and family of the saint.[38] Caterina as a person was utterly exceptional, but she came from a well-to-do citizen family which we may suppose entirely conventional in its outlook—well-to-do, that is, until her prayer for their

[38] Raymond of Capua in *Acta Sanctorum Bollandiana*, April, iii. 853–959 (Eng. trans. G. Lamb, London, 1960). What follows is based on (and partly repeats) Brooke 1982: see references ibid., p. 877 n.

poverty was answered. She dreamed of dedicating herself to the ascetic and celibate life when she was about seven, and when she was a little older prayed that her family might become poor so that worldly involvement should not hinder their path to heaven.[39] So they became poorer and poorer, and she ever richer in heavenly treasure— and thus the strange story of her childhood and family came to be recorded. The fascination of Caterina's story lies in the formation of so unusual a person in such relatively normal surroundings, as we may suppose them to be. It is especially to our purpose to observe the nature of the source. Raymond was a celibate friar; at first sight he might seem to know little of marriage from within. He had access, however, to information normally denied to the historian, and commonly denied to the modern social scientist, through the confessional. Much of Raymond's information came, doubtless in ordinary conversation, from Caterina, from her mother and her friends; but his role as confessor to Caterina herself has evidently coloured his whole approach: he had an exceptional intimacy with the saint's inmost thoughts and memories. His *Life* has been subjected to criticism; and I take it to be widely agreed that this has sometimes been excessive.[40] True, he dwells almost too much on his sources; he seems to us sometimes credulous, sometimes to see events from a different angle from ours. But his honest purpose, and his access both to Caterina herself, and to her mother's reminiscences of her daughter's childhood, give his account, brief though it is, an unusual interest.

The social setting we may take to be normal: the fairly prosperous household, supported by a father who was a dyer, kindly, pious, liberal to his children, and the mother dedicated to child-bearing and to bringing them up to

[39] Raymond of Capua, c. 81, p. 873.
[40] Cf. the many studies in Maffei and Nardi 1982: Fawtier was inclined to be excessively critical of Raymond, valuable as his volumes are.

conventional paths. Lapa wished to breast-feed her own children, but her frequent pregnancies made this rarely possible, and they were evidently well enough off to hire wet-nurses.[41] Evidently too only a proportion of her twenty-five children grew up. Caterina was a twin, and fed by her own mother—not surprisingly it was she and not her twin who survived.[42] These details give us some insight into the social customs of fourteenth-century Siena. More remarkable are the hints of Caterina's own formation. Her mother tried to rear her to domestic arts, which evidently interested her little if at all; and when she approached the age of puberty her mother prepared her for early marriage, striving by every persuasion to instil the idea that early marriage must be her lot.[43] She had an elder sister, Bonaventura, who was married, and who tried to inspire Caterina with her love of clothes and a mild personal vanity; but a harsh fate overtook Bonaventura and she died in childbirth. Next the family tried to enlist the help of a friend who was a Dominican friar, but Caterina convinced him of her vocation, and on his advice, and to her mother's horror, she cut off her beautiful hair and wore a cap over her head. They virtually locked her up and told her she would have to take a husband in the end. We are reminded of the harsh assumption in one of San Bernardino's sermons that when a girl passed into her teens she would be locked up till married; we are also reminded of the evidence that early, universal marriage was the normal destiny of Tuscan girls in the late Middle Ages.[44] When Caterina first met the Dominican Sisters of Penitence—the order which she later joined—they had a strict rule that only

---

[41] Brooke 1982, p. 883, n. 24; cf. Klapisch 1973, esp. pp. 110–11.

[42] For details of the family, see Raymond of Capua, c. 26, p. 860; Brooke 1982, pp. 883–4 and nn. 25–6.

[43] Brooke 1982, p. 884; Raymond of Capua, cc. 41–5, pp. 863–4.

[44] Bargellini 1936, pp. 465, 666; cf. Origo 1963*a*, pp. 65–6; Klapisch 1973; above, p. 17.

widows might be received, and a special concession had to be wrung from them for the saint. Meanwhile it is made clear that she was not brought up to read and write; she learned those skills for herself later.

It is very evident, however, that at an exceptionally early age she had received an impression of the religious life which deeply stirred her imagination, all the more for her being unaware, at any earthly level, of how the impressions had come to her. Thus she had assured Brother Raymond that without the aid of teachers or books she had acquired knowlege and appreciation of the lives of the saints of Egypt and other saints, and in particular of St Dominic.[45] She told her biographer-confessor this story in the context of the enchanting tale of how she set out one day, at the advanced age of six or seven, if we may judge from the context in the *Life*, to become a hermit.[46] Many of us have enjoyed a fantasy world in childhood, and it seems to answer to something deep in human nature—even if it rarely conforms to our adult vocation to anything like the degree of Caterina's. Yet human nature in some measure changes with the centuries; and it is one of the most delicate tasks of historical criticism to determine in what measure we may use our own experience to interpret the minds and development of folk of earlier centuries. Convincing evidence of childhood memories and fantasies is extremely rare from the Middle Ages. I treasure the story in the *De rebus a se gestis* of Giraldus Cambrensis of the late twelfth century: his father was a Norman-Welsh baron whose sons were in the habit of making castles in the sand; but when he observed the young Gerald making churches and monasteries, he called him 'my bishop'.[47] I too have built in the sand, but castles

---

[45] Raymond of Capua, c. 31, p. 861 (cf. c. 33).

[46] Raymond of Capua, cc. 33–4, p. 861. Her age can only be gauged approximately.

[47] Giraldus, *Opera*, i. 21. Such a choice between ecclesiastical and secular

and railway systems, not the materials of ecclesiastical history. One day Caterina set out with a loaf of bread in the direction of her married sister's house—but she went on, through the city gate out into the open country; when there were no more houses to be seen, she judged she was in the desert and found a convenient cave; but after a while she decided it was time to go home—and home, with what she believed to be divine help, she went; and her parents assumed she had spent the day with her sister. A charming tale, reflecting both the eternal nature of imaginative childhood, and the unique qualities of Caterina—for she came soon to reckon (from the age of seven, if Raymond has it right) that she was called to a life of celibacy.[48] Small wonder that the modern reader is astonished to the verge of incredulity by this precocious evidence of single-minded dedication; small wonder too that her mother came to think it was all childish nonsense, and must be knocked out of her by discipline and by every kind of family influence she could command. No doubt the penitent Lapa in her old age lost no opportunity to denounce her own conduct; but the story is none the less piquant for that.

The Sermons of San Bernardino

A valuable indication of the teaching on marriage which was transmitted to the laity may be culled from the English diocesan statutes of the thirteenth century; even more revealing sources are the sermons addressed to married folk by a succession of distinguished preachers in the thirteenth and fourteenth centuries, which have been

symbols is, however, a topos of eleventh- and twelfth-century hagiography: see Ridyard 1988, p. 265.

[48] Raymond of Capua, cc. 33–6, pp. 861–2; for the vow of chastity (aged seven), cc. 35–6, p. 862.

analysed in a very helpful and fruitful article by D. L. D'Avray and M. Tausche.[49] Among the most celebrated and powerful sermons addressed to married women and men are those of San Bernardino of Siena (1380–1444); and these have a special fascination, since many of them were recorded in their original vernacular form.[50] They proceed at three levels. He elucidates the teaching of the Church on marriage, with flashes of personal insight, but essentially in accord with the tradition of marriage sermons of the previous century. Then he scatters his discourse with anecdotes and *exempla* such as medieval preachers used, but in his best stories there is a freshness and vividness which brings to life the society of his time. Finally, there are the famous interjections, when he turns suddenly on his audience and brings us face to face with the ladies of Siena of the early fifteenth century.[51] When he elaborated the theme of 'natural affection' in marriage, he explained how it grew out of the creation of woman from the rib of man—and then he suddenly broke out:

> Oh you ladies, how shameful it is of you, when in the morning, while I am saying mass, you make such a rumpus, that I think I am listening to a pile of bones, you rattle so much! One cries: 'Giovanna!' Another 'Caterina!' Another, 'Francesca!' Oh, what fine devotion you have in hearing mass. To me it just seems a confusion without any devotion or reverence. Do you not recall that here we are celebrating the glorious body of Christ son of God, for your salvation?[52]

---

[49] *Councils*, ii. 2. 1411, 1429, Index s.v. children, marriage; D'Avray and Tausche 1980.

[50] What follows is based on, and partly reproduces, Brooke 1982, pp. 886–9; it also owes much to Origo 1963*a*, ch. 2, esp. pp. 53 ff. See also references in Brooke 1982, p. 886 n. 38—esp. to *Bernardino* 1945, 1976; and other papers in Maffei and Nardi 1982. The sermons used below are in Bargellini 1936, ii. 391–462. On these sermons and their character see esp. Delcorno 1976, pp. 71–107. The translations are my own.

[51] See Origo 1963*a*, chap. 2.   [52] Bargellini 1936, ii. 411.

And he calls them to recollection: by such alternations of mood, by leaping from 'natural affection', and the act of creation itself, to the thoughtless chatter of the housewives, he brings out the solemn message he wishes to implant. Very characteristic is his appeal to temperance between husband and wife, both in punishment and in the marriage-bed. 'And you, husband—do not beat your wife when she is pregnant; that is a great peril, I insist. I don't say—never beat her; but choose your time . . .'. Then comes a sudden twist in his irony. 'One of our doctors said: "*mulier aut mendanda aut ferenda*—a woman should be cured or tolerated". If you have cured her, you have won her, good or bad. If she is good and you give her support, you have won her too. But *I* say—either admonish her or support her: never beat her: set to with good and gentle words . . .'.[53] He passes to the nuptial chamber.

> There was in the city of Verona, a little while ago, an excellent young man, wise and upright, and God-fearing to be sure; and he took a wife, and was not filled with unbridled desire—nor was she the daughter of a mother who put her on the market.[54] When the day came to take her to his house, in the morning he took communion, and had her take communion too, and he led her to his house, held a feast and the marriage celebration. In the evening they entered their chamber, and the husband said to his wife: 'My wife, it has pleased God that you should be my wife and that I should be your husband; and I wish that in honour and reverence to God we stay a while in prayer, and that we pray God that he give us grace to live devoutly in this holy matrimony, that we act to his praise and glory, and at the end may save our souls. And also let us pray that

---

[53] Bargellini 1936, ii. 406; cf. Origo 1963*a*, p. 56.
[54] 'che fusse ruffiana della figliuola'.

if it comes to pass that he gives us grace to have children, they may always prove obedient to his commandments.' And his wife replied: 'I am happy to do all you wish, to the honour and glory of the Lord God.' And so they remained in prayer a part of the night, and in this fashion passed three days and three nights before they consummated their marriage. And when the time came when they wished to consummate it—they had previously slept clothed—they went to bed and with great sighs and devotion and fear of God they consummated it . . .[55]

By this little tale, perhaps from Verona, and certainly from the book of Tobit, he illustrated the merits of a married life regulated, free from excessive excitement, violence, luxury, anger, and so forth; a life of temperance and seriousness.

Characteristic of Bernardino is the mingling of authority and experience, with vivid and sometimes bizarre illustration. St Augustine had deprecated the use of wet-nurses, and Bernardino supports advice to mothers to feed their babies themselves by an analogy with vines.[56] The humour of the wines of Siena is 'clear and subtle'—as too those of Ferrara and San Gimignano. But if you transplant their vines to Siena, the grapes decline in quality since they are growing on the wrong soil. In driving home the true nature of wifely obedience he draws a striking analogy. 'Every time my superior orders me to commit even one venial sin, I am not bound to obey him . . . since I am bound to obey him in doing good not evil: if he commands me to sin and I will not obey, it is he who sins not I . . .'. By the same token if a husband desires his wife with a disordered appetite, she should teach him

---

[55] Bargellini 1936, ii. 439–40. Cf. Tobit 8:4 (Vulgate) and below, p. 43.
[56] Bargellini 1936, ii. 451–2; cf. Origo 1963a, pp. 60–1; Brooke 1982, p. 883 n. 24 and refs., 888–9.

better. 'Oh how noble a thing is a wife chaste and honest in holy matrimony, and how she ought to be cherished!'[57] He can use heavy irony too, in urging husbands to seek wives who are compatible. He attacks families who choose mates without any serious consideration of such matters, and frivolous young men who expect their wives to be virtuous without thinking of being so themselves. He asks them: 'What sort of a wife do you want?—I want her virtuous—and you are not virtuous. You want her peaceable—and you shout your head off when you are thwarted.—I want her obedient—and you obey neither father nor mother, nor anyone: you have not earned such a wife.' And so: 'There are many who desire to have a wife and cannot find her: would you like to know why? It is because they say: I want a wife discreet and wise—and you are a fool. That's not right: a fool should go with a fool [*pazzo con pazza*]!'[58] As we hear the heavy irony, we hear an echo of Bernardino's master, St Francis: 'The Lord said to me that he wished me to be a *new* kind of fool in the world', *unus novellus pazzus.*[59]

The modern reader is struck by the contrast between the conventional nature of the teaching, uttered by a man of learning who was also a stern ascetic, and the penetrating vision of the human predicament which sprang from a temperament naturally kindly and understanding— and above all, from an extensive knowledge derived from the confessional. It is this which puts him in piquant apposition to Brother Raymond, recording the experiences of St Catherine and her mother—and equally to the intimate revelations of married life which we can occasionally glimpse in fifteenth-century correspondence, a very different kind of source.[60]

---

[57] Bargellini 1936, ii. 437–8; Brooke 1982, p. 888. 'Chaste' in the sense of being faithful to her husband.

[58] Bargellini 1936, ii. 408, 407; cf. Brooke 1982, p. 889.

[59] Brooke (R.B.) 1970, p. 288 no. 114.

[60] See below.

1. Approaches

The Letters of the Merchant of Prato

Francesco di Marco Datini was born in Prato near Florence in or about 1335, and died in 1410.[61] He was not born to poverty, but his parents died of the plague when he was young, and he was brought up by a guardian of somewhat straitened means. At the mature age of fifteen, he set off for Avignon to make his fortune in the crowded and stuffy capital of the Western Church—where the popes spent much of the fourteenth century. After over thirty years there, by varied enterprises and partnerships, he had made a large pile of money; and in 1383 he returned to Prato a very wealthy man, with a young Florentine wife Margherita whom he had recently married in Avignon. His story is of remarkable interest—first because it is uniquely well recorded, and second because the record of his correspondence reveals a strained human relationship, the human predicament marvellously preserved. He was a man of conventional piety; and as they had no children it was natural for the greater part of his fortune to be left for religious and charitable purposes. But his closest friend and attorney, Ser Lapo Mazzei—a much more engaging character than either Francesco or Margherita—was both deeply pious and fervently anti-clerical, a common mixture in ages of faith. He was horrified at the suggestion that the clergy be asked to administer the great foundation Francesco planned at the end of his life; and so he established an entirely secular trust. Centuries later, in the days of the French Revolution and the Italian Risorgimento, every religious institution in Italy was secularized at least for a time—and the Fondazione Datini, and its archives, survived as Ser Lapo had foreseen because it was secular, though not quite for

[61] This section is based on and reproduces parts of Brooke 1971, chap. 12 (a lecture given in 1960: see ibid. p. 10); it is deeply indebted to Origo 1963b.

the reasons he had supposed. Thus we have a mighty collection of Francesco's ledgers, and the fascinating letter collection on which our knowledge of the human story—and Iris Origo's biography—are based.[62]

The correspondence of the Merchant of Prato is invaluable to the historian of trade and capitalism; but it is equally valuable as an insight into the attitudes and assumptions of a man of thoroughly conventional outlook—conventional in his love of money, in his religious beliefs, and in his anti-clericalism, bred by the much more original mind of his attorney, Ser Lapo Mazzei. Under the attorney's influence he excluded the Church from the administration of his estate, though he left the bulk of his fortune to support the poor and other charitable purposes; but he summoned five Franciscan friars to his deathbed.[63] In his early years he made a pile of money, and intended to marry, rear a family to enjoy his wealth, then gradually withdraw from business and do his share of good works before he died. None of these plans turned out quite as he intended. The marriage was childless, and not all the best and the worst medical advice of the period could help the couple to legitimate offspring. Francesco had children, though not many; after a while one of them was brought up as his own, with his wife's grudging consent. His wife Margherita's failure to have children set up a barrier between them, and is clearly one of the reasons why he stayed away from home for such long periods. And it is to his absences that we owe the correspondence. Both partners were strong-willed and efficient, and Francesco was a great man of business. Neither was particularly well educated: Margherita learned to write only after their marriage; nor had they any special literary talents. But there emerges from the correspondence a pair of very striking characters, and the vision of a marriage

[62] Origo 1963*b*.
[63] Origo 1963*b*, pp. 326–8, 342 ff., 379–80.

which was by no means happy, and yet far from a total failure. His letters to her are domineering, fussy, suspicious, and full of urgent repetition; in return she gave as good as she got in swift repartee, down-to-earth comment, explanation, and complaint. She was quick-tempered without malice; he full of care, suspicious of everyone, determined to rule his household in every detail, though he rarely visited it.

For all that they had no children and lived apart, there seems to have been a respect which matured into deep affection between them; an underlying strength in the marriage which survived every superficial failure. At one crisis the attorney had written to him: 'Let not the many, many letters you write, to increase your bodily welfare and your riches in this world, make you lose your charity and love for the person to whom you are bound by God's laws. . . . For your rough soul and your frozen heart need to be comforted.'[64] And in the end, in their last years, they lived together; such evidence as we have suggests that their tempers and their affection had mellowed; but as they were together, the letters ceased, and the window was shut again. For the same reason, we can rarely inspect the intimate correspondence of a married couple.

The Calendar of Lady Margaret Beaufort

My final character is a great lady whose name is especially familiar in Cambridge, Lady Margaret Beaufort, mother of King Henry VII, foundress of Christ's and St John's Colleges.[65]

---

[64] Origo 1963b, p. 177; Brooke 1971, p. 236.

[65] This is based on, and partly reproduces, Brooke 1983. I am much indebted to Malcolm Underwood, who has a full biography of the Lady Margaret in train in collaboration with Michael Jones (see p. 312); see meanwhile esp. Underwood 1982, 1987. There is a general account in *DNB*, and much material in Cooper 1874, Mayor 1876, and *CP* x. 826–7.

Among the Royal collection of MSS in the British Library (2. A. xviii) there is a charming book of hours which was evidently for many years the possession of Margaret Beaufort. The book would not be of much distinction as a work of art but for the fact that someone, very likely that strong-minded lady herself, has added to it a handsome group of miniatures from a psalter belonging to the greatest of her enemies, the house of York. Yet it is not the miniatures but the Calendar that gives the book its deepest historical interest. Into it in her later life Lady Margaret bade her chaplains enter the principal events of her family: the landing of Henry VII in 1485, his victory at Bosworth, his coronation, his marriage to Elizabeth of York, the birth of nearly all their children—with special care the very hour of the birth of Princess Margaret, the dowager's namesake and evidently her favourite grandchild, the future queen of Scotland. In 1501 one of the chaplains noted the day when 'my lady princess' (he means Catherine of Aragon) set sail from Spain to become wife of Prince Arthur—the day of their marriage and later, sadly, of Arthur's death. In 1503 Henry VII's wife Queen Elizabeth died, and on 5 July the widowed king, his daughter the queen of Scotland, and a great throng of courtiers, waited on the Lady Margaret at her favourite palace at Colly Weston in Northamptonshire—and so the tale goes on until her death. But for me the interest of all these entries is overshadowed by one that was written by an earlier hand in the Calendar under 31 May. The book had originally been made for her mother, Margaret Beauchamp, duchess of Somerset, and under that day appears a note: 'The birthday of the lady Margaret daughter of the illustrious prince John duke of Somerset, in the year of the Lord 1443'.[66] It is the only

---

[66] BL Royal MS 2. A. xviii, fo. 30. The calendar is on fos. 28–33^v: the other quotations are on fos. 32, 29, 31. On the MS see especially Rickert 1962. The calendar deserves close study and a full edition. Some entries were evidently

precise evidence of the date of her birth; it was entered, evidently, by one of her mother's chaplains and we may believe it to be true; and if so it establishes that she was only seven when she contracted her first marriage—the earliest legal age, though not binding upon her under canon law since she could not be legally tied to any union before she had reached the mature age of twelve. This marriage was dissolved when she was about nine and, in an oft repeated tale told by St John Fisher in his panegyric delivered on her month's mind—at a memorial service a month after death—she was prompted by a dream to accept her second husband Edmund Tudor in 1455; when she was twelve—and this is the most piquant fact established by the date of her birth—she married Edmund Tudor.[67] He died the next year, leaving her pregnant, and in January 1457 her only child was born, the future King Henry VII. She married twice more, but had no further children, and late in life summed up her experience of marriage by taking a vow of celibacy while her last husband still lived. It is clear that Margaret Beaufort accepted that the destiny of an heiress to broad estates, in whose veins the blood of kings flowed, was to be a pawn in the appalling dynastic politics of mid fifteenth-century England. Against all the odds she lived to see her only son a king, and her Calendar is full of his anxieties and triumphs. Among the greatest treasures of Westminster Abbey are the splendid effigies of Henry VII and his

written long after the event. Thus that for Henry VIII's birth (fo. 30ᵛ, 28 June) refers to him as 'postea' prince of Wales, but not as king (i.e. 1504–9). But the entries for Margaret's and Henry VII's births seem contemporary, and are not in hands which occur elsewhere—nor do they use anachronistic titles. The entries in the Royal MS were printed by F. Madden in *Collectanea Topographica et Genealogica*, i (1834), 277–80, who noted that many were copied in a Sarum missal of 1495 in the Douce collection. Exeter College, Oxford, MS 47 has a similar calendar belonging to Margaret's daughter-in-law, Queen Elizabeth of York (cf. Coxe 1852, i, Coll. Exon., pp. 17–18; Warner and Gilson 1921, i. 32–3).

[67] Fisher in Mayor 1876, pp. 292–3; *CP*, x. 826. She married him in 1455, presumably after her twelfth birthday; he died on 3 Nov. 1456.

queen and nearby of his mother, so close to him in age (Pl. 2).[68] We may believe that she was a trial to her daughter-in-law—her surviving letters to her son are full of affection and fuss, and she was evidently a very masterful old lady towards the end.[69] I do not attempt to idealize her, or to attribute to her a great originality of mind. We owe a large part of her munificence to Cambridge to the deep influence of her confessor, John Fisher.[70] Fisher evidently touched chords in her mind already tuned. She was already under the spell of Carthusian devotions which were to lead her to set her name to the translation of Thomas à Kempis's *Imitation of Christ*;[71] and we may be sure that the fearful anxieties of her own childhood and youth, the political necessity (which she evidently fully accepted) that made her a mother at thirteen, were part of the inspiration for her work for later generations of young men—and now at last, in the late twentieth century, of young women too—which has issued in her being the most devoutly remembered of all the greatest benefactors of Cambridge.

The Calendar says nothing about Cambridge. It represents her domestic and her political life—a vision of mutability and constant danger. These concerns and interests and distractions make all the more impressive her efforts to provide a more stable life for young students born in less dangerous eminence or wealth than hers— havens of peace secure from the hazards of fifteenth-century politics. This is the vision which seems to me so clear in Lady Margaret, and it is significant, and remarkable, that as age crept on her, and she was wracked by rheumatic and arthritic pains—not eased by hearing four or five masses on her knees and kneeling for each of

---

[68] Brooke, Highfield, and Swaan 1988, pl. 97.
[69] Cooper 1874, pp. 64, 66–7.
[70] See studies in Bradshaw and Duffy, 1989.
[71] Lovatt 1968, p. 99.

sixty-three Ave Marias a day[72]—and by the ceaseless anxieties of her domestic world, the vision grew on her, and after allying with Fisher to transform God's House into the full College of Christ's, at the very end of her life she gave him warm support also in transforming the ancient hospital of St John into St John's College.

But the Lady Margaret's family has led us out of the dwellings of medieval married folk and past 1500. We must start again.

[72] Mayor 1876, pp. 294–5.

THE INHERITANCE,
CHRISTIAN AND ROMAN

The Early Medieval Inheritance

Medieval marriage was a piquant mixture of notions and customs deriving from the ancient world, from the inheritance of Judaism and the early Church, from Rome and the barbarians. So far as we can discern the fundamental rules and customs, they seem to have derived quite naturally from Roman law: marriage indeed was a secular custom, a part of the world which the Christian Church had inherited; it was part of the law of nations: no one in early days expected it to be directed by the courts of the Church. We shall presently observe the process by which marriage went into church—quite literally, by entering the liturgies and the sacraments of the Church, and figuratively, by falling under the jurisdiction of the courts of the Church. This was a strange manœuvre, very difficult to explain—but not difficult to accomplish, since there was little variance at first between the view of late Roman emperors and of the Christian bishops and popes on what made a marriage.[1]

In Roman law it had been a pact, an agreement, between families and spouses very informally entered into: there had to be consent—whether of the partners

[1] Fundamental for early medieval marriage are Spoleto 1977 and Gaudemet 1980. For a brief summary of marriage customs in the Frankish kingdoms, of exceptional depth and insight, see Wallace-Hadrill 1983, pp. 403–11. For marriage in the Bible and the early Middle Ages, Schillebeeckx 1965 is particularly helpful.

or their parents—there had to be an intent to get married rather than live in concubinage.[2] A certain social formality—especially among the well-to-do—marked off marriage from other relationships; and what the lawyers described as *'maritalis affectio'*, the intent to get married—a phrase which had a nice ambiguity which the twelfth-century popes were to seize on to some purpose.[3] In the heyday of pagan Rome it was almost as easy to leave marriage as to enter it; but the Christian emperors found this to be unacceptable and made divorce, in principle, more difficult.[4] Whether it truly was in practice we cannot tell. As time passed and the barbarian kingdoms of the West came to maturity, there are records of sensational attempts, especially in the ninth century, to prevent kings changing wives:[5] but for centuries the old Roman per-missiveness was in a rough and ready alliance with the traditions of barbarian tribes, which by no means forbade divorce. Even so late as the twelfth and thirteenth centuries the earliest surviving texts of the Welsh laws take it for granted that husband and wife can part for adultery or some lesser causes—and if a woman leaves a husband 'for leprosy, and for lack of marital relations, and foul breath' she does not even lose her dowry.[6] This is a nice mixture of canon law and very secular custom, and there is a great deal of evidence that even after the Church had brought marriage under its courts, many of the older ways survived. Yet the very long period during which the church accepted and in general approved the Roman law of marriage underlines that there was a strong element of

---

[2] See Corbett 1930 and several chapters in Gaudemet 1980; cf. *OCD* 1970, pp. 649–51.

[3] See below, pp. 128–9.

[4] Corbett 1930, pp. 218–48. Justinian forbade divorce, but the ban was eased for a time after his death: *OCD* 1970, p. 651; Dauvillier 1933, pp. 439–43.

[5] For Hincmar of Rheims and the divorce of Lothar II, see Gaudemet 1980, pp. 266–71; Wallace-Hadrill 1983, pp. 273–4, cf. p. 410.

[6] Richards 1954, pp. 69–71, cf. p. 124. See Jenkins and Owen 1980, and esp. for marriage in late medieval Wales, see Davies 1980.

common ground between traditional secular attitudes and practices—shorn of the permissiveness of pagan Rome— and the Christian morality of marriage. In the eleventh century, however, the cult of celibacy among the clergy staged a remarkable revival, and the gap between the sexual morals expected of laity and clergy widened.

The Bible

Meanwhile the clergy and the devout laity alike meditated on the message of the Bible. It has often been doubted that the medieval laity had access to the Bible; but it is plain that in a culture mainly oral well-to-do layfolk at least had ample opportunity through their chaplains or their parish clergy to hear and to learn passages relevant to their life and to their interests. How many grasped these opportunities we cannot tell—in that or any age. The Bible provided not only—as we should see it—the historical roots of Jewish and Christian doctrines of marriage, but stories and prescriptions constantly read in the Middle Ages. Since the Bible enshrines the cultural and spiritual heritage of a whole civilization it is hardly surprising that its texts on marriage both inspired and confused their readers. Right at the outset, in the creation of Eve, one of the authors of Genesis had provided a deeply moving image—that man and wife could be 'one flesh'.[7] The phrase could be interpreted metaphorically and allegorically, so that the union of marriage came to be seen as the type or image of the relation of Christ and the Church—as the author of Ephesians said, 'the husband is the head of the wife, as Christ is the head of the Church'[8]—and though he described a society dominated

[7] Gen. 2: 24.
[8] Eph. 5: 23, in the Douai-Rheims translation. Where in this book I wish to give the precise sense of the Vulgate, I have usually followed this version. Where I wish to come near the original—especially to make clear the precise nuances of

by men, he also gave the union of man and woman the highest compliment which could be imagined. Yet 'two in one flesh'—'*duo in carne una*' (Gen. 2: 24)—is puzzling too. It sits oddly in its context, and it seems to suggest that marriage is primarily a physical thing, a fleshly union; it also seems to imply monogamy, which fitted the text for its fortune in later Jewish tradition and in the Christian centuries; but the folk of the Old Testament were clearly not monogamous. In medieval interpretation the two wives of Jacob, and the seven hundred of Solomon, were interpreted as special dispensations; this was not, however, historically correct. It took many centuries for rich and powerful Jews to come to monogamy; yet on the way they devised and developed a tradition of marriage and family and domesticity of the most inspiring character—as it has remained among practising Jews. From the early prophets comes the tragic story of Hosea and his efforts to cherish an unfaithful wife—and the image of Israel as a child: 'When Israel was a child, then I loved him . . .' (Hos. 11: 1, (AV)). But the finest fruit of the Jewish vision of marriage came later—in the sublime, though remarkably erotic, marriage hymns, the Song of Solomon and Psalm 45—which were also admirably suited for medieval allegorical interpretation; and in the rhapsody on marriage in Ecclesiasticus 40: 18–23 (AV).[9]

> To labour, and to be content with that a man hath, is a sweet life: but he that findeth a treasure is above them both. Children and the building of a city continue a

Pauline thought in 1 Cor.—I have followed the New English Bible. Where I wish to keep both the Greek (or Hebrew) and the Vulgate in view, I have sometimes used the Authorized Version—the most evocative of all, and composed by men who still knew the Vulgate, but who were striving to get close to the original languages. Where there is a significant difference I note it.

[9] For a brief account of marriage in the Old Testament based, however, on a deep learning, see Heaton 1956, pp. 69–71.

man's name; but a blameless wife is counted above them both. Wine and music rejoice the heart: but the love of wisdom is above them both. The pipe and psaltery make sweet melody: but a pleasant tongue is above them both. Thine eye desireth favour and beauty: but more than both corn while it is green. A friend and companion never meet amiss: but above both is a wife with her husband.

Very popular in the Middle Ages was the charming story of Tobias and the archangel—of how the good young man wooed and won his wife, and chased away the devil with the archangel's help—and how, in the Latin version known to all the faithful in the Middle Ages, they spent three nights in prayer before consummating their marriage.[10]

The message of the New Testament was even more inspiring and confusing than that of the Old. The author of the earliest Gospel makes it clear at once that the rules have been tightened up.[11]

And the Pharisees came to him and asked him, Is it lawful for a man to put away his wife? tempting him. And he answered and said unto them, What did Moses command you? And they said, Moses suffered to write a bill of divorcement, and to put her away [thus Deuteronomy 24: 1–3]. And Jesus answered and said unto them, For the hardness of your heart he wrote you this precept. But from the beginning of the creation God made them male and female. For this cause shall a man leave his father and his mother, and cleave to his

---

[10] See below, chap. 7, n. 52.

[11] Mark 10: 2–16 (AV)—the NEB, following some of the best MSS, omits the Pharisees in v. 2. Most scholars have long thought Mark the earliest Gospel; but the passage occurs with some differences (see below) also in Matt. 19: 3–15. Luke 16: 18, 18: 15–17 includes part of it. On this passage see e.g. Beare 1964, pp. 190–3 (incorporating comments by C. R. Feilding); Schweizer 1971, pp. 200–4; Bauer 1970, pp. 551–6; Anderson 1976, pp. 242–4. (I owe help in this region to the kindness of John Sturdy.)

wife; and they twain shall be one flesh: so then they are no more twain, but one flesh.

What therefore God hath joined together, let not man put asunder . . .

And in the house his disciples asked him again of the same matter. And he saith unto them, Whosoever shall put away his wife, and marry another, committeth adultery against her. And if a woman shall put away her husband, and be married to another, she committeth adultery.

And they brought young children to him, that he should touch them: and his disciples rebuked those that brought them. But when Jesus saw it, he was much displeased, and said unto them, Suffer the little children to come unto me, and forbid them not: for of such is the kingdom of God. Verily I say unto you, Whosoever shall not receive the kingdom of God as a little child, he shall not enter therein. And he took them up in his arms, put his hands upon them, and blessed them.

Let us say at once that this is a passage that must bring the warmest echoes to any Christian husband and father—the idea that God makes the union of husband and wife, the delight that even the celibate Jesus took in greeting little children—here is the heart and hearth of Christian marriage—a text to bring endless delight.

But it is also very puzzling. First of all the ideal nature of matrimony is qualified by a saying in St Luke's Gospel.[12]

Then Peter said, Lo, we have left all, and followed thee.

And he said unto them, Verily I say unto you, There is no man that hath left house or parents, or brethren, *or*

---

[12] Luke, 18: 28–30 (AV) (in the Greek 'wife' immediately follows 'house'). Mark 10: 28–30 has a similar passage, but significantly omits 'wife'; so did Matt. 19: 27–9 apparently in the Greek, but in the Vulgate—and in the AV—she is in all three passages. Swete 1898, p. 217, reminds us that Peter himself seems to have left his wife. For omission of 'wife' cf. Nineham 1963, p. 27.

wife, or children, for the Kingdom of God's sake, who shall not receive manifold more in this present time and in the world to come life everlasting.

And Peter was a married man. But it must be owned that Matthew, in the parallel passage, omits the wife, as did Mark, apparently, in the original Greek. She is present in Luke, and in the Latin Vulgate of Mark.

Matthew interpolates, in the passage on remarriage, the famous qualification 'except it be for fornication' (19: 9)—in the Vulgate *'nisi ob fornicationem'*—and in the parallel saying in the Sermon on the Mount, Matthew 5: 32 has: 'Whosoever shall put away his wife, saving for the cause of fornication [*excepta fornicationis causa*] causeth her to commit adultery'. In the original Greek the qualification in 5: 32 could mean something quite different—simply that if the woman has already been unchaste, the man cannot be held responsible for her adultery. But in 19: 9 the exception for *porneia* seems formal and clear, and there has never ceased to be argument whether divorce and remarriage can be justified by the adultery of one of the partners. This ground for divorce was widely accepted in the early Middle Ages—though a more rigorous view was also widely held; and the lawyers and theologians of the central Middle Ages gradually came to exclude it.[13] It reappeared in the debates in the English House of Lords

---

[13] For the possible meanings of the Greek *porneia*—adultery, invalid marriage or premarital unchastity—see Green 1975, pp. 83–4; cf. Vollebregt 1965, pp. 89–90, 114; Zerwick 1960; Hoffmann 1970; Bauer 1970, p. 552. For later interpretation, see Fransen 1977 and Gaudemet 1980. Gaudemet 1980, pp. 257–66, shows with great precision the variety and perplexity of the rulings from popes, councils, and penitentials, between the fifth and the ninth centuries; ibid., pp. 266–71 shows how Hincmar and later writers struggled to interpret the word *sacramentum* in Augustine (ibid., p. 270) and found their deepest ground for indissolubility here—so that it naturally followed that as sacramental doctrine itself developed in the eleventh and twelfth centuries, the rule of indissolubility became firmer; but there was still much debate among the twelfth century canonists (ibid., pp. 279–89). For what follows—the debates of 1670 and later in the Anglican communion—see Winnett 1958, chap. 7.

in the 1660s, with the result that adultery as a ground for divorce was grudgingly accepted in English law for nearly 300 years.

'What therefore God hath joined together let not man put asunder'—this is a marvellously evocative call to the loyalty and the conscience of a husband or a wife. But it will not do in a lawcourt. Who of the witnesses to a marriage can ever say whether or not the couple have been joined by God? Certainly not the medieval Church, which permitted annulment on many grounds.[14] By the same token the argument with Moses starts in common sense and human understanding, but seems to fall into the legalism it condemns before the end. Deuteronomy allowed a husband to dismiss his wife; it did not ensure that he took any responsibility for her—yet that, Jesus seems to say, is just what he must do: if she had been chaste and after her dismissal falls into unchastity, the husband who has deserted her is to blame. This may seem to some a hard saying; but it is of quite a different order from the version in Matthew 19: 9 which seeks to extend the argument with Moses to a formal prohibition of divorce, except where one partner is unchaste—save for adultery (see n. 13). No one doubts that Jesus set a peculiarly high store on marital fidelity, and that the medieval Church correctly descried this, and acted upon it. But it also read into Matthew's phrases a legal statement which inspired it to a ceaseless debate on divorce, its meaning—and the exceptions there might be to its prohibition.

Matthew goes further: he has also interpolated a passage on celibacy, likewise much studied in the Middle Ages. After the passage we have just discussed, he goes on (19: 10–12):

---

[14] Dauvillier 1933, pts. 2 and 3. The commonest ground for annulment was consanguinity (see pp. 134–6); but failure to consummate was also accepted.

His disciples say unto him, If the case of the man be so with his wife, it is not good to marry.

But he said unto them, All men cannot receive this saying, save they to whom it is given. For there are some eunuchs, which were so born from their mother's womb: and there are some eunuchs, which were made eunuchs of men; and there be eunuchs, which have made themselves eunuchs for the kingdom of heaven's sake. He that is able to receive it, let him receive it.

Medieval ascetics did not, in the manner of Origen, suppose that this justified castration; but it was taken—like a similar hint by St Paul of the benefits of celibacy—to set a high store by the ascetic, celibate life. It is not possible for a Christian who reads these passages carefully wholly to reject marriage. Even the greatest of the ascetics, even the desert fathers or St Peter Damian himself, who reckoned marriage very much worse than a second best, could not escape Jesus' clear statement that though marriage was not for all—and not for him—it was a true and lifelong vocation for many.[15] For an ascetic writer influenced by Damian, this was a painful concession; he wished to be orthodox; he even saw marriage as a sacrament. But he could count, not two or seven but twelve sacraments, and marriage was the twelfth.[16]

Two more visions of marriage from the gospels must suffice. In John 2, very early in Jesus' ministry, we are taken to the marriage feast at Cana in Galilee; and although the miracle which provided wine for the wedding guests out of the water jars is commonly interpreted as a prefiguring of the eucharist, the Church has always taken comfort from the countenance Jesus gave to wedlock, in Abelard's words, 'by the first of your miracles'.[17]

[15] See below, p. 73.
[16] *PL* cxliv. 902, where it is attributed to Damian himself: but see Lucchesi 1983, p. ix.
[17] See p. 115.

2. The Inheritance, Christian and Roman

In Mark 12: 18–25 (a pericope also in Mathew and Luke) the Sadducees state the case to Jesus of seven brothers all of whom, in turn, following the counsel of Deuteronomy 25: 5, marry the widow of the first: 'In the resurrection . . . whose wife shall she be . . .?'. It was a debating question concerning the resurrection; and Jesus gave it a debating answer: 'When they shall rise from the dead, they neither marry, nor are given in marriage; but are as the angels which are in heaven'.[18]

There is much about the practice of marriage in the epistles, but in two passages especially Paul entered deeply into the nature of the union.

To the Corinthians (1 Cor. 7: 1–16 (NEB)):

And now for the matters you wrote about.

It is a good thing for a man to have nothing to do with women; but because there is so much immorality, let each man have his own wife and each woman her own husband. The husband must give the wife what is due to her, and the wife equally must give the husband his due. The wife cannot claim her body as her own; it is her husband's. Equally, the husband cannot claim his body as his own; it is his wife's. Do not deny yourselves to one another, except when you agree upon a temporary abstinence in order to devote yourselves to prayer; afterwards you may come together again; otherwise, for lack of self-control, you may be tempted by Satan.

All this I say by way of concession, not command. I should like you all to be as I am myself; but everyone has the gift God has granted him, one this gift and another that.

To the unmarried and to widows I say this: it is a good thing if they stay as I am myself; but if they

---

[18] See pp. 262–3.

cannot control themselves, they should marry. Better be married than burn with vain desire.

To the married I give this ruling, which is not mine but the Lord's: a wife must not separate herself from her husband; if she does, she must either remain unmarried or be reconciled to her husband; and the husband must not divorce his wife.

To the rest I say this, as my own word, not as the Lord's: if a Christian has a heathen wife, and she is willing to live with him, he must not divorce her; and a woman who has a heathen husband willing to live with her must not divorce her husband. For the heathen husband now belongs to God through his Christian wife, and the heathen wife through her Christian husband. Otherwise your children would not belong to God, whereas in fact they do. If on the other hand the heathen partner wishes for a separation, let him have it. In such cases the Christian husband or wife is under no compulsion; but God's call is a call to live in peace. Think of it: as a wife you may be your husband's salvation; as a husband you may be your wife's salvation.

Paul seems to be between two fires.[19] He is not aware of legislating for hundreds or thousands of years: he is saving a precious institution in a world in turmoil, for the brief interval till the trumpet sounds. He honours celibacy; he safeguards marriage; he hammers home that marriage is better than immorality—'Better be married than burn . . .'. It has not always seemed to ardent married Christians an entirely happy thing to be dictated to by a bachelor Apostle: but it was paradoxically a most salutary passage for a medieval celibate theologian. For Paul was a celibate too—yet he did the estate of marriage great honour. In Ephesians 5: 21–33—whether it be by Paul himself or by another hand under his inspiration makes

---

[19] For Paul's problem in a mission church, see esp. Jeremias 1954.

little odds—the relations of the secular world of the first century AD are sanctified by the apostolic blessing.[20]

In this passage the author sets side by side a contemporary view of the relation of men and women in society—'the man is the head of the woman'—with a dazzling vision of the union of marriage as a figure or symbol of the union of Christ and the Church. To the modern taste there is too much emphasis on male superiority, but it must be seen in a social context in which a different statement could have seemed wholly unreal—and it must be set beside the words of Galatians 3: 28, undoubtedly Paul's, that in Christ Jesus all are equal—'there is neither male nor female'.

> Be subject to one another out of reverence for Christ.
> Wives, be subject to your husbands as to the Lord; for the man is the head of the woman, just as Christ also is the head of the church. Christ is, indeed, the Saviour of the body; but just as the church is subject to Christ, so must women be to their husbands in everything.
> Husbands, love your wives, as Christ also loved the church and gave himself up for it, to consecrate it, cleansing it by water and word, so that he might present the church to himself all glorious, with no stain or wrinkle or anything of the sort, but holy and without blemish. In the same way men also are bound to love their wives, as they love their own bodies. In loving his wife a man loves himself. For no one ever hated his own body: on the contrary, he provides and cares for it; and that is how Christ treats the church, because it is his body, of which we are living parts. Thus it is that (in the words of Scripture) 'a man shall leave his father and mother and shall be joined to his wife, and the two shall become a single body [Gen. 2: 24]'. It is a great

[20] On the authorship of Ephesians, see esp. Mitton 1951; but there is a vast literature, defending a variety of views.

truth [*sacramentum* in the Vulgate] that is hidden here. I for my part refer it to Christ and to the church, but it applies also individually: each of you must love his wife as his very self; and the woman must see to it that she pays her husband all respect (Eph. 5: 21–33 (NEB)).

The Interpretation of the Bible

I have quoted these passages at length, for they must be ever to hand as we search the cupboards and the passages of the mansion of medieval marriage. These words, and the whole New Testament, lay in the minds of theologians, canonists, and popes—and many others too, including many devout layfolk—as they handled the marriage problems and disputes of medieval Europe. Two examples will show the force of this.

In the middle of the twelfth century the English pope Adrian IV was confronted with the problem of whether the marriage of slaves was valid. The Church had always accepted slavery and lordship as consequences of the fall—and as part of the society of the Roman Empire in which the Church was born. It had neither condemned slavery nor attempted to restrict a lord's rights over the slave's person. It had always been accepted that a slave could not marry—perhaps could not marry at all; certainly not without his lord's permission. But to Adrian and his advisers marriage was a Christian sacrament. They fully accepted the hierarchical nature of society: was not the pope himself the greatest hierarch of all? But they equally accepted, without question, Paul's great saying in Galatians 3: 28: 'There is neither Jew nor Greek, there is neither bond nor free, there is neither male nor female: for ye are all one in Christ Jesus'. 'Just as in Christ Jesus there is neither a free man nor a slave, who may be prevented from receiving the sacraments of the Church, so too ought not marriages between slaves to be in any way prevented.'[21] Thus spake Pope Adrian. Christendom gasped, and some modern historians have declared his decretal a forgery; but recent scholarship has vindicated it and even the canonists came eventually into line.

Following a respectable tradition in the fathers, the great canonist Gratian (c.1140) declared that heathen marriages were valid, and converted heathen not free to desert their heathen spouses.[22] In two very remarkable decretals Pope Innocent III (1198–1216) sent a deeply considered answer to questions on heathen marriages. In the first, addressed to an Italian bishop, he quoted 1 Corinthians 7: it is better for the Christian partner in a marriage to preserve the marriage; but if the heathen partner wishes for separation, the Christian cannot be bound—he or she is free, says the pope, to marry again. In the second, addressed to a bishop in the Holy Land, he pondered the case of a non-Christian who had married within the forbidden degrees or had several wives: according to the Apostle all could be deemed valid marriages, but in Christian law only one could stand. Yet the children of all four—conceived in heathendom—were legitimate. The decision was related to the doctrine of putative marriage: that a child born of parents reasonably supposed to be married could be reckoned legitimate even if the marriage was later annulled. In the rubric to this Decretal in the official collection of Gregory IX, Raymond of Peñaforte answered the one question not specifically handled by the pope—of the four marriages, only the first might survive.[23] In both these instances one word from Paul was definitive; and in the first, it cancelled a long tradition.

[21] Adrian IV's bull as quoted in Landau 1967—the article which vindicated the bull and Adrian's authorship of it, and set it firmly in its place in the history of canon law: see esp. p. 517 n. 16.

[22] *Decretum* C. 28 q. 2. See p. 210 n.

[23] *Decretals of Gregory IX*, iv. 19. 7–8. Cf. Noonan 1967, pp. 506–7.

Thus the New Testament offered a rich, inspiring, and confusing tradition which the medieval Church could never escape. Least of all could it ignore the holiest of marriages, that between Mary and Joseph. In Matthew 1 the medieval Church read that Jesus was conceived by a virgin betrothed to a man called Joseph. When he found that she was pregnant he wished to have the contract set quietly aside, to avoid any public exposure; but it was revealed to him in a dream that 'it is by the Holy Spirit that she has conceived this child' (1: 20)—and that he was to take her as his wife. 'He took Mary home to be his wife, but had no intercourse with her until her son was born.' It was almost universally believed from the fifth century—and by some before—that the marriage to Joseph was never consummated, that the brothers of Jesus mentioned in the New Testament were in fact cousins.[24] There was a strand in medieval thought which claimed that the marriage of Mary and Joseph was the perfect marriage. This could have an ascetic, wayward tendency: it was thought by many devout readers of Bede that it was wholly admirable that St Etheldreda, in seventh-century England, was married for twelve years to the king of Northumbria (her second husband) without losing her virginity—without consummating either marriage—though Ecgfrith thought otherwise.[25] Much later it was believed that Edward the Confessor remained childless owing to a pious agreement with his wife to avoid consummation—though others might think that it was his first duty to beget a son to succeed him, who could have saved England from the chaos which

---

[24] For a general account and bibliography, *ODCC*, pp. 882–4, esp. 882. On the doctrine of Mary's perpetual virginity, and for the view that the marriage of Mary and Joseph was perfect, see below, p. 131; Peter the Lombard, *Sententiae* iv. 30. c.2 (Peter the Lombard 1971–81, ii. 439–41). See discussion in Le Bras 1926, cols. 2144–5 (Hugh of St Victor), 2150 (Gratian), 2153 (Peter the Lombard).
[25] *Historia ecclesiastica*, iv. 19, ed. B. Colgrave and R. A. B. Mynors (OMT, 1969), pp. 390–1. Cf. Ridyard 1988, pp. 53, 85–6.

followed Edward's death in 1066.[26] This tradition was most movingly defended by the eminent twelfth-century theologian Hugh of St Victor in his popular tract *On the Virginity of the Blessed Virgin Mary*. He quotes Ephesians—with Genesis behind it—'The two shall become one flesh: this mystery is a profound one, it refers to Christ and the Church'; and with delicate logic he says that this must also mean—one soul. After marriage 'Henceforth and for ever, each shall be to the other as a same self in all sincere love, all careful solicitude, every kindness of affection, in constant compassion, unflagging consolation, and faithful devotedness. . . . Such are the good things of marriage and the happiness of those who love chaste companionship.'[27] The marriage of Mary and Joseph 'illustrates perfectly that marriage is contracted by consent and not by consummation'.[28] Hugh was adding a spiritual dimension to a perception which lay at the root of all medieval marriage law, and went back to a famous saying of the Roman jurist Ulpian: 'It is not consummation but consent which makes marriages.'[29]

Augustine

But though many medieval theologians and canonists agreed that the union of Mary and Joseph was perfect in its own kind, there was another line of argument that denied that it was in this respect a model Christian marriage. A powerful tradition stemming from Judaism

---

[26] F. Barlow, *Edward the Confessor* (London, 1970), pp. 81–5, who views the belief with a sceptical eye; and also refers to the similar tale about the childless Emperor Henry II and his wife Kunigunde (both subsequently canonized).

[27] *PL* clxxvi. 859–60, translated in Leclercq 1982, p. 26, slightly adapted. Celibacy as a normal ingredient in marriage is as alien to us as to most medieval theologians: but Hugh defended it as a *possible* ingredient most persuasively. See pp. 278–9.

[28] Leclercq 1982, p. 25.   [29] See p. 128.

put carnal union at the centre of marriage, and Paul had been very specific that husband and wife should not deny themselves to one another. When Hugh spoke of 'the good things of marriage' he was much aware that he was echoing the title of St Augustine's fundamental tract *De bono coniugali, On the Good of Marriage*; and Augustine had made the procreation of children the first good fruit of marriage.[30] In Augustine's capacious mind it was possible to hold together the notion of woman as the temptress, inferior to man—'If man perchance were weary of being alone, how much more suited for common life and good conversation would have been two male friends living together than a man and a woman'; Eve was created to have children[31]—though he strongly disapproved of St Jerome's much more extreme denunciation of female wickedness. He left a curious legacy to medieval theologians in his view that carnal union after the fall cannot avoid 'some taint of cupidity',[32] which becomes much worse as passion enters deeply into it. But he accepted the need for it, faced it squarely, and set it in the forefront of the good things of marriage—along with marital fidelity and the binding obligation or 'sacramentum' that prevented the partners dissolving their marriage. Augustine saw the difficulty in making marriage wholly indissoluble in the light of Matthew 5: 32 and 1 Corinthians 7, but came steadily to a fairly 'strict and rigorist position'[33] in his later life which deeply affected his medieval successors. He accepted in principle that it was consent not consummation which made a marriage—and the prime purpose of his book was to

[30] Written in 401: St Augustine, *De fide et symbolo etc.*, ed. J. Zycha, Corpus Scriptorum Ecclesiasticorum Latinorum, xli, Vienna, 1900. The core of Augustine's teaching in this book is summarized with subtle precision in Chadwick 1986, pp. 112–15, in the context of Augustine's wider views on sexual relations.

[31] *De Genesi ad litteram*, ix. 5 (ed. J. Zycha, Corpus *ut supra*, xxviii(1), Vienna, 1894, p. 273): cf. Chadwick 1986, pp. 89, 114.

[32] Chadwick 1986, p. 114. On this legacy, see p. 73.

[33] Chadwick 1986, p. 114.

convince the ascetic nuns to whom it was addressed that marriage was no inferior state. Yet when all was said and done his voice was heard to say that the first aim of marriage was to have children—and so, that there was something incomplete about marriage unconsummated; and the book itself is deeply concerned, not to say obsessed, with the sexual element in marriage.

The Eleventh and Twelfth Centuries

If we look forward to the eleventh and twelfth centuries when the main themes of this book are under way, we may see marriage most clearly defined under five aspects. First, there is a liturgy of marriage: although custom and practice clearly varied much, already in the regions of France and England bordering on the English Channel a complete ritual of marriage covering every stage from betrothal, exchange of promises, through the nuptial mass to the blessing of the bridal chamber, was encompassed in a single text or texts.[34] Next, the Church has full jurisdiction over marriage, or claims so, and the claim is widely accepted—and it seeks a uniform, clear, enforceable definition of what lawful and valid marriage may comprise.[35] Third, the theologians are drawing up lists of sacraments, which include marriage and seek to define the nature of the act and its symbolism—in what the sacrament consisted.[36] Beside the theologians, the poets were developing doctrines of human love in which marriage, and various attitudes to it, are set in apposition or opposition to the other kinds of human affection.[37] Most strikingly, marriage is sought by the nobility and landed folk of Europe as the key to the inheritance of their estates and kingdoms.[38] William, duke of Normandy and

[34] See chap. 11. [35] See chap. 6. [36] See pp. 273–6.
[37] See chaps. 7–8. [38] See chap. 6.

conqueror of England, was illegitimate. The succession of a bastard to any throne or any great estate in the late Middle Ages was a very rare event, and the conqueror's great-grandson, Henry II, built up a great empire out of the alliances of his ancestors, his wife, and his children.

How much of this was new? The essence of marriage law and doctrine in the twelfth century lay in the reaffirmation of positions already established in earlier times. Consent not consummation made a marriage—yet children were of its essence. What is new is the attempt by the Church with great sophistication and subtlety to define and enforce its law of marriage. Marriage is a sacrament—and here, in the definition of sacraments, we have something clearly original; yet the elements of the doctrine may largely be found in the New Testament and St Augustine; and the devout paradox—that marriage is holy, and yet inferior to virginity—was nothing new. Peter Dronke has warned us against seeing in courtly or romantic love a wholly new sentiment in twelfth-century Europe—by reminding us both of its earlier career and of how much of the characteristic oral literature of the early Middle Ages has been lost.[39] Yet there is no doubt that the romance poets created an elaborate world of sentiment and doctrine, and a literature, which have many new features; and they prepared the way for one of the greatest of medieval poets, Wolfram von Eschenbach, who displayed a deeply original gift in the exposition of married love. And finally, few would dispute that it is significant that William the Conqueror was born out of wedlock; in the eleventh century legitimacy was not essential, but he represents the passing of an old world, the coming of a new: it really mattered much more to the European nobility in the twelfth century than in the tenth that their marriages were secure and their heirs legitimate.

[39] Dronke 1968, i. 1–56.

2. The Inheritance, Christian and Roman

If we go back into the seventh or eighth centuries we can certainly discern a remarkable difference. Various forms of nuptial blessing are well recorded by the second century, and may well have a distinguished ancestry in the nuptial ceremonies of the Jewish synagogues and the early Church.[40] But marriage was still fundamentally a civil institution and could be entered without any such blessing; nor was it normally accorded to second marriages after a first spouse had died; nor have we any trace of a complete ritual of marriage in service books earlier than the eleventh century.

The Church had inherited marriage customs from Rome, and from the barbarian tribes under Roman influence, with many congenial features. But the civil courts made no attempt to curb matrimonial abuses; some churchmen were content to leave the affairs of married folk alone—so long as they did not involve violent scandal or legal irregularity; others tried to dictate rules of practice and morality to married folk, sometimes all the more noisily because they had no legal sanctions. Councils and penitentials thundered against infanticide, abortion, and even contraception;[41] they set heavy penances on adulterers and fornicators, and on those who broke their rules, some of which were candidly bizarre. Women might not enter church during menstruation, nor for forty days after giving birth. Sexual intercourse, even between spouses, was forbidden in Lent and Advent and at certain other times. A man might not marry a woman with whom he had committed adultery. More substantial than any of these prohibitions was the extension of the rules of incest.[42] A man might not marry his second cousin—so the rules ran from the sixth century on; but in

---

[40] Stevenson 1982, chaps. 1–2; and for what follows, Molin and Mutembe 1974.
[41] Wallace-Hadrill 1983, p. 409; for other literature see above n. 1.
[42] See esp. Goody 1983, pp. 134–46.

the eleventh Peter Damian was to use all the power of his deep and eccentric learning to extend the prohibition to sixth cousins—and this extension the reformed papacy tried to take on board. For the rest, as the Church became more influential in the law of marriage, and—from the twelfth century—presided over the settlement of innumerable marriage suits, many of these more extreme or improbable restrictions were pared away. Partly, perhaps, this was because Christendom became for a time more civilized. Infanticide rarely figures in the volumes of *Councils and Synods* for the English Church after the early eleventh century: and by the thirteenth the very numerous references to marriage in diocesan instructions and statutes relate mainly to ensuring an orderly entry to marriage, with some advice to mothers to treat their children carefully so that they are not smothered accidentally—and to have a baby-sitter if they leave their children alone.[43] The prohibitions on consanguinity were gradually pruned. The Church was facing the facts of life.

But the harsher side of the teaching of the fathers was not forgotten. St Jerome's diatribes against the wickedness of women were eagerly copied and read; and the letters and treatises of his most eloquent disciple in the central Middle Ages, St Peter Damian, were immensely popular—230 manuscripts or more survive, the highest score for any of the literature discussed in this book written after the year 1000.[44] The early Middle Ages left a legacy of love and lust and high asceticism, of venom and sweet reason, of sin and sublimity, to set beside the normal play of human emotion and of human nature. Men and women

---

[43] See *Councils*, i. 2, index, p. 1117; ii. 2, index, p. 1411, and esp. ii. 1. 137, 632 (exposure of children), 441; 2, 1073 (infanticide); ii, 1, 70, 183 (safety precautions). For the later penitentials, see Ziegler 1956. For what follows, see pp. 61–3, 72–4.

[44] For Jerome, *Adu. Jouinianum* see *PL* xxiii; and for an instance of its influence, James, Brooke, and Mynors, 1983, pp. 288–9 n. For Damian, see Peter Damian, *Letters*, ed. K. Reindel, i. 33–9, where 235 are listed, including some seventeenth-century transcripts.

may be at one moment more passionate and perverse than any other animals—at another a little lower than the angels. Human affairs are full of paradox; and the inheritance of eleventh- and twelfth-century marriage was infinitely rich.

3

THE CULT OF CELIBACY IN THE ELEVENTH AND TWELFTH CENTURIES[1]

Preamble: Peter Damian, Heloise, and St Jerome

Two generations separated Peter Damian in the mid eleventh century from Heloise in the early and mid twelfth; but there is a greater gulf than that, for Damian hated all sexuality and barely allowed marriage to be a legal cover to sin, while for Heloise her marriage to Abelard was the central experience of her life. That said, they had this in common: each was or became a notable leader of the religious life, and each had a special fondness for St Jerome's tract against Jovinian. So with Jovinian let me start. He was a monk who, about 390, was so rash as to issue a tract modestly claiming that virginity as such was not superior to marriage.[2] To this Jerome gave answer with such violence that even Augustine was embarrassed, and felt bound to reply to Jerome's onslaught on women and marriage by assuring a group of holy nuns that virginity was not all, that marriage had its good uses, in his tract *De bono coniugali*.[3] Jerome's *Aduersus Iouinianum*

---

[1] In this chapter I look afresh at themes which I studied forty years ago—see Brooke 1951, 1956, 1957; for all that relates to the English cathedral chapters and especially St Paul's I owe much to Diana Greenway: see esp. Greenway 1968; see also Greenway 1985.

[2] See Jerome, *Aduersus Iouinianum*, lib. i, *PL* xxiii. 211–82; cf. Chadwick 1986, pp. 112–15; *Lexikon für Theologie und Kirche*, v (Freiburg, 1960), cols. 1147–8 and refs.

[3] See p. 55.

became the basic medieval textbook for antifeminism, Augustine's *De bono coniugali* for the theology of marriage. Jerome's book is, as Augustine evidently saw, only a hair's breadth from the Manichaean view that marriage itself is evil. 'The distance between marriage and virginity' says Jerome 'is the distance between avoiding sin and doing good, or to speak more lightly between good and better'—but he does not go on to speak lightly; marriage gets many knocks. 'Marriage fills the earth, virginity heaven [*Nuptiae terram replent, uirginitas paradisum*].'[4] Jerome had to answer the charge: if all became virgins, how could the human race survive? He laughed it off: if we all became philosophers, who would till the fields? It won't happen: 'virginity is difficult, and so, rare . . . many are called, few are chosen'.[5] He was embarrassed that St Paul in Ephesians (5: 32) had called the union of husband and wife *sacramentum magnum*—and a disciple of Peter Damian was even more embarrassed, since he lived in a world in which sacramental theology was blooming, in which the sacraments were being counted and defined. He had to put it in his list, but it was a long list, and marriage came at the end. But Paul went on to liken the union of husband and wife to that of Christ and the Church—and that gave Jerome a let-out: Paul was not talking about sexuality; the union he had in mind had nothing to do with sex.[6] Most of the way Jerome was indeed concerned with virginity, and so almost as much with men as with women—though he cannot avoid swipes at the posterity of Eve from time to time. But at the end he comes out openly in antifeminine satire of a rather heavy

---

[4] i. 13, 16, *PL* xxiii. 232, 235. Kelly (J.N.D.) 1975 gives a thorough and sympathetic account of Jerome: on his relations with his women disciples, see esp. pp. 91–103; and see esp. p. 273: 'marriage and child bearing were excusable provided their fruits were consecrated virgins'.

[5] i. 36, *PL* xxiii. 259.

[6] i. 16 (see n. 4). For marriage in the list of sacraments, see *PL* cxliv. 902 and above, chap. 2 n. 16. Jerome, of course, assumed that Eph. was by Paul.

kind, based on a lost book attributed to Theophrastus of which Walter Map, reworking Jerome, made much more entertaining use than Jerome himself.[7] The essence of it is that wives are a pest to philosophers, a view Jerome reinforced from his wider reading with such stories as that of Socrates. 'One day when he had withstood infinite abuse from Xanthippe from an upper room, and she then drenched him with dirty water, all he did was to wipe his head and reply: "I knew that would happen, that a shower of rain would follow such a thunderstorm." '[8] By a curious compensation not uncommon in human affairs, Jerome's most devoted followers in his own lifetime were women—it was a part of their ascetic vocation, no doubt, to relish his diatribes against their sex—and I fancy that *Aduersus Iouinianum* has often been particularly favoured reading by women, especially those of lively mind and sense of humour. It certainly appealed to Heloise. When Abelard described in his *Historia Calamitatum* how he offered her marriage after he had made her pregnant, he gives a detailed account of her arguments against the fatal step, mostly based precisely on this passage in Jerome and quoting specifically the story about Socrates.[9] Now there has been a lot of argument about the authenticity of the letters of Heloise and Abelard; but we cannot view it, or the condition of marriage in twelfth-century Europe, until we have given due space to celibacy.

Celibacy and Concubinage

In the eleventh and twelfth centuries marriage found a place among the Christian sacraments in a world of

[7] i. 47–9, *PL* xxiii. 276–82; James, Brooke and Mynors 1983, pp. 288–313, esp. pp. 310–11.

[8] i. 48, *PL* xxiii. 278–9. For what follows, see Kelly 1975, pp. 91–103, 129–34, 273–82.

[9] Monfrin 1962, pp. 75–9; Radice 1974, pp. 70–4.

religious sentiment dominated by the celibate ideal as never before or since. The history of marriage is indeed full of paradoxes. The historian of marriage in the twentieth century will have to explain how a period which witnessed unprecedented divorce rates and a determined assault on the whole concept by many of the younger generation, and especially by the freed female slaves of our era, should yet have been presented at many levels and from many sources with an ideal of marriage unknown to most of our ancestors. Of course we can see some of the links: it is evident enough that we enter marriage today expecting far more than our grandparents commonly did, and we may be correspondingly disappointed; if we are not, we have an opportunity for partnership of a kind which would have surprised them—and surprised even more the great theologians of celibacy of the early Middle Ages from St Jerome to St Peter Damian.

In a similar way we can see some of the links in our theme from the start. In the early Middle Ages members of the clergy married. The law forbade it; custom, in a fashion, sanctified their unions. The campaign for celibacy, from the eleventh century on, led to a much sharper distinction between the status of the married woman and the concubine. It could never be admitted in orthodox Catholic, Christian theology that marriage and concubinage were exactly the same;[10] marriage had always been an honourable estate, even if often thought of by literate ascetics as a second best. Downgrading the concubine therefore meant upgrading the wife.

But we have been talking as if the campaign for celibacy, the ascetic movement, the distinction of wife and concubine, were somehow novelties in the eleventh

[10] See Brundage 1975; Brundage 1987, esp. pp. 98–103, 245, 297–300, 341–3, 444–7, 514–17, who shows how long some measure of legal tolerance for concubinage lasted.

century. How can this be? Peter Damian himself would have hotly denied it. As for clerical celibacy, it had been the law of the Church for many centuries—as we know, since the fifth century, though many of the elements go back to the fourth and the inspiration for it right back to the primitive Church.[11] If we wish to understand why the distinction between wife and concubine could be regarded as wholly traditional, we need look no further than Augustine. To a modern reader there are few more jarring passages in that most attractive of human revelations, Augustine's *Confessions*, than his references to his concubine.[12]

> In those years I knew a girl who was my comrade, not in that kind of marriage which is called lawful, but one whom I had found by a wandering passion, empty of wisdom . . . in whom I experienced in my own person the distance between the restraint of the marriage alliance, a treaty made for the sake of procreation, and the contract of love based on lust, where a child is born against the parents' wish . . .

Augustine was as yet unconverted, but his Christian mother found a suitable heiress to be his wife; she was two years under marriageable age—which presumably means that she was about ten years old—so the thirty-one-year-old professor of rhetoric had to wait for his bride. Meanwhile the family circle of his fiancée were determined to ensure that their girl would not be the second woman of the household, and Augustine was made to dismiss his concubine, who had lived faithfully with him for a number of years.

[11] For earlier literature see Brooke 1956, p. 1 n; E. Vacandard in *DTL* ii. 2068–88 (1923); Denzler 1973.
[12] *Confessions*, iv. 2, 2; iv. 4, 7–9; vi. 15, 25. This passage repeats Brooke 1978, pp. 5–8, 12; cf. Brown 1967, pp. 61–3, 88–9. On Augustine's doctrine of marriage, Noonan 1965, pp. 119–39; Chadwick 1986, pp. 114–16.

3. The Cult of Celibacy

Meanwhile my sins were multiplying, and she with whom I had been living was ripped from my side as a hindrance to my marriage. She was still part of me and my heart was torn and wounded; her loss drew blood from me. She had returned to Africa, vowing to you, O God, not to know any other man, leaving with me my natural son by her.

This pathetic story opens to us a strange world of fourth-century custom and marriage law. By social convention, normally accepted by the Church, a man might have a concubine, so long as he only had one and they were faithful to each other. The difference between a concubine and a wife was one of social and legal status: the wife was a social equal, the concubine a servant. Both could be companions of a kind, though Augustine and his like rarely looked to their womenfolk for true companionship: friendship as we understand the term was to be found between man and man. Yet we would be wrong to suppose that his life with the concubine and the separation from her made little impact on him.

Everything is offensive to our taste in Augustine's references to his concubine: first, how little he can find to say of a woman who had lived with him for a number of years and was evidently devoted to him; he does not even name her; second, that he took it for granted that when his mother found a suitable heiress to be his wife, he had to send the concubine away; and third, that he talks more of his own sorrow in this event—and how it put him under the necessity, since his wife to be was not yet of marriageable age, of taking another mistress for a time—and says little of hers.[13] All this seems very unattractive to us; yet it was normal social custom at the time, and Augustine was breaking the rules, and showing unusual consideration, at least to his own feelings, in mentioning

[13] *Confessions*, vi. 2, 2.

her at all. Christian marriage grew up within the world of late Roman society, in which marriage was a graded thing, from full union carrying with it the whole galaxy of legal consequences, to informal relations of various grades; but Roman Law recognized established concubinage as a real relationship; and so did canon law down to the twelfth century, not without prevarication.[14] This made the notion of marriage as a religious union not too clear, and should underline for us the force and power of some of the statements on it in the New Testament.

Similarly with celibacy. In its fullest sense it was an inherent part of the ascetic movement, and from the moment when ascetic celibacy became a recognized institution it was a substantial and formidable part of the life of the Church—whenever we reckon that was, say with Origen in the third or the great monks of the desert in the fourth century; certainly no later.[15] Yet when it was reduced to legal forms a crack appeared. What of the married man who wishes to be ordained, or become a monk? Or again, if marriage is forbidden to the clergy, may they not take concubines from time to time so long as the relationship is not permanent? And thirdly, a subtler point: if you have been ordained and married, which takes preference?—can you repudiate your wife on the ground that the two are incompatible, or must you renounce your orders and cleave to her? In human terms these were living issues at every period of the Church's history; but in law and social custom they were not more than ripples on the surface till the eleventh and twelfth centuries. The answer to my third question came at a particular period of time, though obviously after a millennium of preparation: we can date its solution to the early 1120s.[16] From then on (though the decree does not

---

[14] See references in n. 10.   [15] See n. 2.

[16] The decree attributed to the First Lateran Council (c. 21) in the older texts and Brooke 1956, p. 5, is now known not to belong to 1123; but it was evidently

exactly say as much) it could be assumed that a married couple could only enter religion if both partners took vows simultaneously, as did Heloise and Abelard in 1117. Under no other circumstances could a validly married man take orders till his wife died; similarly, if he was in major orders—that is to say, under the classical definition of celibacy law by Pope Leo the Great, subdeacon, deacon, priest, or bishop—no marriage contract he might enter could be valid.[17] Broadly speaking, the law was clear from the 1120s on; before that date it was far from clear.

This helps to illustrate the way in which the movements of the eleventh and twelfth centuries sharpened the edge of the celibacy laws. And they had to, for all sorts of reasons; above all because in an age with strongly enhanced consciousness of canon law far larger numbers of men and women than ever before, or at least since the fifth century, were vowing themselves to celibacy.

In general terms this is a very familiar feature of the religious sentiment of the eleventh and twelfth centuries. Deep in the currents which flowed from the popular religious movements of the late tenth and eleventh centuries, and very visible upon the surface of the papal reform movement which assumed its leadership from the mid eleventh century, was the call to the ascetic life. The papal reformers, though often disagreeing among themselves, evidently enough in the end stood for a platform with three planks: the abolition of simony—the sale of Church offices, and with it of lay interference in the government of the Church; the establishment of celibacy; and the establishment of the practical supremacy of the Holy See, the papal monarchy. Each had its roots

in circulation as a variant in the 1120s or 1130s, and was attributed, very likely correctly, to Pope Calixtus (II) by Gratian (*Decretum* D. 27 c. 8): see Brooke 1980, p. 342 n. 21. From Gratian on it was regarded as definitive. For the date of the marriage of Heloise and Abelard (1116–17) and their entry into religion (1117), see Bautier 1981, p. 56 n. 1.

[17] Brooke 1980, p. 342 n. 21; Brooke 1956, p. 4 n. 9; Brooke 1980, pp. 341–2.

in a thousand years of Christian history; each had its precedent in the New Testament; each was profoundly conservative; but they added up to a social revolution, one of the most dramatic in the history of Christendom.

The ascetic ideal affected the lives of men more than of women in this age: not perhaps so much because it was more attractive to men, as that most women lacked opportunity to fulfil a celibate vocation. There were far fewer openings for women in the religious life than for men, and this remained so except in Germany and the Low Countries, where the twelfth and thirteenth centuries witnessed an astonishing transformation hardly paralleled elsewhere.[18] This disproportion is very surprising to us, for in the modern world there are two or three times as many female religious as men; the wheel has gone full circle. None the less, the proportional growth of women religious was much the same as for the men; the urge to convert distaffs into wimples was perhaps as strong as that to convert spades or swords into cowls; perhaps, but hardly stronger.

The male predominance in the ascetic movement had many grounds, difficult for us fully to penetrate. At the very heart of the movement lay the notion that women were a temptation and a danger—weak, and so a danger to themselves; but wheedling, and so a danger to men. 'The woman . . . gave me of the tree, and I did eat.' This curious doctrine is of the essence of the struggles of the fathers of the desert; nothing new in our period. Yet there was evidently a new edge to it. This comes out clearly enough in the story of the papal reform. The earliest accounts of Pope Leo IX's Council of Rheims in 1049, the first major statement of the platform, make it clear that the centre of the papal initiative was an attack on simony in

---

[18] See Southern 1970b, pp. 318–31 (on the beguines); Bolton 1973, pp. 83–95; Rosin 1943; for foundations of Cistercian nuns, see index to Van der Meer 1965, corrected by Vongrey and Hervay 1967.

the sense of corruption in episcopal appointments: Who here has committed simony?, said the papal chancellor in well simulated innocence.[19] A frisson of embarrassment greeted his words, for most of the bishops present were guilty. This was simony in its literal sense; as Leo himself was the protégé and devoted colleague of the emperor, it could not include the flight from lay control which was to follow. It may well be that decrees against clerical marriage were included in the council's canons, but it was not until the arrival of Peter Damian in the papal curia a few years later that celibacy can be seen in the forefront of the battle.

Peter Damian's writings contain many of the most eloquent statements of ascetic doctrine the Middle Ages produced. He attacked the issue from two sides. On the one hand he had an exceptionally acute sense of the sinfulness of mankind, a revulsion from everything that savoured of the world and the flesh.[20] To Peter Damian the life of the ordinary world is mud and dung. On the other hand there is a positive element in his teaching, for he was the first great propagandist of the new movement to establish canons regular: new only in a limited sense, for it is at least as old in its essence as the Carolingian period, when Chrodegang and Amalarius had tried to infiltrate a good deal of the spirit and the rule of St Benedict into the life of the ordinary clergy.[21] But as in all the trends we are examining the mid eleventh century saw a quickening of the pace. It lived very evidently in the wider context of Damian's view of the world and its destiny. First of all, very few would be saved, and only

[19] See esp. Southern 1953, pp. 125–7, citing Anselm of Rheims, *Historia dedicationis ecclesiae s. Remigii, PL* cxlii. 1417–40.

[20] See esp. his *Liber Gomorrhianus (Opusculum* vii, *PL* cxlv. 159–90) and his ascetic writings, e.g. *Opuscula* xvi–xviii (ibid. cols. 365–424).

[21] On Damian, see Miccoli 1959–62, and other studies in Mendola 1959–62; Dickinson 1950, pp. 29–42, esp. 34–6. On the Carolingian reforms, Wallace-Hadrill 1983, pp. 174 ff., 264 ff.

monks had more than a sporting chance;[22] under this circumstance it was evidently right and reasonable to make as many folk into monks as possible. But Damian's mind was broad and rich: he was an intellectual, one of the pioneers of the twelfth-century renaissance.[23] The sanctity and unworldly character of the Church's sacraments was a strong theme with his generation and the next; and it seemed to him of the essence that the hands which held the Sacrament of the Altar in which God was present in some special and particular sense, should be unsoiled by the world; and to Damian the world and its filth meant above all money and women[24]—a doctrine shared by many of the holy women of the Middle Ages. In a very positive way, he was passionately devoted to virginity, both in women and in men: he fervently believed that both Mary and Joseph had avoided all sexual intercourse, and that Jesus had entered the world without breaking Mary's hymen—a bizarre doctrine which he combined with the view that virginity, even if broken, could be miraculously restored.[25]

This may seem relatively liberal. Yet as one reads Peter Damian, or the pitiless analysis of a modern scholar such as M. Bultot, one sees him coming ever nearer to the Cathar doctrine, the old Gnostic dualist doctrine, if you like, that the material world is wholly evil, even in its creation; that the only hope of good in this life is to escape from the flesh into the spirit. Something like this was

[22] This is implicit e.g. in Damian's spirited attack on the bishop who allowed a layman who had been clothed as a monk to return to secular life: *Opusculum* xvi, *PL* cxlv. 365–80; cf. Bultot 1963, p. 132. Cf. the similar view of St Anselm (Southern 1963, p. 101).

[23] Knowles 1963, pp. 18, 20, 28–9, on his classical learning and Latin style. For another branch of his learning, in canon law, see Ryan 1956.

[24] Bultot 1963, pp. 100–11. On money and its evil effect on monks, see *Opusculum* xii, *PL* cxlv. 251–92, esp. cc. 1–8, cols. 253–60. On medieval misogyny, see e.g. Brundage 1980, pp. 376–7; Brundage 1987, esp. pp. 324 and n. 318, 425–8.

[25] See Resnick 1988; and, for Mary and Joseph, esp. *Opusculum* xvii, c. 3, *PL* cxlv. 384–5.

indeed common talk among the monks: the much more tolerant and kindly Orderic Vitalis in the early twelfth century will talk of knights escaping from the 'deep pit of worldly temptation' in which they were trapped into the cloister, as if ordinary secular life was, quite literally, hell on earth.[26] In its fullness the doctrine that the material world was wholly evil was heretical; and it was clearly known to be heretical since it had been denounced with the errors of the Manichees by St Augustine in some of his most outspoken pages. Nor can we be sure that it was held by anyone in its fullness in Western Christendom in the eleventh century. It became a widespread popular doctrine again only with the Cathars in the middle of the twelfth century, and this partly under the influence (I am convinced) of Bogomil missionaries from the Near East. But the rapid and spectacular success of the Cathars is unthinkable without a large foundation; and this was evidently provided by the eleventh- and early twelfth-century ascetic movements. Here and there in the early eleventh century, and again and more widely in the early twelfth, these movements were partly heretical. It is a well known oddity of the history of heresy that we have no evidence of such heretical movements in the late eleventh century; and although this may well be partly by default of evidence, it is hard not to think that it is also because the ascetic, puritanical, pessimistic currents in popular religion in this age had found leaders within the papal curia itself, the most vivid and powerful of whom was the hermit-preacher Peter Damian, for a time cardinal bishop of Ostia.[27]

Peter Damian was a man of learning, and of very acute mind, and no heretic. He understood that marriage was

[26] Bultot 1963, *passim*, esp. p. 140; cf. Brooke 1971, p. 153. For 'the deep pit' see Orderic, iii. 226–7: 'in . . . profunditate mundialis illecebrae'. For married life as a *naufragium* cf. Ridyard 1988, pp. 90–1.

[27] See Brooke 1968; Moore 1975, 1977.

permitted, even blessed, by some curious and incomprehensible mystery of the divine providence. Without it the human race would die out; and so not only could human couples live in domestic comradeship, but they had to be allowed to sleep together. Yet the sexual act was the essence of everything abhorrent to Damian. He shared Augustine's repulsion for it and rejoiced in his teaching that it could only primarily be justified by the need to procreate children. From this Damian and all known theologians before Abelard, and most before the great thirteenth-century scholastics, took it for granted that the act of the marriage-bed was only just and righteous if the parties took no pleasure in it.[28] In Damian the propriety of marriage is a very reluctant concession; he really thought that even those who married ostensibly to bear children usually did so for reasons of pride or egotism, with lust at best barely disguised. And the most polite thing he could ever find to say to married folk was: 'I specially address you my brothers now, who have not yet reached high ground in the spiritual life, are still given over to worldly acts, bound by the chains of marriage—be instant and vigilant in works of piety and mercy, give aid to brothers struggling in poverty, strive to show a life as chaste, as sober and as good as your order allows, so that to preserve your posterity you may be able to bear children worthy to serve God.'[29] Significantly, the context was a sermon on St Alexius; and Damian goes on to describe how Alexius abandoned his wife on their wedding-day and fled to lead a life of impoverished chastity. In a famous letter to Pope Alexander II he claimed that 'The whole world at this time is nothing else but greed, avarice and lust'—and went on

[28] See Brundage 1980. However, 'Augustine judged it "pardonable" if married people enjoyed conjugal union without the intention to procreate . . .' (Chadwick 1986, p. 114). See now Brundage 1987, esp. pp. 80–7, 240–1.
[29] Peter Damian, *Sermo* 28, in Lucchesi 1983, p. 162; also in *PL* cxliv. 653, cited Bultot 1963, p. 103 n: cf. n. 6 above. For what follows see cols. 654–5. On Alexius see Molk 1981.

to denounce the lustful habits even of married couples. Domestic animals behave less culpably; better still the elephant, who turns his face away when compelled to the marriage act; best of all the vulture and bees, who (so Damian supposed) bore offspring without it.[30]

In the twelfth century the population of heaven grew larger. The torments depicted by the great sculptor Gislebertus at Autun are no less terrifying than eleventh-century dooms; but there was a more optimistic breeze blowing, and just as the world offered more opportunities for men, so the gates of heaven seemed more widely open to those who were not devout monks. We might expect to find a growing optimism united with a decline in the appeal of the ascetic life. In fact we find the opposite. In the fourth century the popular monastic and ascetic movement had flourished in opposition and criticism and fear of a Church grown (in the eyes of the ascetics) too lax and worldly; and so the growing living standards of the twelfth century doubtless led many to rebel and react against the world. Hence in part the flight to the monasteries; hence too in part the popularity of heresies. Nor must we exaggerate. Very likely even at the end of the twelfth century the proportion of the population engaged in the religious life was not sensationally high, though higher than we are accustomed to. But the growth had been spectacular, far surpassing any reasonable estimate of general growth in population. David Knowles and Neville Hadcock, in their *Medieval Religious Houses, England and Wales*, deploy figures which suggest that the number of religious houses in England increased ten fold in the ninety years following the Norman Conquest in 1066, and the number of religious seven or eight fold.[31] But the true significance of this rise must have been far

---

[30] Peter Damian, *Ep.* 1. 15, *PL* cxliv. 231–2. For what follows Brooke 1984, pp. 146–55.

[31] Knowles and Hadcock 1971, pp. 488–95.

greater than these figures suggest. If one reads the monastic customs of Lanfranc, or Eadmer's *Life of Anselm*, one is made to realize how large a part in monastic life in this era was played by the child oblates.[32] Though no monk could legally be kept in his community if he did not give his own consent when he was of age to do so, in effect this was not a real choice; they had come not by their own vocation, but by their parents' decision; there was little opening for them in the world outside. It was commonly a decision quite happily accepted in the long run—it was from the end of a contented life that Orderic Vitalis looked back to the bitter moment at the age of ten when he had parted from his father—'Weeping he gave a weeping child to Rainald the monk, and sent me into exile for your love—nor ever after saw me.'[33] But for our present purpose the significant thing is that in the new orders, and after a while in the old too, it came to be emphasized that monks must enter the novitiate of their own vocation; and the child oblate was rejected by the new and declined in the old, till in the thirteenth century the practice would be formally condemned. And this means that the increase in vocations to the ascetic life—or at least to a life of celibacy—increased even more than any statistics could reveal.

This change reflects a society in which men of middle or high rank were expected to have far more freedom of choice in their calling than before. Choice could sometimes be awkward. Henry I of England, trying desperately (as I would suppose) to legitimize his grip on the throne in 1100, sought a wife of the Old English royal line, only to meet the objection that Edith-Matilda wore a nun's veil. In that case even St Anselm allowed himself to be

---

[32] See Knowles 1967, pp. 126, 131, 141, s.v. infans, infantes, magister, puer; Southern 1962, pp. 37–9. Cf. Brooke and Swaan 1974, p. 88 and pls. 142–3 from the *Liber Vitae* of New Minster, Winchester.
[33] Orderic, vi. 552–3; trans. from Brooke 1987, p. 14.

convinced that she had worn it unwillingly and only because Aunt Christina made her, to protect her from 'the lust of the Normans'—when the aunt's back was turned, the pious princess assured the Church council met to consider the problem, she tore the veil off and jumped on it.[34] This seems intelligible to us, though it provoked murmurings at the time; and we have no means of knowing how the more startling case of another nun of Romsey later in the twelfth century was justified. For it turned out in 1159–60 that the future of the counties of Boulogne and Flanders demanded that the heiress of Boulogne, Mary of Blois, should marry the count of Flanders, even though she was abbess of Romsey.[35] These cases reflect occasional strains in high society, and in neither case was the lady a nun by her own choice, so far as we know. Far commoner no doubt were the lesser arguments and struggles of those who sought the religious life against resistance. If we compare the known facts of recruitment in France, Germany, and England we may suspect, indeed strongly suspect, that the English aristocracy were more averse to their sons and daughters taking to religion than their Continental neighbours.[36] But this can hardly be documented. There are a number of cases of quite a different type of resistance: of a pope or some other church leader telling a bishop he must not resign, as St Francis was later to tell Cardinal Hugolino, the future Pope Gregory IX, not to become a friar.[37] But these cases are in the margin of our theme; it is well to remember that the most marked characteristic of the twelfth century as against the eleventh was growing variety, and this included variety of opinion and outlook; a place for the heretic, the worldling, the ascetic, the devout layman, or what have you.

[34] Eadmer 1884, p. 122.   [35] Heads, p. 219 and refs.
[36] Brooke 1974–7, p. 545 and n. 35; for France and Germany cf. Guillemain 1971–4; Brühl 1974–7.
[37] If we may believe Bartholomew of Pisa, Analecta Franciscana, iv (Quaracchi, 1906), p. 454.

It would be a nice question to determine whether the ascetic or the worldling was more truly the drop-out in that society. In a similar kind of way in all ages rebellion has been the duty of conformists of certain age groups. If we could interview Peter Damian and Hildebrand, and ask them, 'Are you revolutionaries?'—and succeeded in explaining to them what that means to us in modern terms—we might get a very ambiguous answer. They were extreme traditionalists enforcing the law; they were also preaching social revolution. In the end they and their colleagues stopped short of saying that all masses performed by simoniac or womanizing priests were invalid—but not with a united voice or clear conviction.[38] Gregory VII even encouraged a kind of half-way position: the faithful should absent themselves from the masses of unsuitable priests: a dangerous practice.

Even more ambiguous must have been the position of those who defended the old order. Yet there are several lively defences of clerical marriage and of the legality of ordaining the sons of priests and concubines, to show that old-fashioned views could be vigorously and ingeniously defended. 'The apostle laid it down that "a bishop should be the husband of one wife". He would hardly have made this ruling', observed the Anonymous of Rouen or York, 'if it were adultery, as some assert, for a bishop to have at one time both a wife and a church—two wives, so to speak. . . . For the Holy Church is not the priest's wife, not *his* bride, but Christ's.'[39]

---

[38] Gilchrist 1965.

[39] Pellens 1966, p. 204; (cf. fac. edn., Pellens 1977); Brooke 1971, pp. 88–9. The relevant tract is in Pellens 1966, pp. 204–9 ('*De sancta uirginitate et de sacerdotum matrimonio*'); cf. pp. 116–25 and 209–12 for priests' sons. For other literature see Brooke 1971, pp. 88–9 n. 44.

3. The Cult of Celibacy

Secular Canons

Cathedral chapters could be served by canons or monks, and canons could be regular or secular. The word secular conjures a way of life much like a modern cathedral chapter in England and elsewhere, with canons living in separate houses in the cathedral close, supported by separate incomes, united in a chapter whose presiding dignitary is a dean or provost. The individual income which fed the canon in the Middle Ages was his prebend—the word is cousin to our 'provender'—and so a canon was a prebendary. The nineteenth-century reforms in the provinces of Canterbury and York stripped most of the prebendaries of their incomes and created the modern prebendary, who is commonly a canon without a prebend. The regular chapter was a community under a rule—of monks under the rule of St Benedict or canons under the rule of St Augustine. Augustinian chapters were common on the Continent, but in England only Carlisle was Augustinian—and Carlisle was hardly established as a cathedral before the thirteenth century. Benedictine chapters were rare on the Continent, though not unknown; there were four in England in 1066, nine by 1109, a striking increase.[40]

Yet another of the remarkable features of the Norman settlement of the English Church was the appearance of a new kind of very secular cathedral chapter. This provided for a sizeable group of canons with individual prebends. There are other striking features: a proportion of the canons were from the beginning absentees in the service of king or bishop or some other potentate; many in all

---

[40] In general, see Edwards 1967; Knowles 1963, chap. 36; and for Carlisle, Greenway 1971, pp. 19–21; see also Brooke 1957, esp. pp. 15–26; Greenway 1985. Before the late eleventh century regular chapters had often followed the rule of Chrodegang or the like.

probability spent part of their time in the close, part elsewhere; there were strenuous efforts made to build up cathedral schools; and, from our point of view the most interesting feature, there was an element of married canons with concubines and children, and in many cases the sons were to inherit the canonry and even the dignity. There is no evidence for such a chapter in England before about 1090. On the Continent it is far older, but its history has been remarkably little studied.[41] The model is in general terms north French—though in its elements it spread much more widely than that. Its most prestigious centres (at least in our eyes) in the late eleventh century were at Chartres and Paris. In Normandy something of the kind had evidently existed at Rouen and perhaps elsewhere from at latest the middle of the century; the chapters of Bayeux and Coutances were remodelled in this fashion by the Conqueror's two most worldly bishops, Odo of Bayeux and Geoffrey of Coutances.

No doubt ardent reformers and ascetics regarded these chapters as abuses, as Augean stables of old corruption; but their formation in England seems to have been an act of deliberate foundation. It has long been seen that there was some collaboration among the English bishops in founding or refounding secular chapters about 1090.[42] By a curious chance the annals of Holyrood in Edinburgh have preserved a series of annals clearly deriving from Salisbury in the late eleventh century, and one of these tells us that in 1089 'Bishop Osmund established 36 canons in the church of Salisbury', that is, in Salisbury cathedral.[43] Diana Greenway's brilliant study of the

---

[41] But see Barrow 1987, and Dr Barrow's forthcoming comparative study of English and German chapters. For French chapters, cf. Becquet 1975; for Bayeux and Coutances (below), see Brooke 1974–7.

[42] Edwards 1967, pp. 12–21; cf. Brooke 1957, pp. 17–19; but cf. the cautions in Greenway 1985.

[43] Anderson 1938, p. 110, quoted Greenway 1985, p. 80 n. 13. See Anderson 1938, pp. 22–3, 110–11 for the Salisbury annals.

Institutio of St Osmund has established that the description of the chapter dignities and customs which had long been thought to enshrine the principles of Osmund's foundation in the late eleventh century was actually devised in the mid-twelfth; but she has confirmed that the foundation charter of St Osmund dated 1091 is sound in wind and limb.[44] By the same token the 'prebendal catalogue' of St Paul's cathedral establishes that some remarkable change took place at St Paul's about 1090.[45] Hugh the Chanter of York tells us that Archbishop Thomas I, from Bayeux, first rebuilt the common refectory and dormitory and appointed a provost to govern the canons—and only much later reconstructed the chapter with prebends, dean, treasurer, and precentor.[46] We know that this happened before 1093 and probably not long before 1093. There are similar indications at Lincoln that the final decision to establish a large secular chapter belongs to the last years of Bishop Remigius, who died in 1092.[47]

But the other chapter which bears a date as precise as that of Salisbury is the most curious of all. Between the 1090s and the early thirteenth century the bishops of the province of Canterbury claimed a share in or the whole task of electing their archbishop.[48] It was a highly rational claim in a world in which electoral procedures were being formalized and clarified; and it is rather surprising that it had no imitators, so far as I know, elsewhere in Europe. At first the bishops and the monks of Christ

[44] Greenway 1985, esp. pp. 79–80, 97–100.

[45] Brooke 1951, esp. pp. 114–15. The full evidence for the first generation of dignitaries and canons is laid out in Greenway 1968.

[46] Hugh the Chanter 1961, p. 11; new edition for OMT by M. Brett, C. N. L. Brooke, and M. Winterbottom (1990), pp. 18–19; meanwhile, on this passage, see Hill and Brooke 1977, pp. 25–6; Phillips 1985, pp. 4–6.

[47] Hill and Brooke 1977, p. 25 n. 93; the study by Kidson referred to there will be part of the new *History of Lincoln Cathedral*, ed. D. Owen; on the foundation of Lincoln, see meanwhile Owen 1984.

[48] For what follows, *GF*, pp. 227–9.

Church Canterbury collaborated (sometimes very uneasily) in electing an archbishop who was in effect a royal nominee.[49] But as time went on the election became less of a formality; and eventually, in the great battle over the Canterbury election of 1206—which issued in seven years of interdict and the acceptance of Stephen Langton in 1213–14—Pope Innocent III finally quashed the claims of the bishops and confirmed those of the monks.[50] It was a pyrrhic victory, since they were hardly ever allowed to exercise them freely or at all; and just a little survived of the bishops' pretensions, in the title still borne by the bishop of London of dean of the province. The title 'dean' first appears in Eadmer's account of the events following St Anselm's death in 1109 written in the 1120s; but there are clear indications that the bundle of claims and rights of which the title 'dean' came to form part went back to the long vacancy at Canterbury after the death of Lanfranc, before Anselm became archbishop, from 1089 to 1093.[51] Thus at Salisbury, Lincoln, York, and London, and in the province of Canterbury at large, the notion of the secular chapter was evidently much under discussion at this time.

We may reasonably doubt if these new chapters came out of a clear sky; and yet all the evidence converges to suggest that in some sense the secular chapter had been kept at bay over the previous years. Strongest of all seems to be the evidence from Salisbury; for unless the foundations of St Osmund's cathedral, as they now lie open to inspection on the hill at Old Sarum, grossly deceive us, Osmund can hardly have conceived a chapter

---

[49] For the elections of 1161–2 and 1173–4, see *Councils*, i. 2. 843–5 and Barlow 1986, pp. 64–73, 292–5; *Councils*, i. 2. 956–65 and refs.

[50] Cheney 1976, pp. 147–54, 294–356.

[51] *GF*, pp. 228–9; Eadmer 1884, pp. 42, 211. The precedence of London and Winchester goes back to the 1070s, but the titles 'dean' and 'precentor' may be an anachronism of the twelfth century.

of thirty-six canons when he built its east end.[52] Lanfranc was an old reformer of independent mind;[53] there were elements in the papal reform he disapproved of. He sat lightly to papal monarchy, not in principle but in practice; he evidently disapproved of Gregory VII's encouragement to the faithful to vote with their feet—to absent themselves from the masses of incontinent priests. His own decree at the Council of Winchester in 1076 had provided for gradual reform—for acceptance of concubines for parish clergy *in esse*, but a determined effort not to ordain any more clergy who intended to marry or had wives or concubines; and for canons there is no compromise: a canon may not have a wife.[54] This was relatively liberal, and seems to have been the occasion for rumours spreading in Normandy that Lanfranc was soft on the celibacy issue; this he denied, and we may be tolerably sure that his aim was the practical elimination of clerical marriage by building up the institutions of celibate clergy; that he disapproved of secular chapters. Doubtless secular canons could then be, as often in the future, sworn to celibacy. But Lanfranc and those who thought like him could well suspect, and not without reason, that secular chapters were often in practice havens of concubinage.

Doubtless the full story was more complex, and there are signs that Lanfranc hesitated between this kind of chapter and that at the outset of his reign, in the early 1070s. There are hints that he at first showed doubts about the chapter of monks in Christ Church itself; and Walkelin, the first Norman bishop of Winchester, is said to have laid serious plans to replace his monks by

[52] If the plan in Clapham 1934, facing p. 22, is correct: it was based on excavations by W. H. St John Hope recorded in Hope 1913–14, pp. 102–3, 105–10. It shows a tiny choir from Osmund's time replaced by an ample choir under Bishop Roger in the early twelfth century.

[53] He was clearly sympathetic to the movement to establish regular canons, though not (as used to be thought) himself present at the crucial Roman council of 1059 (Bates 1982, pp. 200–1; for the council, Miccoli 1959–62).

[54] *Councils*, i. 2. 616–19.

canons.[55] But early in his pontificate Lanfranc had a letter from Pope Alexander II (formerly his pupil), urging him to defend the monastic chapter at Canterbury; and all the indications are that he gave it warm support, in the event, at Winchester, Canterbury, and elsewhere. With his support Bishop William of Saint-Calais introduced monks into Durham Cathedral in 1083, and monastic coups may have been fostered elsewhere, even though the establishment of monastic cathedrals at Bath, Norwich, Coventry, and Ely came shortly after his death.[56]

Thus the foundation of secular and monastic cathedrals bears witness to a lively debate in the episcopate on their rival merits; and the outbreak of secular chapters at or near the death of Lanfranc strongly suggests that the old man had kept this secular drift in check. It is hard to tell how secular it really was. Such chapters could contain devoted celibates, foster liturgy and devotion, provide patronage for schools. But it is also manifest that they could harbour the concubines and children of canons. The papal reformers condemned such practices; but it is perfectly clear that they were widely tolerated and still in some sense respectable. Godwin, the pious precentor of Salisbury early in the twelfth century, regarded himself as subject to a rule; he reckoned the difference between regular and secular as a small matter—but he flourished under Bishop Roger, who peopled the chapter with his sons and nephews. When St Paul's cathedral in London fell under the sway of a monastic bishop in the 1140s there was for a time a quasi-monastic movement in the chapter.[57] It did not spell the end of the canons' families;

---

[55] Eadmer 1884, pp. 18–21 (also for what follows); cf. Knowles 1963, p. 130 and n. But Knowles needlessly doubts the validity of Alexander II's letter.

[56] See Knowles 1963, p. 169, for Durham; for the rest, Brooke 1967; Knowles 1963, pp. 621–4.

[57] For Godwin, see Edwards 1967, pp. 4, 7, 183 n.; Kealey 1972, p. 110; for his tomb, Hope 1913–14, p. 113 [and T. Webber, *Scribes and Scholars at Salisbury Cathedral* (1992), pp. 123–8]; for St Paul's in the 1140s, see Brooke 1957, pp. 24–8.

they can be traced down to the end of the twelfth century. Hugh du Puiset, bishop of Durham from 1153 to 1195, lived with at least three women, and passed one of them on to a lesser baron of the neighbourhood.[58]

But the heyday of the married canons was in the period 1090 to 1130, when the clerical concubine at St Paul's enjoyed, along with the hereditary succession to canonries, passing from father to son or uncle to nephew, an Indian summer. When in the 1950s I first studied the St Paul's prebendal catalogue, which is our chief evidence, I hoped that similar documents could be found for other cathedrals in northern Europe in this age; but none have so far come to light—although the substantial new work on cathedral chapters which Diana Greenway, Julia Barrow, and others have undertaken may well throw more new light on these problems. St Paul's still provides one unique ray of light on the role of clerical marriage in this period.[59] Yet there are other documents of a very different character which complement it in a remarkable way.

First of all, the *Liber Vitae* of Durham cathedral priory includes among its confraters: 'Ralph son of Algot and his brother Edmund and Mahald his concubine [*socia*] and Thomas his son and William and the mother of Ralph Leoverun'.[60] Now the prebendal list for Rugmere in St Paul's contains Ralph son of Algod and William his son, and that for Chiswick Edmund who may well be an Edmund son of Algot who occurs in Domesday Book.[61] All this is unlikely to be coincidence, and we may be tolerably sure that we have lighted on a family from the chapter of St Paul's—an unlikely union of a married

---

[58] Brooke 1956, p. 20 n. 67; Scammell 1956, pp. 311–13. Some of these married clergy may have had families as laymen, but this possibility only slightly affects what follows.

[59] See nn. 1, 41. For the prebendal catalogue, and for details of the chapter, see Brooke 1951 and esp. Greenway 1968.

[60] Thompson 1923, fo. 42+ ʳ, quoted in Brooke 1951, p. 123 n. 66, with other details. It is possible that Mahald (Maud or Matilda) was Edmund's concubine.

[61] i. 127b.

canon and his family with the monastic celibacy of Durham in the first flush of its revival.

The prebendal catalogue survives in two copies of later centuries; but detailed analysis has shown that they provide reliable lists for all the prebends from *c*.1090 on, and full critical lists of all the dignitaries and canons of St Paul's between 1066 and 1300 were published by Dr Greenway in 1968.[62] It has long been known that the most remarkable feature of these is their family complexion. The see of London was occupied twice in the twelfth century by members of the family of Beaumais or Belmeis: by Bishop Richard I from 1108 to 1127, and by Richard II from 1152 to 1162.[63] Something like eleven of their family are known to have had dignities and prebends in St Paul's in the course of the century—most of them in the first half. The principal known members of the family may be tabulated as in Fig. 1.[64] We find other family groups: Ranulf Flambard, the celebrated minister of William II and bishop of Durham (1099–1128) with two sons and two brothers; Anger or Anskar of Bayeux and his two more celebrated sons, Audoen bishop of Evreux (1113–39) and Thurstan archbishop of York (1114–40).[65] But the most remarkable feature of these lists is the number of cases in which a dignity or a prebend passed from one member of a family to another in a quasi-hereditary succession. In the first half of the twelfth century the dignitaries were

[62] Greenway 1968; cf. Brooke 1951.

[63] Greenway 1968, pp. 1–2 (and *passim* for what follows); Stubbs 1876, i, esp. pp. xxi–xxxviii; *GF*, pp. 43–7, 204–6.

[64] References in Fig. 1 are to Greenway 1968, except as indicated. It is not certain that the two Richards were sons of Richard Ruffus I (see *GF*, pp. 272, 280). The youngest of the family seems to have been Richard Junior, who succeeded to his father's prebend, probably in 1167, when his distant relative Gilbert Foliot was bishop—but possibly in the 1150s, and if so most probably under the patronage of his uncle Bishop Richard II (Greenway 1968, p. 53).

[65] Brooke 1951, p. 114 and n. 71, 130 and n. 18, corrected (for the Flambard family) by Greenway 1968, pp. 97–8; see ibid, pp. 43, 47, 77, for the other members of the families; for the family of Thurstan of York see new edn. of Hugh the Chanter (n. 46 above).

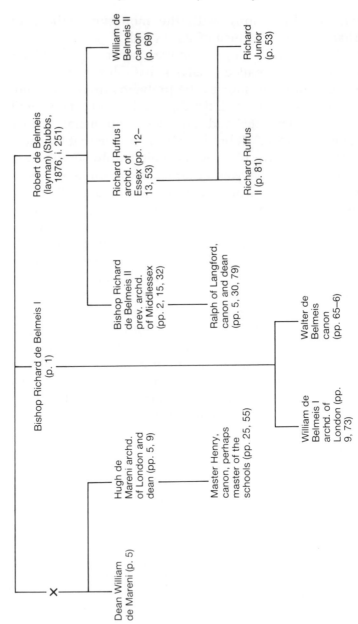

Fig. 1. The Belmeis family.

the dean and the four archdeacons: the deanery and the archdeaconry of London enjoyed two Belmeis each in this period, the archdeacon of Essex only one; Middlesex and Colchester both passed from a father to a son at the first change in the century—Colchester from Quintilian to his son Cyprian.[66] In a similar way the lists reveal to us that in thirteen out of the thirty prebends, either certainly or very likely, son succeeded father—in one case nephew followed uncle—at the first or second change in the century[67]—and in a majority of the prebends we meet either such a succession, or one or two Belmeis, or the brothers of other canons. The impression is overwhelmingly domestic.

The bulk of this evidence relates to the first third or so of the twelfth century; but not all. A few such successions occurred down to *c*.1150 and a thin trickle of the Belmeis survived till the end of the century. In 1163 Bishop Richard II was succeeded by his relative Gilbert Foliot, a monk by origin, but a man of many nephews, whom he proceeded to endow with archdeaconries and prebends.[68] It was partly to make space for the nephews, no doubt, that the hereditary canons had to give way. There were also royal clerks like Thomas Becket to be accommodated.[69] But indeed, they were nothing new, for several of the married canons of the early twelfth century, including Flambard and his brothers, Richard de Belmeis I and the Bayeux clan, had been royal clerks.[70] The difference

---

[66] Greenway 1968, pp. 5, 9, 12–15, 18.

[67] Greenway 1968, pp. 34, 36, 45, 53 (not certain), 55, 57 (the first name is Algar son of Dereman, and Dereman seems to have been a canon connected with Islington), 59, 61 (uncle and nephew), 67–8, 69, 74–5, 83, 85–6. It is possible that Ailward, son of Sired, first in the list for the prebend of Newington, was son of a canon—but there is no specific evidence to link Sired with Newington (Greenway 1968, pp. 65, 89).

[68] *GF*, pp. 44–6. All the four archdeacons appointed in Gilbert Foliot's tenure of the see of London were his nephews (ibid., pp. 272–4).

[69] Greenway 1968, p. 73.

[70] Brooke 1951, pp. 123–4.

was that Becket was not married. For at the end of the day, however much we may attribute to rival sources of patronage and other good cause, the gradual disappearance of the family element from the chapter must reflect in some measure the campaign against clerical marriage.[71] This decline may be exaggerated by these figures: there are copious signs that less obtrusive paternity occurred still among the higher clergy into the late twelfth century and beyond; among the lower clergy it never ceased. But the figures themselves are minimal: there may well have been more, even far more, domesticity in the chapter of St Paul's than they reveal to us. Granted the chances of infertility and early death—and that not every son might be willing to enter the family business—there must have been far more than thirteen canons living with concubines to produce these figures.[72]

The unique survival of the prebendal catalogue opens a window nowhere else discovered. But it suggests profound reflections on the significance of the secular chapters in the late eleventh and early twelfth centuries. They formed a reaction in more ways than one against the campaign for celibacy and for regular canons. Nor have we any reason to suppose that St Paul's was either unique or unusual. How widespread such arrangements were is quite unknown; but it would be surprising indeed if they had not been paralleled in Normandy and elsewhere in northern France—perhaps over a much wider area.[73] In Normandy lay Bayeux from which came Canon Anger,

[71] Brooke 1956; but see also the evidence cited in Cheney 1980, pp. 69–78, which shows hereditary benefices, including hereditary prebends, as an active problem in the third quarter of the twelfth century in the see of Worcester.

[72] How many of the 'married' canons were resident we cannot tell: a fair number do not witness the chapter's charters, but these are not so numerous as to make any conclusion based on them cogent, and even the royal clerks might well find a base in London convenient.

[73] On the Norman church see Brooke 1956, esp. p. 11; Bates 1982, pp. 189–235, esp. pp. 215–16. For a valuable study of Angers, see Robin 1970. For what follows, above, n. 65.

and perhaps his concubine Popelina, known to us from York historical tradition. From Normandy came Bishop Roger of Salisbury (1102–39), and perhaps his amazonian concubine Matilda of Ramsbury.[74] And outside Normandy, but not far away, lay the two chapters most obviously in contact with the Anglo-Norman world, Chartres and Paris.[75]

Paris and Heloise

The cathedral chapter of Paris in the opening decades of the twelfth century has been brought into the light of day in a fascinating study by R.-H. Bautier.[76] The canons formed a small, privileged community on the Île de la Cité, living in about fifteen houses within and without the old enclosure of Notre-Dame, dominated by the factions led at the opening of the century by two powerful archdeacons, Étienne de Garlande, eminent royal official, a great political figure, accused by Ivo of Chartres of being illiterate, frivolous, and a womanizer; and William of Champeaux, Abelard's teacher, who became a canon regular at Saint-Victor and later bishop of Châlons. William represents a spirit of reforming zeal in the chapter; and the same spirit re-emerged with Bishop Étienne of Senlis in the late 1120s, who attempted to colonize the chapter with canons regular from Saint-Victor.[77]

In the *Historia Calamitatum*—'the tale of my calamities'— Abelard set in the forefront his quarrel with William of Champeaux, his first teacher. This led to Abelard's first

---

[74] Kealey 1972, esp. pp. 3–10, 22–3, 186, 272, 274; Brooke 1956, p. 16 n. 53.
[75] On Chartres see Clerval 1895; Southern 1970a, ch. 5, 1982; and the Chartres cartularies cited ibid., p. 125 n. 31; Molinier and Longnon 1906, pp. 1–178 (obituaries).
[76] Bautier 1981, esp. pp. 29–30, 53–77.
[77] Bautier 1981, pp. 53–77, esp. p. 69.

departure from Paris, and even after he had returned, when William, soon to be bishop of Châlons, was still teaching in Saint-Victor, he managed to have Abelard ousted from a short-lived scholastic post in the cathedral school.[78] When Abelard quarrelled with William, on each occasion he went to teach at Melun, still within the royal domain; but twice it happened that Abelard found it expedient or necessary to leave the royal domain altogether—once in 1105–8[79] and again in the 1120s after his affair with Heloise and a spell as monk at Saint-Denis. These exiles corresponded in some measure with the ascendancy in Paris of Bishop Galon (1104–16) and Bishop Étienne de Senlis (from 1123), the first of whom gave Abelard no favour, the second of whom was his particular enemy; and his exile in the 1120s coincided with the rise of another enemy, Abbot Suger of Saint-Denis. In these and later events there is more than a hint that Abelard had sided with the faction in the cathedral chapter led by Étienne de Garlande, who was in the ascendant when Abelard returned in 1108, in disgrace when Abelard was exiled in the 1120s, in the ascendant again when Abelard returned once more to Paris in the 1130s.[80] If so, Abelard was supported by the more secular faction against the more regular.

It was in the cathedral chapter at Paris that the young Heloise was reared. We do not know who her parents really were, but Bautier has found evidence to associate her with noble families of the region who were at loggerheads with Suger, and perhaps supported Étienne de Garlande.[81] She grew up with her uncle Fulbert in a

---

[78] Monfrin 1962, pp. 64–7; Radice 1974, pp. 58–62.

[79] Bautier 1981, p. 54 n. 7.

[80] Bautier 1981, pp. 53–71.

[81] Bautier 1981, pp. 75–7. Both Abelard (Monfrin 1962, pp. 71–9; Radice 1974, pp. 67–75) and the obituary of the Paraclete (Bautier 1981, p. 75 n. 5) call Fulbert Heloise's *avunculus*. This could have been a euphemism for father, but this seems unlikely: Abelard was not squeamish, and in the contemporary English chapters fathers and sons were commonly called such.

society, we may suppose, not fundamentally different
from the chapter in London. Fulbert witnesses a number
of documents of the cathedral chapter in Paris between
1107 and 1124.[82] In the first of her celebrated letters to
Abelard, Heloise put forward with telling eloquence her
preference for being Abelard's 'concubine or whore';[83]
marriage was not for her, because it would ruin his career;
but in any case marriage can be a corruption of love,
chains rather than freedom. These statements, issuing
from a holy abbess in her maturer years—in her thirties,
to be precise—have proved very shocking to some
modern readers. For one modern scholar they have
proved a significant ground, for another a main ground,
for supposing her letters to be spurious—to be later
inventions.[84] They seem to M. Silvestre to belong to the
world of the *Roman de la Rose* and the late thirteenth
century. Undoubtedly they were gathered like fragrant
flowers by Jean de Meung for his contribution to that
interminable allegory. But the arguments of Heloise
belong to a different world: they are compounded of
learning and eloquence and dialectic; they speak of a love
of argument; they echo a world in which there was a real
choice between being a wife and being a concubine.
M. Silvestre finds it astonishing that such sentiments
should have been written by a woman, when nothing of
the kind has been uttered by a female author since the
dawn of time. Now Heloise on any showing was one of a
rare breed: the world of learning was a man's world. But
there was one milieu in the early twelfth century in which
ladies freely mingled, where many or most clerical
households contained concubines and children—and that
was in the cathedral closes; and nowhere was education
more advanced and more effective than in Paris. If we had

---

[82] Bautier 1981, p. 76 n. 1; for what follows, see below, pp. 111–13.
[83] Below, chap. 5, at n. 16.
[84] Muckle 1953, esp. pp. 62–4, 67; Silvestre 1985, esp. pp. 194–5.

to look for a learned lady who uttered such sentiments in the whole realm of medieval social life and intellectual experience, we should look for her precisely in the opening decades of the twelfth century, and in Paris.

4

THE CORRESPONDENCE OF HELOISE AND ABELARD[1]

The letters of Heloise, and to a slightly lesser degree, those of Abelard, illustrate in a remarkably vivid way the conflicts and paradoxes we have been exploring. Many of the best minds of the eleventh and twelfth centuries were dedicated to chastity and asceticism. For the ascetic, the path to heaven lay through the cloister or the hermitage; in the mingling of the sexes lay an instant and inescapable threat of hell. Yet every monk had human parents and a human family; many had passed on to their cloister from a happy married life; many of the monks of whom we have any extensive knowledge had married friends for whom they showed an extraordinary sympathy. Dom Jean Leclercq has laid out in two delightful books the happier side of the monastic commentary on marriage in the twelfth century.[2] There is a deep paradox here: the ascetic ideal and the ideal of marriage marched hand in hand, often in conflict, often in harmony. Of this paradox we have a unique witness in the letters of Heloise and Abelard, if they are authentic documents of the early twelfth century.

[1] Earler discussions of the authenticity of the letters were resumed and answered in Gilson 1960, pp. 145–66. The next, and more serious, stage in the argument is brilliantly analysed — with many important comments — in Luscombe 1980 [and see now especially Luscombe 1988]; another admirable survey, also supporting authenticity, is Zerbi 1981; and there is a summary of the case in Luscombe 1979, pp. 25–8. Southern 1970a, chap. 6, remains a very just appraisal of the correspondence. For an elaborate discussion of the letters as autobiography, see Misch 1959, pp. 545–627.

[2] Leclercq 1979, 1982.

4. Heloise and Abelard: Correspondence

But are they? Before the 1970s a variety of attempts were made over a long period of years to find grounds for doubting the authenticity of the letters.[3] These were answered by Étienne Gilson in an appendix of his justly famous *Heloïse and Abélard,* and most scholars reckoned he had settled the matter.[4] Yet doubts remained and were expressed from time to time;[5] and since 1970 there has been a flurry of literature presenting all manner of different views; John Benton and Hubert Silvestre have argued for a late thirteenth-century forgery, based on earlier materials—for Benton the *Historia Calamitatum* was of the twelfth, the rest of the correspondence thirteenth; Peter von Moos reckoned the letters a work of literature, whatever may lie behind them.[6] Some writers have admitted perplexity or changed their ground; a number, while conceding that there are problems, have continued to propound powerful arguments for their authenticity. Conspicuous among these have been Peter Dronke, Don Pietro Zerbi, and David Luscombe.[7] The argument is serious, and depends on a mass of detailed analysis, some of it textual. This can only be conducted effectively in the context of a critical edition of the corpus of letters: J. Monfrin has one in hand, and David Luscombe—who has already contributed some of the most important discussions to the argument—another.[8] Meanwhile no

[3] Most powerfully in Schmeidler 1914 and Charrier 1933.

[4] See n. 1.

[5] See esp. Muckle 1953.

[6] Benton 1975 (for other contributions by Benton see Luscombe 1980, nn. 33, 41); Silvestre 1985; Von Moos 1971–2; Von Moos 1975; cf. Von Moos 1980. Benton 1980 expresses very honestly and honourably doubts about Benton 1975: but for clarity it is necessary still to cite the arguments as they appeared in 1975. Benton's argument depends on the assumption that we have no evidence that the correspondence was known to any but the 'authors' before the second half of the thirteenth century. But see n. 32.

[7] For Luscombe, see n. 1; for Zerbi, Zerbi 1981; for Dronke see esp. Dronke 1976.

[8] Luscombe's will appear with English trans. by B. Radice (a revised version of Radice 1974) in OMT. See meanwhile Monfrin 1962; Muckle and McLaughlin 1950–6. For a more detailed analysis of the letters see chap. 5.

scholar who wishes to use the letters as evidence can ignore these discussions: the letters are central to my account of twelfth-century marriage, and I must justify their use.

The dossier opens with Abelard's autobiography, the *Historia Calamitatum*—the story of my calamities—in form a letter of consolation to a suffering clerk.[9] One of the major calamities, and the one described in greatest detail, was his affair with Heloise—calamitous, not in its inception, but in its consequences for the hero—and for this and other reasons the next letter, purporting to be by Heloise, takes Abelard severely to task for his treatment of her. It analyses their life together and their relationships, and demands his spiritual guidance and his prayers. To this, if we take the documents at face value, Abelard replied, and the next two letters continue the dialogue; then Heloise changed tack, abandoned the confession of her love for him, and turned in earnest to the demand for advice: she requested in considerable detail a treatise on holy women and the origin of the order of nuns, and a Rule. These Abelard provided.

In an ideal world a study of authenticity should follow not precede the close analysis of the argument of the documents; but all real historical arguments are circular, and a full deployment of the argument must equally follow, not precede, some assurance of its status as evidence. The curious reader may therefore read Chapter 5 twice, if he or she has the patience—once before, once after Chapter 4.

The detailed arguments are numerous and difficult to assess.[10] One does not have to go the whole way with Newman in saying that a thousand difficulties do not add up to a doubt to be perplexed by an amassing of tiny

---

[9] Monfrin 1962; Muckle 1950.
[10] They are conveniently listed in Silvestre 1985; and most persuasively argued in Benton 1975.

particulars. More serious, perhaps, is the fact that almost every detail has been thought by one scholar or another to point both ways. Earlier critiques made much play with Heloise's claim that since her conversion to the religious life Abelard had neglected her—'nec . . . vel sermone presentem vel epistola absentem consolari tentaveris'. 'You have not attempted to console me either by talking to me in person or sending me a letter from afar.'[11] This appears to be in direct contradiction to the *Historia Calamitatum*, where he describes frequent visits to the Paraclete, and all likelihood; but only if it is taken to mean there were no visits, no letters at all. As Sir Richard Southern has said, 'only a very solemn critic would think the point very serious'.[12] The context makes clear that she wanted personal consolation, advice that would lead her out of her perplexities—and since Abelard's first letter shows he had no notion of her perplexity, it would have been true that he had not consoled her. As some critics have seen, the demand is more intelligible from the historical Heloise—if such really was her predicament—than from a forger, especially from one who had any knowledge of, perhaps had even composed, the *Historia Calamitatum*.

Arguments of an apparently more objective nature were propounded in the most elaborate and (in my view) the most important of the onslaughts, that by John Benton in a lecture at Cluny delivered in 1972 and published in 1975. In particular he showed that there were remarkable discrepancies between Abelard's Rule and the *Institutiones* of the Paraclete, which, he argued, represented custom at the Paraclete, Heloise's own abbey, in her later years.[13]

[11] Muckle 1953, p. 70.

[12] Southern 1970a, p. 98. Cf. Gilson 1960, pp. 148–55; and esp. Monfrin 1962, p. 101; Radice 1974, p. 98. Another very good example is the discussion of a cross-reference in letter 5, which has been supposed to be to a different letter—as if both were part of the same book or treatise—but which Luscombe showed to be within the same letter after all: Luscombe 1980, p. 28.

[13] Benton 1975, pp. 474–83, 503–6, esp. 474–5, and references. See now the full edition and commentary in Waddell 1987.

4. Heloise and Abelard: Correspondence

Luscombe has expressed caution about Benton's use of these documents.[14] But in any case the two most dramatic divergences can undoubtedly be interpreted in support of both points of view. Abelard laid down that the abbess should be under the ultimate control of a male abbot, as Heloise herself claimed to be under the direction of Abelard himself; and he contradicted the rule of St Benedict by permitting the eating of meat.[15] But the *Institutiones* (and all other evidence) seem to indicate that Abelard had no successor—that like Fontevrault but unlike Marcigny an abbess ruled supreme—and also that meat was forbidden. Both have to be seen in context. In her own letter to Abelard which elicited the Rule Heloise went into detail as to what it was to contain. The letters (if genuine) show that she thoroughly enjoyed the opportunity of dialogue with him; but they suggest fairly forcibly a yet more potent motive for the details she gave. Like many a submissive wife she knew better than her husband and was determined that he should instruct her to do what she wanted. In many passages we can hear the distant echo of St Francis instructing Peter Cathanii what to order him to do.[16] There is an extremely lively discussion of the merits and demerits of St Benedict.[17] This may or may not have been a common theme among twelfth-century nuns—perhaps we shall know more of the matter one day. But it was certainly unconventional. It is not at all surprising that Heloise, or her community—in other respects undoubtedly devout and ascetic—grew more conventional, more respectful to Benedict, as time went on. In this as in other cases Abelard takes up her own line

[14] Luscombe 1980, pp. 30–1.

[15] Benton 1975, pp. 475–8, 503–6; cf. Luscombe 1980, pp. 30–1. Benton 1975, p. 477, argues that the eating of meat was the subject of livelier debate in the thirteenth than the twelfth century; but the issue arose in every century in which the Rule of St Benedict was observed in such matters.

[16] Brooke (R. B.) 1970, pp. 126–7: 'I am going to tell you the penance that I wish to do for it so that you can confirm it for me, and not contradict me at all.'

[17] Muckle 1955, pp. 243–8; Radice 1974, pp. 161–70.

of thought and labours it ceaselessly. But on the relation of the abbess to outside authority she had been silent, and he could well have thought that she wished to perpetuate the external authority, especially as she expressed herself very freely on the benefits of a retired life.[18] Yet if the Heloise who emerges from these letters was in any sense a historical character, it would not be at all surprising if she refused to let Abelard have a successor. Abelard she worshipped—and yet felt it necessary to put her ideas into his head. She might well have thought it intolerable to be under the direction of another man, reserving her respect for great monastic potentates like Peter the Venerable of Cluny, who deeply respected her, and submission for the properly constituted authority of the Church at large, that is, for the pope.

It will not have escaped notice that in all these cases the interpretation which favours authenticity is related to a view of Heloise's personality. There has indeed been a plea from this scholar and from that to avoid the supposedly subjective evidence of human nature and the character of Heloise—and Abelard—in favour of more objective criteria.[19] This has led some to reject such arguments in favour of textual and stylistic analysis, and others to look on the letters as products of literature rather than life. But in this context the notion of objectivity is deeply suspect: none of the arguments is independent of human nature and human values, nor should it be if there is anything in the themes developed in this book. We await a really precise word-count and computerized analysis both of the style of Abelard's works and of the letters; and meanwhile various propositions have been made with varying degrees of dogma: that the style

[18] Muckle 1955, pp. 242–3; Radice 1974, pp. 160–1.
[19] Jolivet 1977, p. 311, cited Luscombe 1980, pp. 23–4. Von Moos 1975b, pp. 462–3 has a very pertinent criticism of those who argue in the name of historical objectivity, which, he suggests, is just another ideology.

of the letters shows that they are the work of a single author; that the author is or is not Abelard; or again that the style reveals two authors, one clearly Abelard, the other probably Heloise.[20] I do not deny that there are very close resemblances, that many of the same quotations and arguments are in works attributed both to Abelard and to Heloise.[21] But Heloise was one of his most brilliant pupils, and enjoyed an intimacy with the master beyond that open to any of her colleagues: she was soaked in his ideas and his words and works. It is inherently probable that she wrote with the pen of Abelard; and the criteria by which one would decide the value of word-counts are not based on scientific facts, but on human judgement. By the same token, if this is a genuine correspondence, both Abelard, when he grasped the opportunity to write of his calamities, and Heloise, when she started to write to him, had a unique opportunity for self-expression. She in particular seized the chance to develop an argument with her master. The result might or might not be moving personal letters—it was bound to be work of the highest art known to the authors, work of literature.

Some of the earlier arguments turned on the notion that the love story of Heloise and Abelard, in its details and its quality, had only been known from this dossier, and that such deployment of an idyll between a monk and a nun was unthinkable in the early twelfth century. This has

---

[20] For extremely interesting stylistic analysis, see esp. Dronke 1980, 1984. Monfrin 1975, pp. 423–4, foreshadowed the completion of a computer-aided analysis; [see now J. F. Benton, 'The Correspondence of Abelard and Heloise', in *Fälschungen im Mittelalter*, v (*MGH Schriften* 33, v, Hanover, 1988), 95–120]. For discussions of the vocabulary of the letters see the comments and references in Luscombe 1980, pp. 23–4, 34–5. It was the contention of Schmeidler 1914 that Abelard wrote all the letters, and for letter 6 at least his view has been revived in Benton 1980.

[21] It has often been observed that when Abelard describes Heloise's arguments against marriage in the *Historia Calamitatum* he is citing some texts he himself quoted elsewhere (e.g. Benton 1975, p. 501). Naturally: he is summarizing a discussion they must have gone over and over—the sources they quoted were a common possession.

been an exceptionally fruitful argument, since it has stimulated Peter Dronke and David Luscombe to show how far from true both propositions are.[22] They have shown that most of the story could be reconstructed from other evidence—not without discrepancies, which still remain to be fully elucidated and explained; but sufficient can be known from scattered sources to make it very difficult to understand how a thirteenth-century forger could have had the information needed to compile the dossier with such little error.[23] Especially striking is the evidence of the *Carmen ad Astralabium*, Abelard's strange song of instruction to their son, which puts these words into the mouth of Heloise:

> If I can not be saved without repenting of what I used to commit, there is no hope for me.
>
> The joys of what we did are still so sweet that, after delight beyond measure, even remembering brings relief.[24]

This confirms a major theme of her second letter, which Father Muckle found so shocking in a holy nun that the sentiments could hardly be authentic.[25] Some have defended her by denying she ever said them; others have claimed that she was later converted, that they represent an interim stage while she was still struggling to find a vocation based on God's calling and not just on Abelard's. Some conversion we must believe took place.[26] The successful foundation of a religious order (albeit a small one), and the deep respect shown by Peter the Venerable, no mean judge of personality—and not a ladies' man—is

[22] Dronke 1976; Luscombe 1980, pp. 21–2, 25–6.

[23] Of the recent contestants, only Silvestre seems to place the *Historia Calamitatum* in the thirteenth century. Indeed, if it is not authentic, it is an astonishing achievement to have discovered by research or intuition so much that is authentic.

[24] Dronke 1976, p. 43; cf. Luscombe 1980, p. 26. Now in Rubingh-Bosscher 1987, p. 127 (ll. 381–4).

[25] Muckle 1953, pp. 62–4, 67.   [26] Luscombe 1980, p. 31.

incompatible with a persistently secular, sensual outlook.[27] Simply to argue that this reveals an unconverted secular woman is to miss all the nuances of the case, and the extraordinary force of Heloise's personality.

My plea has been that judgement, in the end, be made on the basis of large arguments more than on small; and the two most massive seem to me to have been least in evidence in recent debates: the intellectual arguments waged between the protagonists in the letters, and the personalities of Heloise and Abelard which emerge. My view of both will, I hope, become clear in due course. Let me just say here that the deployment of the argument from intention—the heart and core of Abelard's *Ethics*—in her first letter is brilliantly ingenious.[28] It is a debating argument: *he* could not have used it to defend her innocence, for it involved setting him almost in the place of God. It is hard to imagine how it could have arisen save between Abelard and one of his most devoted and ingenious pupils—or in the work of a modern novelist as imbued as Umberto Eco with the byways of medieval thought. By the same token, the power and subtlety of Heloise as she is portrayed—or portrays herself—in the letters is something quite other than the characters in medieval epics or romances.

The central paradox of the early letters is that human love, like the love of God, is eternal. Marriage is not: it may indeed in its very inception be a corruption of love; it cannot survive legal separation or the death of one of the partners. Thus she accepts that their marriage is a thing of the past—but not their love; and since it was that love and the obedience stemming from it which made her a nun, it is an inherent part of her religious life. Yet she still cannot think of him without remembering the sublime delights which had made them one flesh. It was not a

---

[27] See chap. 5, at n. 2.
[28] See p. 112.

paradox which could be exorcized by any simple process of conversion.

Nor yet could it have been invented by Jean de Meung or any other medieval author: least of all by Abelard, who is cut down to size more effectively than ever St Bernard did it. The contrast between the ebullient, self-centred egoist who struts the stage in the *Historia Calamitatum* and the blundering male subjected to Heloise's rapier thrusts in her letters, makes it inconceivable that Abelard wrote them— unless the portrait of the *Historia* gravely misleads; but on the point of his vanity and arrogance we have clear corroborative evidence.[29] I find it hard to conceive of any imaginative writer before the great novelists of the nineteenth century who would have attempted such a character as Heloise. There is much of her in the best seventeenth and eighteenth-century interpretations, especially in Pope's *Eloisa*; but there is much that is missing.[30] Gilson and his Benedictine friend thought the human story too beautiful to be false, and Benton and others have rightly pilloried them for the argument:[31] assuredly a great novelist could have created such a character. I could well imagine Tolstoy or George Eliot making the attempt. But the manuscripts are peremptory: the whole dossier, as we know it, was in existence in the thirteenth century at latest.[32]

On these grounds I believe the letters of Heloise and Abelard in this dossier to represent, in all essentials,[33] an authentic correspondence.

[29] Thus Otto of Freising in Waitz and Von Simon 1912, pp. 68–9, '*tam arrogans . . .*'.

[30] For the cult of Heloise and Abelard in the seventeenth and eighteenth centuries see esp. Charrier 1933 (bibliography on pp. 613–16); see also McLeod 1971.

[31] Gilson 1960, pp. xii–xiii; Benton 1975, pp. 471–2.

[32] Very recently, Helen Laurie has argued (Laurie 1986) that the correspondence was known to Chrétien of Troyes. Some of the parallels are striking, but I am not convinced they establish a knowledge of the text: however, there is evidence here to throw doubt on the confident assumption hitherto held that the letters were not known at all in the twelfth century.

[33] The precise extent of revision which may have taken place—if such can be established—must await Luscombe's edition for OMT.

5

THE MARRIAGE OF
HELOISE AND ABELARD[1]

Heloise

A few months after the death of Peter Abelard in 1142, Peter the Venerable, the courtly and charming abbot of Cluny, wrote to Heloise abbess of the house of the Paraclete, and formerly Abelard's mistress and wife, a long letter of friendship and comfort. The first part of the letter warmly commends Heloise and her community; he likens the abbess to Penthesilea queen of the Amazons and to the prophetess Deborah. Next he describes the last months and edifying end of Abelard, as a monk of Cluny. Finally, an eloquent word of sympathy and understanding. 'God fosters him, my venerable dear sister in the Lord—him to whom you have been attached, first in carnal union, then in the stronger, higher bond of divine love; under whom you have long served the Lord—God fosters him, I say, in your place, as your other self, in his bosom; and keeps him to be restored to you, by his grace, at God's trumpet call . . .'.[2] It was a very special occasion: even the kindly, diplomatic Abbot Peter was not greatly given to scattering compliments to abbesses, and no one but Heloise could have extracted from an

---

[1] This chapter is a revised and extended version of Brooke 1987, pp. 457–66. The story has been told a thousand times: I am particularly indebted to Gilson 1960, Southern 1970, chap. 6. There is an exceedingly sensitive study of Heloise as an author in Dronke 1984, pp. 107–39, published after this chapter was drafted. See also Dronke 1980.

[2] Constable 1967, i. 303–8, esp. 307–8, no. 115.

austere churchman of the early twelfth century so lofty and inspiring a view of the marriage bond.

The secular society of Europe was feudal and military; its interests and activities, outside the boudoir, were male; and although Penthesilea queen of the Amazons was doubtless a familiar figure in that society, it was firmly patriarchal. The spiritual and intellectual world, furthermore, was inclined more and more to study and to take literally what St Paul had said, and although some of it could be interpreted in two ways, none can doubt that he (a confirmed bachelor) thought men the senior partners in marriage.[3] An intelligent woman born in the late eleventh century might well think that inspiring claim in the Epistle to the Ephesians that the union of husband and wife was the image of that of Christ and his Church was an idle mockery; for marriage as she knew it was compounded of four temporal notions, in whose company a Christian sacrament must feel ill at ease. One tradition ancient in European society claimed carnal union as the essence of marriage; another, canonized by ancient Roman law, made a stated consent the heart of the institute; another made mock of this consent by the assumption that a girl was always in her father's gift; the fourth, increasingly powerful in this age, made marriage the key to the passage of estates and kingdoms. It can have been little compensation to Matilda, daughter of Henry I of England, that the fate of the greatest kingdoms in Europe turned on her marriages, for she was a tiny child when the first was arranged, and even though she was an empress at the time of the second, she had no more freedom of choice than at the first.[4]

---

[3] See Col. 3: 18; cf. Eph. 5: 22–3.

[4] For her first marriage, see Orderic vi. 166–9 and notes; Leyser 1960, esp. pp. 62–70; for her second, William of Malmesbury, *Historia Novella* (ed. K. Potter, NMT, 1955), pp. 3–5.

There has never perhaps been a time in the Church's history between the chaos of the first century reflected in 1 Corinthians and the chaos of the twentieth, when marriage law and custom was in such disarray as in the childhood of Heloise; and such a situation was perhaps well suited to the forming of new ideas. Heloise was a child of the cathedral close at Paris (whoever her father and mother may have been), and she was brought up there by her uncle, Canon Fulbert.[5] She was also quite exceptionally well educated for a lady of her day, even before she was set to her lessons under Abelard. Three aspects of the relations between men and women must have been particularly well known to her: first the union of the cathedral close, of canons and concubines, socially accepted though condemned by the Church's law—a union which must commonly have been a well established type of matrimony, but also freely terminable; second, she was aware that celibacy was the Church's law for canons, and for all clergy in the orders of subdeacon and above— and in practice necessary for any cleric ambitious to be admired as well as promoted beyond a canonry;[6] and thirdly she knew that in current theology marriage was coming increasingly to be spoken of as a sacrament, as a union blessed by God and the Church, specially countenanced and blessed by Jesus's presence at the marriage feast at Cana in Galilee.

The outline of her story is well known.[7] As a girl in her teens she had already won a reputation for learning unusual in a woman; and Abelard, who had also ascertained (in his own curious phrase) that 'she was not ill-endowed with looks', determined to seduce her. Such was his reputation for chastity that Fulbert had no

[5] See above, Chap. 3 n. 81, and below.
[6] See below, n. 9; Brooke 1971, pp. 74–5 n.
[7] What follows is mostly based on Abelard's *Historia Calamitatum*, Monfrin 1962, pp. 71–82, 100–1; Radice 1974, pp. 66–7, 96–8, and the sources discussed in Dronke 1976.

hesitation in accepting Abelard as a lodger and her tutor. In due course the hours of teaching gave cover to love-making; he became so preoccupied with her that his lectures in the schools languished; he could devise no new ideas but only songs in her honour. Eventually even Uncle Fulbert learned what was going on and Abelard had to flee the house. But presently Heloise wrote to him in great delight that she was pregnant, and asked him what she should do. His answer was to steal her away by night, and take her to his sister's home, where their son Astralabe was born. Abelard then proposed to marry her; but she at first refused—and in their correspondence Abelard tells us, and she confirms, the powerful arguments she mounted from St Paul, St Jerome, and their own wide reading to dissuade him from the fatal step. It would hinder his intellectual life and prevent ecclesiastical preferment. Bad enough for learning and its paraphernalia to get entangled with maidservants, distaffs, and spindles; worse still for a philosopher to be disturbed by the babble of children and the commotion of nurses and infants; worst of all for a clerk and a canon to set carnal pleasures before the divine office. It was not, needless to say, that Heloise wished to be rid of him; on the contrary, it was the measure of her total surrender to his true interest that made her prefer to be his strumpet (*meretrix* is her own word)[8] to being his wife. Abelard had by now learned enough of her own quality from this extraordinary woman to override her objections; and the couple were married, in church, in the presence of a priest. The marriage was quite illegal, since he was a canon and probably (though we cannot be certain) in higher orders; but as the law then stood it was valid and unbreakable, save only by death or by one of the current forms of

---

[8] Muckle 1953, p. 71; for the rest of this passage see Monfrin 1962, pp. 75–8, 70–4. Heloise tries out the words *amica, concubina, scortum,* and *meretrix*—Abelard confines himself to *amica*.

annulment that the legal system of the Church reckoned it had to devise to dissolve unions which God had clearly not blessed.[9] There is a special piquancy about this marriage. Heloise argued that it was respectable for a canon and a teacher to have a concubine—impossible to have a wife; and Abelard seems to have overborne her out of a romantic and pious vision of the sacrament which bound them. But very soon after, the pope—conceivably in knowledge of this case; more probably not—closed the loop-hole, and made the marriage of a cleric invalid as well as illegal.

Fulbert was not appeased, and while the marriage was still officially a secret, and Heloise in hiding among the nuns of Argenteuil, he supposed that her husband was disposing of her for good, and so a group from his family circle conspired to have Abelard castrated. Abelard felt this as a divine judgement, and in the reaction which followed he insisted that their union be dissolved spiritually as well as carnally, by both partners entering religion. Many years later, Abelard recalled the moment when Heloise took the veil.

> And she, as I recall, when many full of sympathy for her youth were vainly endeavouring to deter her from submission to the monastic Rule as though it were an unbearable punishment—she, I say, breaking out as best she could amid her tears into Cornelia's famous lament [to her husband Pompey after his defeat, as recorded by the poet Lucan], cried aloud: 'O most renowned of husbands!—so undeserved a victim of my

---

[9] For the legal issue see above, p. 105, and Brooke 1971, pp. 74–5 n.; Brooke 1980, pp. 341–2 and n. 21. Gilson imagined on flimsy grounds that Abelard was not in major orders (Gilson 1960, pp. 9 ff.) but he accepted that he was a canon, and canons were forbidden by current canon law to marry, whatever their orders. Much of Gilson's discussion seems to me, however, irrelevant: Heloise clearly perceived and argued (Muckle 1953, p. 71; Radice 1974, pp. 113–14) that it was perfectly respectable for a canon to have a concubine—a wife was another matter.

marriage! Had fortune, then, power thus far over such a one as thee? Why did I marry so impiously, only to make him unhappy? Accept from me the penalty which I pay of my free choice.' And with these words she hastened to the altar, and took from it the veil blessed by the bishop, and before all bound herself with the monastic vows.[10]

Many commentators have raised their hands in horror at this pagan vocation; for myself, for reasons which we shall presently consider, I think it is rather an assertion that her will was wholly subject to Abelard's—as on current reading of Ephesians 5: 22–3 a wife's should be— and so that she was called, not directly by God, but by him.

However this may be, she proved a very successful nun, and Abelard, at first, a very unsuccessful monk. She took the veil at Argenteuil *c.*1117, he at the great abbey of Saint-Denis, just outside Paris.[11] Presently she rose to be prioress of the community at Argenteuil; and when the community was dispersed owing to a lawsuit, Abelard established her in the oratory of the Paraclete, the Holy Ghost the Comforter, near Troyes, where he had been for a time himself a hermit; and there she remained until her death in 1163–4, abbess of a growing community which came to be the centre of a small Order; from the start respected by her neighbours and by the great figures of the contemporary monastic world, especially by Peter the Venerable of Cluny and even St Bernard of Clairvaux himself, notorious for his persecution of her husband.[12]

---

[10] Monfrin 1962, p. 81; the translation is by David Knowles (Knowles 1963, p. 23) slightly adapted; in Radice 1974, pp. 76–7; the quotation is from Lucan, *Pharsalia*, viii. 94–8 (I owe help from Professor Charles Brink in the interpretation of *indigne*: see *Oxford Latin Dictionary*, fasc. iv, ed. P. G. W. Glare, Oxford, 1973, p. 884, s.v. indignus 5b.) Cf. Von Moos 1975.

[11] For the date, see Bautier 1981, p. 56 n. 1.

[12] On her relations with Bernard, see McLeod 1971, pp. 126–8, 272–4. For Heloise's death (16 May 1163 or 1164), see McLeod 1971, pp. 225, 287–9. For the

Abelard meanwhile had quarrelled with the monks of Saint-Denis, and after the interlude when he presided over a hermit school at the Paraclete, he wandered again, and returned with Heloise to the Paraclete; then, as his presence at her side threatened scandal, he fled to Brittany to take up the abbacy of Saint-Gildas, whose monks (so he alleges) presently tried to poison him. Once again he wandered, returned to Paris to teach; suffered his last condemnation (inspired by St Bernard) at the Council of Sens and the papal Curia in 1140–1, and retired to Cluny, to spend his last months under the sympathetic and kindly guidance of Peter the Venerable. After a dramatic reconciliation with Bernard of the kind both Bernard and Peter loved, Abelard was left to die in peace, and somewhat later Peter the Venerable himself travelled to the Paraclete so that the abbey and its abbess might have the body of their founder and her husband buried in their midst.

Abelard was immensely gifted, an immortal teacher and the towering intellectual figure of his age. He was restless, unquiet, disturbing, as many great teachers are; and he was exceedingly self-centred and arrogant. He collected enemies with the abandon of a philatelist. Early in the 1130s he wrote a letter to a clerk who needed comfort: my calamities, he said, are far worse than yours; drown your sorrows in mine. And he listed his own many persecutions, by his early teachers because he pointed out their errors, by Fulbert for his love of Heloise, by the authorities of the Church for his supposed heresy, by the monks of Saint-Denis, the neighbours of his hermitage, the monks of Saint-Gildas—and finally by those who envied his relations with the Paraclete and its abbess. So

earlier chronology, see Van der Eynde 1963, and confirmation and revision in Bautier 1981, esp. pp. 55–7 and 56 n. 1. Attempts to revise it e.g. in Benton 1975 do not seem to have succeeded, but there are problems which can only be sorted out when Luscombe's edition of the correspondence has been completed.

powerful are the woes of Abelard that many who read the *Historia Calamitatum* are inclined to doubt if the poor clerk who is supposed to be receiving consolation really existed; certain it is that the letter was not written for the eyes of Heloise. For it describes the affair in some detail, yet as if it were something past and distant, confessed and shriven. 'There was in the city of Paris a girl called Heloise, niece of a canon named Fulbert; her uncle doted on her and on that account sought every means to improve her learning. She was not ill-endowed with looks, but supremely well-endowed in letters.'[13] He then tells the story we have been following, culminating in their marriage. There is a curious edge to the story in the care this highly unconventional couple took to ensure as much obedience to the law as was open to them. They were married; clandestinely, as I have said, illegally, but validly. The tragedy of Abelard's castration and sudden flight from the world rapidly followed. Thus Heloise came to make her profession as a nun, not through any vocation, but at his command; and even under the veil his efforts to help and guide her were prevented by gossip and scandal.

Heloise and Abelard in their Letters

The *Historia Calamitatum* seems scarcely designed for the eyes of Heloise, but Abelard must have been very naïve if he supposed she would not read it. In the opening of *Mansfield Park* Jane Austen explains how all intercourse between Mrs Price and her sisters came to an end because she wrote a letter which 'bestowed such very disrespectful

[13] Monfrin 1962, p. 71; this and the quotations which follow are my own translation (cf. Radice 1974, p. 66). This is the only precise evidence about Heloise's family—there is no basis for conjectures that Fulbert was her father, although it is not impossible (see p. 90 and n. 81).

reflections on the pride of Sir Thomas as Mrs Norris could not possibly keep to herself'. By the same token someone—'*quidam*' says Heloise[14]—felt he must show it to her. It greatly distressed her; but also gave her the opportunity to make new demands on her former husband.

In her first letter Heloise gave three reasons why Abelard was bound to write the letters she asked for, and give her community the advice she sought. First, because he was its founder; and then 'Know that you are all the more deeply in my debt, as you are the more fully tied by the bond of the nuptial sacrament, and *more* indebted to me in that I have always encompassed you, as is known to all, with a love beyond measure.'[15] She then proceeded to unfold how selfless, how complete, how sacrificial, her love for him was. She had asked nothing from him but himself—she never looked for marriage or dowry, only for him. 'If the name of wife seems holier and stronger, sweeter ever to me was the name of mistress, or if you can bear it, concubine or whore.'[16] She is expounding the viewpoint of a lady of the cathedral close, as well as the paradox so brilliantly paraphrased by Pope:

> Should at my feet the world's great master fall,
> Himself, his throne, his world, I'd scorn them all;
> Not Caesar's empress would I deign to prove;
> No, make me mistress to the man I love;
> If there be yet another word more free,
> More fond than mistress, make me that to thee![17]

There is a kind of social comment here—astonishingly modern in some respects—utterly remote from our world

---

[14] For some curious textual evidence—including the observation that four MSS read '*quidem*'—see Dronke 1976, pp. 33–4 n. 18.

[15] Muckle 1953, p. 70 (Radice 1974, pp. 112–13).

[16] Muckle 1953, p. 71 (Radice 1974, p. 113). For the words she uses, see n. 8.

[17] Pope, *Eloisa to Abelard*, 85–90.

in others, anyway to someone like myself descended from many generations of married clergy. The clerical concubine was socially respectable, however virulent the thunder of reformers against her. Marriage implied take as well as give; a contract; the word sacrament in this context echoed the idea of an oath or vows; all these things weakened the utter selflessness of giving as Heloise had known it. 'I call God to witness that if Augustus, the emperor who rules over the whole world, deemed me worthy of the honour of marriage and confirmed to me the whole world as a possession for ever, dearer to me and worthier would it seem to be called your whore than his empress.'[18] Strong words from a highly respectable abbess.

She goes on: 'A woman who prefers a rich to a poor husband, or who yearns for his goods rather than himself, may not reckon herself other than corrupt [*venalem*]'— this sort of marriage is for money and is a kind of prostitution. And so she develops a dazzling argument that her love for him was pure: 'I have been wholly astray—wholly innocent too, as you know. For crime consists, not in the outcome of the deed, but in the mind and attitude of the doer; and justice weighs, not what is done, but the spirit in which it is done.'[19] And he knows what that was.

We can see the glint in her eye as she reminds him of one of his own most famous arguments—the doctrine of intention which was the basis of his *Scito Teipsum*, his *Ethics*.[20] Undoubtedly she is enjoying an argument with him—she was not one of his most brilliant pupils for nothing. Clearly too the letter is a work of great literary art. Nor does the literary effect make it any less a real letter: he was not only her former lover and husband, he

18 Muckle 1953, p. 71 (Radice 1974, pp. 112–13).
19 Muckle 1953, pp. 71–2 (Radice 1974, pp. 114–15).
20 Luscombe 1971.

was her teacher, the great master of logic and rhetoric; she was seizing a supreme opportunity—only the best would do. This is indeed a crucial moment in the first letter, for she is leading him by flattery and self-abasement to see how supreme was *her* self-sacrifice: while as for *him*—it was lust not love that brought him to her, for as soon as he had lost the lure of the marriage bed he began to neglect her. 'How much more righteous now to rouse me to God's service than then to our lusts?'[21]

Abelard's reply is a feeble thing; it seems very likely that he failed to grasp her urgent need for comfort, and that he was embarrassed by her efforts to shock him. In his own first letter he had told his clerkly friend how exemplary a nun and superior Heloise had proved—loved by bishops, abbots, and layfolk as well as by her sisters, retreating ever further from the world, and ever more sought out. So she does not need his help—rather it is he who needs her own and her community's prayers; and he produces a number of edifying cases of wives who helped their husbands. Occasional words of comfort break through, but Abelard was too deep in his own anxieties to give much attention to hers. 'But if the Lord gives me into the hands of my enemies, so that they prevail over me and kill me—or by whatever fate I arrive at the way of all flesh while separated from you, . . . I beg you to have my body carried to your cemetery . . .'.[22]

The abbess's reply is justly celebrated as the masterpiece of the collection; a bitter, heart-rending lament, one of the most moving passages in twelfth-century literature. The very idea of his death had filled her with intense wretchedness, and set in sharper relief the unhappiness and injustice of the world—unhappiness, since she could be lowered from such heights of bliss to such despair, and injustice, since divine vengeance spared them while they

[21] Muckle 1953, p. 73 (Radice 1974, p. 118).
[22] Muckle 1953, p. 76 (Radice 1974, p. 125).

enjoyed the delights of love—'to use a baser, but plainer word, revelled in fornication'—but when they were honourably married, it fell on them unjustly. Oh, the misery of being the cause of such a crime; and a misery from which there was no respite or consolation, for while Abelard could no longer feel the lure to the marriage-bed, Heloise was as she had ever been. How could she expect forgiveness, since she still delighted in her sin?

> So delectable were the lovers' joys which we sought together, that they still cannot seem displeasing to me, nor can I yet forget them. Whichever way I turn, I always see them calling to me, luring me. They do not even spare my dreams at night. Even in the celebration of Mass, when prayer should be wholly pure, the obscene phantoms of those pleasures thus utterly encompass my wretched soul, that my time is spent more in such wicked thoughts than in prayer. It is not only the actions, but places and times when we enjoyed each other are so instilled in my mind's eye that I go over them again and again even in my sleep. O I am wretched indeed, and truly that plaint of a soul in torment is mine: 'Unhappy that I am—who will free me from the body of this death?'[23]

The consequence of sin and the presence of Hell were very close, especially to a highly intelligent lady who was deeply read in the ascetic literature of her own and previous ages, and knew, or thought she knew, in at least a part of her mind, that women were the weaker sex and their salvation particularly precarious. 'I seek no crown of victory: it is enough for me if I can escape from peril. Safer to flee from peril than to join battle; in whatever corner of heaven God may place me, that is sufficient . . .'.[24]

---

[23] Muckle 1953, pp. 79–81 (Radice 1974, pp. 130–3).
[24] Muckle 1953, p. 82 (Radice 1974, pp. 135–6).

Most of Abelard's response makes to a modern reader fairly disagreeable reading. He tried to answer her arguments and in his turn shock her out of her line of thought. But in the end he rose to the occasion. Heloise in her first letter had argued that it was her love that was selfless—marriage could be just a legalized corruption, could not add to the purity of her motive. Abelard now responds: it was precisely because they were married that God revealed to them the true path to the holier life they were now leading—he had made their marriage an instrument of their salvation. But he goes beyond this and expounds something like a doctrine of marriage—marking it as a holy union. Christ is a better groom than I. I have suffered, truly; but for my lust, not for you; he suffered for our sins. 'We are one in Christ; one flesh by the law of marriage. Whatever is your possession I reckon no whit alien to me. But your possession now is Christ, since you have become his bride. Now you . . . have me for servant whom before you knew as lord, more closely bound to you by spiritual love than before you were bound to me in fear.' And so he has ground for hope for them both, which he sets in a finely worded prayer. 'God, who from the beginning of man's creation, formed woman from the rib of man, who has sanctified the mighty sacrament of the union of marriage, and has held it up on high by doing it tremendous honour, first in being born of a woman espoused, then by honouring a marriage by the first of your miracles, and who once of your goodness gave this cure to the weakness of my incontinence, despise not the prayers of your handmaid!'[25]

---

[25] Muckle 1953, p. 93 (Radice 1974, pp. 154–5): 'in being born of a woman espoused' renders '*de desponsata nascendo*'—but '*desponsata*' cannot be rendered adequately in modern English, for it combines the notions of engagement, betrothal, and marriage: see pp. 137–8.

5. Heloise and Abelard: Marriage

Their Religious Life

The rest of the correspondence tells us nothing more directly about their marriage. Indirectly, it is very revealing about their relations. For Heloise sets Abelard to work to give her useful advice about the example of holy women from the past, and to provide a Rule for her community; but being a strong-minded woman with a clear view of her own, she takes the precaution of telling him with some vigour what to say—and he duly obeyed her at inordinate length. But he did not always understand what was in her mind—nor did she always foresee the more conventional stand she would adopt as she grew older. Hence (I am convinced) the discrepancies between his Rule and hers. At the conscious level she regarded Abelard still as her god, as the great monk-theologian, and it was natural for her to ask for his instructions. She also enjoyed dialectical discussion with him, as she obviously had done in earlier days. Intuitively, she can hardly have been unaware that she knew more about the monastic life than he did, and in particular had far better notions of how to look after sisters and daughters in religion, and was a great deal the more practical of the two. For all these reasons, we may conjecture, she took the precaution of telling him what to say in his Rule.

The essence of the matter is that she wanted him to make up for the deficiencies of the Rule of St Benedict, which was written for men and took no account of women's special needs in clothing and so forth, nor of their physical weakness: Who lays such burdens upon an ass as he deems fitted for an elephant?—she asks.[26] Her demands are mostly for a retired life—free from the inconvenience of having to entertain men, who were

---

[26] Muckle 1955, p. 243 (Radice 1974, p. 162).

dangerous company, and gossipy women of the world, who were worse—austere and practical.[27] She had her eccentricities, as we should expect, but all very rationally explained. St Benedict, though a very holy man and spiritual adviser, was occasionally silly; thus he refused to allow meat although every one knows that fish is often more luxurious and expensive than meat, and allowed wine which is dangerous stuff ('wine and women make the wise to fall away', Ecclus. 19: 2) even if women can hold their wine better than men.[28]

Abelard dutifully did what he was told, dug out all he could from the New Testament and the early fathers about the devout life of widows and nuns, and lots of good commendable references to holy women; then he finally provided her, at great length, with a Rule. It is fascinating to observe the way in which he picked up every hint in her letter and solemnly carried her own arguments to their logical conclusion—occasionally misinterpreting wishes not fully expressed. Abelard, in one of his own comparatively rare contributions, prescribes that the abbess or deaconess (as he calls the head of the community, following Heloise's description of herself) shall always be under male control and not leave the community to do business.[29] He probably thought this would be congenial to her, and in any case much of the rule is evidently designed to make sense in later times, when Heloise and he had departed; and thus he prescribed a rule similar to that at Marcigny.[30] Following her own use of 1 Timothy, he instructs that widows should not become deaconesses till they are old, even though Heloise herself is generally reckoned to have been

[27] Muckle 1955, pp. 242–3 (Radice 1974, pp. 160–1).

[28] Muckle 1955, pp. 245–53 (Radice 1974, pp. 165–79, esp. 168–9).

[29] Muckle 1953, p. 77; McLaughlin 1956, pp. 258–9 (Radice 1974, pp. 127, 210–12; cf. McLaughlin 1956, pp. 252–8, Radice 1974, pp. 199–210 on the abbess).

[30] Wollasch 1971, esp. pp. 165–6; Hunt 1967, pp. 186–94.

under 35 at the time![31] Heloise was undoubtedly a very masterful woman, and she is not the only wife in history to have ruled over a man she promised to obey. Peter the Venerable likened her to the Queen of the Amazons, and to Deborah.[32] Abelard she would obey, in her own way, to the end; but it was not in her nature to place herself at the disposal of any other man. Heloise survived this period of anguish, survived Abelard's death in 1142, to die herself many years later, in 1163 or 1164, a widow of sixty or more and an abbess of unblemished reputation. It is not at all surprising that this respected abbess should grow a little more conventional, and a little more respectful to St Benedict, as the years advanced.

Thus she remained both wife and abbess, subjecting herself and her sisters to a severe discipline; whether she achieved any measure of serenity is quite unknown. Her distress elicited from them both a doctrine of marriage of the deepest interest, and to this we shall return.[33] All that we can be sure is that she hoped and worked to avoid peril, so that she might find reconciliation in heaven in the end. And one cannot but think that a single sentence from Peter the Venerable was worth to her all the eloquence and learning of Abelard in her search. 'God fosters him, my venerable dear sister in the Lord—him to whom you have been attached, first in carnal union, then in the stronger, higher bond of divine love; under whom you have long served the Lord—God fosters him, I say, in your place, as your other self, in his bosom; and keeps him to be restored to you, by his grace, at God's trumpet call . . .'.[34]

---

[31] McLaughlin 1956, p. 252 (Radice, p. 199), quoting 1 Tim. 5: 9–11.
[32] See n. 2. For what follows, see McLeod 1971, esp. pp. 225, 287–9 for Heloise's death.
[33] See pp. 259–64.
[34] See n. 2.

6

MARRIAGE IN LAW AND PRACTICE[1]

Marriage, Kingdoms, and Estates

Studies of the medieval aristocracy used to be dominated by an endless semantic debate on two concepts: on feudalism and on nobility. The concept of feudalism has spread a thick mist over many areas of medieval law and society, and it is the constant aim of scholars who really wish to understand medieval institutions to escape it, and to search for more intelligible regions of experience to explore. The discussion of nobility—of what it comprised, of how it was transmitted, of inheritance, of primogeniture, of chivalry, of snobbery as it was understood by medieval knights themselves—has been the subject of a rich literature, especially on the Continent.[2] But in the view of numerous social historians these approaches have been replaced, in the forefront of their studies, by enquiry into marriage and the family, and family structure, fields of study at once more appealing and more intelligible than 'feudalism'.

They have been particularly illuminated in two recent books by Georges Duby, *Medieval Marriage* and *Le*

[1] An abbreviated version of this chapter appeared in Brooke 1987, pp. 444–57. Brundage 1987 came to hand only in the final revision: it is a rich mine of valuable information and insight on the church's teaching on sexual practices and on many aspects of marriage law.

[2] Brilliantly distilled in Reuter 1978. See also Holt 1982–5, esp. 1982, pp. 199–200 and n. 23 for studies of the shift from clan to lineage. This is a highly contentious subject, which I avoid, since the lineage (on any showing) was well established by the eleventh century; but it is, as many historians have emphasized, an important part of the process whereby the aristocracy came to accept and to favour the kind of inheritance we are considering here.

6. Marriage in Law and Practice

Chevalier, la femme et le prêtre—The Knight, the Lady, and the Priest.[3] They bid fair to be among the most influential works of one of the greatest of living social and economic historians, and to canonize for a generation many students' attitude to their theme. I start with a text from Duby's later book. He observes 'that all the witnesses' to marriage in the early and central Middle Ages 'are ecclesiastics. They are men, males'. There is only one reference in the book I can find to Heloise.[4] These references underline the difference between his approach and mine. It is easy to pick holes in a book of this kind, and my purpose is not at all to engage in polemic. With all its faults it is an enchanting book, full of rich and brilliantly presented evidence; and I shall myself return again and again to the delectable passages in which he invokes St Arnoul, patron saint of worried wives, and St Godelive, the living hope of the deserted ones.[5] The errors are not such as to vitiate most of the marvellous canvas which he paints of the many facets of medieval marriage.

One fundamental element in the books—explicitly and lucidly expounded in *Medieval Marriage*, implicit in the more elusive and *nuancé* book which followed—is the doctrine of the two models, or sets of attitudes to marriage: that of the French kings of the eleventh and twelfth centuries, and that of the clergy of the early medieval church. The kings sought marriage above all to provide themselves with male heirs and for personal satisfaction; if the wife was unsatisfactory she was changed. He could in fact have gone even further than he did—Robert sometimes called the Pious (996–1031) had two divorces, and every king from Philip I (1060–1108) to Philip II (1180–1223) had one at least.[6]

---

[3] Duby 1978, 1983–4.   [4] Duby 1983–4, pp. 20, 158.
[5] Duby 1983–4, pp. 127–35.
[6] What follows is a revised version of the fascinating account in Duby, 1978 and Duby 1983–4, chaps. 1, 4, 10, from a rather different point of view. The

What is not so clear are the motives in some of these cases: there seems to be an extraordinary tangle of personal and political grounds for changing wives; and popes and bishops were often at loggerheads as to the extent and nature of the breach of canon law involved. Robert the Pious married first an Italian princess, Rozala or Susanna, widow of the count of Flanders—and presently repudiated her, on what ground we do not know; it was alleged that she was too old for him, and that he was nineteen at the time.[7] His second wife was Bertha daughter of the king of Burgundy and countess of Blois, a lady in whose veins flowed Carolingian blood. This marriage seems to have aroused the anxiety of the Emperor Otto III, who perhaps feared a French claim to the kingdom of Burgundy, and it seems likely that he encouraged the pope in his strenuous efforts to annul the marriage on the ground that Robert and Bertha were second cousins—and Robert godfather of one of her sons; perhaps too because Robert was already married—although the archbishop of Tours had blessed the new marriage.[8] Robert paid little or no attention to the ban until about 1004. By then his first wife had died and he was doubtless troubled that Bertha had born him no children: like Henry VIII of England he was the second king of a new dynasty and a flow of male heirs was his first duty. So he repudiated Bertha and married Constance of Arles, cousin of the count of Anjou. From then on till

details are often obscure, and I frequently differ from Duby; but more often I accept his account wholeheartedly and the story bears repetition. The wives and children of the Capetian kings are conveniently laid out in Mas Latrie 1889, cols. 1521–2. I have tried to check all the details of marriages given below in the sources, since there is much divergence in some modern accounts.

[7] Richer, iv. 87 in Latouche 1930–7, ii. 286–9 and notes; cf. Pfister 1885, pp. 43–6. She died in 1003. For Robert's marriages see also Dhondt 1964–5.

[8] Pfister 1885, pp. 47–60 (for the archbishop's blessing, p. 51); Duby 1978, chap. 2; Duby 1983–4, pp. 45–54, 124–7, esp. p. 49 n. for the relationship of Robert and Bertha; Lot 1903, esp. pp. 107–8, 127 and n., 147; Lot 1891, pp. 358–69; Hallam 1980, pp. 71–2.

6. Marriage in Law and Practice

Bertha's death a curious *régime à trois* subsisted. Robert was the prey to faction, and when Blois was in the ascendant, Bertha returned; when Anjou, then Constance resumed her sway.[9] Bertha seems to have been the more congenial companion, for Constance was extremely quarrelsome and masterful—this at least seems well attested—but Constance was a plentiful source of children. For all their difficulties they reared five children, including four sons.[10] At the end of his life Robert, poor man, repented of his wives and won a belated reputation for piety. Small wonder that the son who eventually succeeded him, Henry I (1031–60), after losing his first wife, sought a wife in whose union no pope could find any possible ground or suspicion of incest: to whit a Russian princess, Anna of Kiev. They had three sons and Henry was content.[11] But when the eldest, Philip I, was on the throne, it all started up again. By his first wife, Bertha of Holland, he had Louis VI and three other children—but Louis was the only boy to grow up and the succession must have seemed precarious. He was also attracted by Bertrada, wife of the count of Anjou, and married her. Once again he found an archbishop and a notable gathering of bishops ready to bless his wedding.[12] But the great canonist Bishop Ivo of Chartres, a man of dauntless integrity, fervently objected: both partners had living spouses and the marriage was adulterous; Philip and Bertrada were distantly related, and the marriage was incestuous.[13] The charge of adultery was complicated by

[9] Pfister 1885, pp. 61–9; Hallam 1980, pp. 71–2; Duby 1985, pp. 80–5.

[10] Pfister 1885, pp. 70–84, correcting Mas Latrie 1889, col. 1521. Constance survived him, and the impression that he finally wearied of her may not be well founded.

[11] See n. 10. Henry's first wife was Matilda niece of the Emperor Henry III (Dhondt 1964–5, pp. 53–60); he had previously been betrothed to another Matilda, daughter of Conrad II (Dhondt loc. cit.).

[12] For what follows, see Fliche 1912, chap. 2; Duby, 1983–4, chap. 1; corrected by Moule 1983, pp. 32–47; Ivo, *Epp.* 13–15, 23, 211. On Ivo and marriage, see also Labonté 1965. [13] Ivo, *Ep.* 211 laid out the details of their relationship.

the question of whether Bertrada was in any sense married to Fulk, who had two wives living—and went away when Bertha died in 1094.[14] Ivo remained deeply concerned about the charge of incest and for a time won the ear of Pope Paschal II, who made the couple do penance. But they continued to live together, reared three children at least, and in the end won some measure of recognition even from the pope.

After these adventures what follows must be anticlimax. But the divorces went on. Louis VI quickly repudiated the first girl to whom he was betrothed—though we have no reason to suppose it was a mere engagement; and won a reputation for irregularity of life.[15] In 1115 Bishop Ivo, at the very end of his life, urged Louis to marry Adelaide of Maurienne;[16] and Louis may well have felt that a testimonial from Ivo made all safe: he complied, and they reared a family of six sons and one daughter at least. Louis VII was married at about seventeen to Eleanor heiress of Aquitaine, and fifteen years later their marriage was annulled on the usual ground that they were related: they were reckoned to be third cousins once removed. Eleanor then instantly married Henry II of England, by the same token reckoned her fourth cousin.[17] If the rules of consanguinity had been

---

[14] Bautier and Gilles 1979, p. 136; Fliche 1912, pp. 40 and n. 6, 547. Orderic, vi. 54–5, tells the story of Bertrada's attempts to poison her stepson Louis VI.

[15] For this marriage, arranged in 1104 and dissolved in 1107, see Luchaire 1890, nos. 32, 50, pp. 20, 27. Suger in Waquet 1929, pp. 40–1 (cf. pp. 42–3) states that Louis married her—*'matrimonio solempni reciperet'*; Orderic, vi. 156–7, says *'desponsauit'*; and although Suger indicates she was too young for the marriage to be consummated, and Orderic also indicates she remained a virgin, the grounds for annulment were consanguinity, not any informality in the vows (Suger in Waquet 1929, pp. 40–1; cf. the Chronicle of Saint-Pierre-le-Vif in Bautier and Gilles 1979, p. 146). The Chronicle of Saint-Pierre describes a dissolution authorized by Pope Paschal II, *'quia dignitati regię indecens erat et consulibus regni displicebat'*. Orderic (vi. 156–7) simply says Louis gave her to Guichard of Beaujeu—*donauerat*.

[16] Ivo, *Ep.* 239; Luchaire 1890, no. 187, pp. 94–5; cf. p. 97; Previté-Orton 1912, p. 281 and n. 3.

[17] See the table in Warren 1973, p. 43; cf. ibid., pp. 42–4; Vacandard 1890, p. 417, calls it *'peu certaine'*. Louis VII was probably born in 1120; Luchaire 1890

strictly applied, the bar to her marriage to Louis applied equally to Henry—though doubtless the facts were not fully known or calculated at the time. In any case Pope Eugenius III had made a serious attempt to reconcile Eleanor and Louis a few years before, of which we have a moving account from the pen of John of Salisbury.[18] Pope Eugenius set more store by marital fidelity than by the remoter forms of incest: the shift in opinion is very marked. But after fifteen years of marriage, two daughters and no son, the tender conscience of Louis VII was stirred, or so we may reasonably suppose. His second wife likewise had two daughters, and then died; and from his third, at last, in 1165, came Philip II—'a son of faith, by God's gift, and an heir to his kingdom, whom he would have asked for if he had been given the choice of anything he might wish to have'.[19] Philip himself had a son, his future successor Louis VIII, by his first wife; repudiated his second, the Danish Ingeborg, after a brief marriage— it was said that he took a dislike to her on the day after their wedding-day.[20] A council of French bishops dissolved the marriage in 1196, but Pope Innocent III (1198–1216) refused to accept the divorce, and after a long dispute and the death of a third wife, Philip restored Ingeborg to her throne.

no. 300, p. 139. The marriage of Louis and Eleanor took place in July 1137 (ibid. no. 589, p. 268; cf. no. 580, p. 264). On this marriage see Duby 1983–4, pp. 190–8.

[18] John of Salisbury, *Historia Pontificalis*, pp. 52–3, 60–2. This curious account, disrespectful to both Louis and Eleanor, was none the less written when she was reigning queen of England and John an exile under the protection of Louis (in or after 1164); it makes no mention of her failure to produce sons—but by 1164 she had born Henry II four—too many, as events were to prove! On Eleanor and Louis VII, see also *HF* xii. 117.

[19] John of Salisbury, *Letters*, ii. 358–9 (no. 215).

[20] Cf. Luchaire 1890, pp. 248–60; Cartellieri 1899–1922, iii. 57–68; iv. 352–4. The beginning and the end of the affair are equally mysterious: see Cheney 1976, p. 343. At the council in 1196 which attempted to annul the marriage— presided over by William aux Blanchesmains, archbishop of Rheims, a man of the highest reputation—evidence was produced (which was later challenged) that they were fourth cousins.

The notorious saga of the French kings has been variously interpreted. First of all, it is clear that many perfectly conscientious French bishops assumed—as Thomas Cranmer was to assume in the 1530s—that royal authority and a king's wishes were not lightly to be set aside. Secondly, the extreme rules of consanguinity established in the eleventh century were at once a marvellous excuse for cynics and a sad burden on tender consciences.[21] But even in societies in which kin and lineage were so central, it baffles the wits of a man to know who his sixth cousins may be; and it seems clear that these abstruse calculations were and could be only applied to the very great. When the twelfth-century popes witnessed a stream of marriage causes flowing into their court, they became acutely aware that the stability of Christian marriage was threatened by the rules of consanguinity; and without condoning incest as they understood it, they doubted if it should be sought in regions too remote. When Pope Innocent disputed with Philip II over Ingeborg, he gave notice to Christendom that the easy divorces of the French kings were to cease. But he could not entirely destroy their causes. In the tangled story we have been contemplating, the details are frequently obscure and the motives confused: political conflict and domestic discord often played a major role. But one theme is evident in the anxieties of most of these kings: the need for male heirs, and plenty of them, to counter the effects of illness and sudden death. An ardent desire for legitimate heirs brought the kings and nobles of Europe themselves to seek monogamy, and a curious alliance of dynastic ambition, nature, and Christian teaching resulted. But nature will not produce an unbroken flow of sons strong and fortunate enough to resist the chances of this fleeting world.

[21] See pp. 134–6.

6. Marriage in Law and Practice

The Ecclesiastical Model

After exploring this French royal secular model Duby proceeds to a summary of the deposit of ecclesiastical lore: that marriage was a second best to virginity; that it was none the less instituted by God to provide for children and as a cure for lust; that men should have only one wife at a time; that the sexual act was only good if there was no pleasure in it—and so forth.[22] No one doubts the French royal dynasty behaved in that way; no one doubts these clerical views were widely and deeply held—and lasted long. Nor is Duby content with his model: there is an abundance of rich evidence presented which shows many of the depths and strange corners in this fascinating and difficult subject. He sees the link between the weighty insistence by St Augustine and his successors that children are the fundamental justification for marriage and the aspirations of his kings. But the basic effect of his two models is to give the impression that the medieval lay nobility and the medieval clergy had doctrines of marriage so fundamentally opposed it is a miracle that they ever agreed on anything. And this is strange, because it was precisely in this period that the lay aristocracy of Europe allowed the Church to take over almost completely the jurisdiction of the law of marriage.[23] This is one of the central facts of medieval social and legal history and it requires a great deal of explaining.

Fundamentally the Church aimed to establish Christian monogamy for life; and the central point of the story seems to be that as the generations passed the lay aristocracies of western Europe, and even their monarchs, came to see a great advantage to themselves in monogamy.

[22] Duby 1983–4, chap. 2; cf. above, chap. 2; and many passages in Brundage 1987.
[23] See below, p. 127; cf. Duby 1983–4, p. 133.

The two laws, of the Church and the kingdoms, sat side by side for centuries; the advance of the Church was not sudden and can hardly be descried. Already in the ninth century an archbishop or a pope might thunder on a matrimonial scandal.[24] But he rarely did. By slow stages the Church became more active, more involved. To point to an exact date when the Church assumed competence in marriage suits is impossible. A good case has been made for the ninth or tenth centuries; but cases rarely came to court before the twelfth. Richard Helmholz goes as far as to say:[25]

> The establishment of the Church's exclusive control over marriage was a long and disputed process. Fixing the date it occurred has exercised scholarly minds.[26] But in my view the effort is wasted: worse, it is misleading. The struggle was not between competing court systems. It was not a question of competition between secular and ecclesiastical jurisdictions. The problem was to ensure that ordinary marriage disputes went to court at all. The real hurdle was the persistent idea that people could regulate marriages for themselves.

Even in the twelfth century, the popes were not in a hurry to legislate for marriage cases or seek them out before the suitors themselves sought the curia. Innocent III at the turn of the twelfth and thirteenth centuries could explain to Philip II of France that he appeared to treat the matrimonial tangles of John of England more leniently than his, only because he did not intervene in cases

---

[24] See G. Picasso in Spoleto 1977, i. 222–6.

[25] Helmholz 1978, p. 5. Helmholz's book is a most valuable study of the England ecclesiastical courts at work: as for twelfth-century papal decretals, so for fourteenth- and fifteenth-century lower courts, English cases are exceptionally well recorded. See also Sheehan 1971.

[26] Helmholz cites Daudet 1941. See also the important study, based on canonical collections, of G. Picasso in Spoleto 1977, i. 191–231, esp. pp. 230–1; and the careful words of G. Fransen, ibid. ii. 626–30. For all that follows Esmein 1929–35 is still useful.

unless they were brought to him; and elsewhere he observed that patience could be exercised if cases were not brought to judgement—a patience which would not be acceptable if they came to court.[27]

For all this we can discern clearly enough that by the middle of the twelfth century it had happened: the lay courts might determine all the details of an inheritance, but the church courts settled first the issue of marriage, its validity and its qualities.[28]

In earlier centuries the Church might influence, or attempt to influence, the practice of the courts, but the law of marriage generally recognized was secular, Roman law. Under the Roman Empire marriage was entered by consent: by mutual consent between the partners, or between their parents, or whoever had *patria potestas*, parental authority, over them. A principal purpose universally recognized was to have legitimate children. But in the words of the great Roman jurist Ulpian: 'It is not consummation [*concubitus*] but consent which makes marriages'—or again 'It is not consummation [*coitus*] but the intent to get married [*maritalis affectio*] which makes a marriage.'[29] The whole history of marriage might be written round these concepts of *consensus* and *maritalis affectio*. For in Roman law they both had a significance which seems remote and formal to us: consent and mutual

[27] Cheney 1976, p. 100 n. 9, quoting Innocent III in *PL* ccxiv. 1015 and *Decretals of Gregory IX*, iii. 5. 18.

[28] As late as 1160 John of Salisbury—or Archbishop Theobald, in whose name he wrote—still found it worth saying in a letter to the pope: 'Since a question of matrimony was involved, and matrimony is annulled or confirmed in accordance with ecclesiastical law, the court of our catholic sovereign Henry II, king of the English, decreed that the case should return for judgement to an ecclesiastical court, where the question of marriage might be duly determined in accordance with canon law, which the clergy know, whereas the common people do not [*clerus nouit, uulgus ignorat*]' (*Letters*, i. 227–8, no. 131; see below, pp. 148–52, for this case).

[29] See above, p. 54; Gaudemet 1980, esp. pp. 338–78: Ulpian is quoted from *Digest* 35. 1. 15, 50. 17. 30, and 24. 1. 32. 13, ibid., p. 344 n. 15. For *maritalis affectio* see esp. Noonan 1967.

giving were often simply matters for the families, in which the partners might have little say; in many cases there was a genuine mutual giving, but the word *consensus* covered both situations. Similarly, *affectio* is a word of very obvious ambiguity: from it springs our own 'affection'—and to us 'married affection' has very different overtones from 'intent to get married' which puts no human emotion into the mind at all, though it does not forbid it. The marriage of convenience and the love-match might equally be covered by these phrases. Notoriously, both types of marriage have flourished in every century of recorded history. But if the language of Roman law survived, its meaning was subtly adapted as the centuries passed. From the ninth century at latest— and doubtless in many minds much earlier—*consent* in the eyes of leading churchmen came to mean consent by the partners themselves; and *maritalis affectio*, by slow and delicate stages, was given an aura of sentiment and feeling, even of romance, by the celibate canonists who modified the ancient doctrines of the married Roman jurists.[30]

No responsible lawyer or theologian ever supposed that consent or *affectio* made a marriage in any profound sense. If its main purpose was to have children, consummation must count for as much as the mutual consent, the mutual giving, the exchange of promises or oaths, which were covered by the term *consensus*. A tradition which owed much to the experience of the Old Testament made of consummation the central event in the entry to marriage. As facts of ordinary experience consent and consummation seem equally important. But the great difficulty of defining and applying acceptable rules to the entry to marriage is that it is both a very private, intimate, personal bond between a man and a woman, and a public

[30] Noonan 1967.

act from which all sorts of consequences which concern many folk besides the partners may flow. Its definition is too intimate a matter to be left to the crudities of the law; yet it is also too public a matter to be left to the private convictions of the partners. The outward and the inward views of marriage have always been, and must be, in some degree of tension, even conflict.

Down to the twelfth century the Church's leaders might stress the importance of consent, but they were not compelled to produce a wholly watertight definition of marriage to cover all cases, for all cases did not come their way. Marriage was so much a matter for local and variable custom that it would have been very unwise to propound universal definitions. But in the twelfth century the church courts—and increasingly the papal court itself—had squarely to face the problem of definition; and the popes, and most leading canonists, settled for *consensus* as the basis of the entry to marriage.[31] It not only represented the heart and core of the Roman law on which the practice of earlier courts had been based, but presumably—and in this region we have little concrete information, and must make do with inference—it reflected a widespread custom. It must often have been the case that a couple once firmly betrothed, who had given their mutual consent, were reckoned free to cohabit; and this the Church, while preferring and promoting more open, formal, and visible ceremonies, felt bound to respect.

No one doubted that consummation, sexual partnership, and the procreation of children, were normal parts of marriage. But the question arose whether consummation

---

[31] An extremely interesting variant is represented by Vacarius' *Summa de Matrimonio* (mid twelfth century), which makes of mutual *traditio* by husband and wife the central, definitive act of marriage, thus remarkably uniting the legal and theological trends of the time. See Maitland 1897. For Gratian's views, which emphasize both consent as the basis of marriage and the role of consummation in making it perfect, see esp. Moule 1983, pp. 137–89; see now also Brundage 1987, chap. 6. For the development of the distinction between consent *de futuro* and *de praesenti*, see below, pp. 151–2.

was essential to the fullness of marriage. This is a region in which perfect consistency was impossible: for it is the point at which the public and the private faces of marriage most obviously look in different directions. Even allowing that most folk lived in circumstances of much less privacy than we are accustomed to, only the partners themselves could ultimately bear witness as to whether effective consummation had taken place;[32] and this left ample space for doubt and collusion where marriage had broken down and no children been born. It was a widely received opinion that marriage without consummation was incomplete, and the Church felt compelled to accept the view that when one or other partner was or appeared to be incapable of consummation the marriage could be annulled.[33] Yet it was the universal doctrine of the medieval Church that the Blessed Virgin Mary was always a virgin—that she had never consummated her marriage to Joseph; and it was widely held that the marriage of Joseph and Mary was perfect, the most perfect marriage of all—and that it could not be incomplete.[34] This opened a chasm in the opinions of churchmen on the married state. It was felt by many that virginity was better than marriage, and by some that it was specially virtuous to be a virgin within the married state. Yet there was another strand of opinion, which we can well understand, which condemned such behaviour, and insisted (as St Paul had said) that husband and wife owed each other a debt—that mutual giving involved sexual union as much as any other kind of partnership; that this was an obligation of marriage; that husbands and wives had *rights* to the partnership of the marriage-

---

[32] Cf. Kelly 1976, pp. 225–36, for doubts still subsisting among fifteenth- and sixteenth-century canonists about the precise definition of consummation.

[33] Oesterlé 1953. For the problems this raised for Alexander III see Dauvillier 1933, pp. 285–99; but see esp. their resolution in Moule 1983, pp. 333–9. See below, n. 37.

[34] See above, pp. 53–4.

bed.[35] In the early and central Middle Ages clerical moralists reckoned that sexual union nearly always had some element of sin in it, that it was only justified by the desire to have children; that it was only moral so long as there was no pleasure in it. In the mid and late Middle Ages the whole atmosphere slowly changed; the union of marriage came to be much more sacramental in the eyes of the theologians; and although the medieval Church forgot very little and had to accommodate all these various strains—and few theologians doubted that virginity was in the end a higher calling—sexual union was more readily accepted as of the essence of marriage.[36]

The refusal of one partner or the other to consummate a marriage left it incomplete, and somehow or other annulment on the grounds that a marriage had not been consummated remained a part of the labyrinth of marriage law. There are in fact two strands in Alexander's decretals, which it took the ingenuity of St Thomas (two generations later) to reconcile. On the one hand Alexander accepted mutual consent as the basis and essential minimum of marriage, as in Roman law; on the other hand he also accepted Justinian's ruling that securely proved impotence could lead to the annulment of a marriage—and that the incapacity to consummate was an impediment to marriage. Here he showed hesitation: the Roman tradition had been to encourage impotent partners to stay married and enjoy the other blessings of the state; the Gallican tradition had been for parting them. Alexander was torn three ways: he was determined not to disrupt existing custom where it was tolerable ('we shall patiently tolerate' Gallican custom said he) and cause chaos; he reckoned that promises were truly binding; and yet he was also deeply conscious of the phrase 'una

---

[35] See pp. 48, 133.

[36] There is an admirable conspectus of the views of many leading theologians in Le Bras 1926. For the twelfth century, see also Leclercq 1982.

caro', 'one flesh', and assumed that this meant that consummation was somehow *essential* to the true character of marriage.[37] St Thomas observed that consent to marriage could not be genuine consent if it turned out to be consent to a manner of life of which either partner was incapable; and impotence therefore made it null. Behind all this area of reasoning lay Paul's words to the Corinthians: 'The husband must give the wife what is due to her, and the wife equally must give the husband his due. The wife cannot claim her body as her own; it is her husband's. Equally, the husband cannot claim his body as his own; it is his wife's' (1 Cor. 7: 3–4). *Must give*—a biblical imperative which dominated this area of medieval theology and law. Thus Alexander was

---

[37] On *una caro*—Matt. 19: 5–6, Mark 10: 8, from Gen. 2: 24—see Moule 1983, pp. 333–9; and on these details and for what follows, Oesterlé 1953, cols. 1263–5; on the Roman law relating to impotence, see Corbett 1930, pp. 245–6. The attempt to devise a chronology in Alexander III's doctrine of marriage, first posed by Dauvillier 1933, and developed e.g. in Donahue 1982, essentially fails as Moule 1983 has shown (pp. 306–64) and is emphasized below. Of the three elements, consent *de praesenti* was upheld by Alexander throughout his pontificate (see esp. pp. 169–72 below; Moule 1983, esp. p. 328); the possibility of annulment for non-consummation was always present (Oesterlé 1953, cols. 1263–5); marriage *in facie ecclesiae* was always encouraged, but never essential (Moule 1983, esp. pp. 318–20).

Brundage 1986, esp. pp. 70–4, argues, especially on the basis of the decretals upholding the annulment of marriages not consummated, that 'sexual relations, according to the decretals examined thus far, were intrinsic to marriage in Alexander's view' (p. 71), and in n. 51 seems to challenge Donahue 1976, p. 252 n. 2, who reckons that Alexander's decretals on impotence 'do not form a coherent whole'. But he admits that in this region Alexander was evidently struggling with divergent local customs—and, one could add, trying to avoid breaking perfectly acceptable human situations. One must agree with Brundage that sexual relations mattered deeply to Alexander as to Gratian in this region; but that does not blunt the force of the inconsistency. He upheld purely consensual marriages, as in both the cases considered here; but admitted the possibility of annulment for lack of sexual relations under certain special circumstances. The problem will perhaps be clearer when we have fully critical texts of all the relevant decretals (for his firmest statement of the importance of sexual relations, Brundage cites John of Salisbury, *Letters*, i. 231—but this represents neither the pope nor John, but John's very careful reporting of Mabel's advocates, i.e. of the view which Alexander ultimately rejected). See also Brundage 1987, pp. 333–4. The problem is very well discussed in Moule 1983, pp. 333–9. [See now Brundage 1988: see below p. 312.]

compelled a little reluctantly perhaps to accept impotence as a ground for annulment.

The other chief ground for annulment was that the partners had been too closely related to one another. In the fifth and sixth centuries the Western Church had come firmly out against the marriage of cousins, though it was never entirely clear how distant the cousins were you might not marry.[38] What is certain is that the Western tradition slowly increased the extent of these prohibitions, until by the late eleventh century the prohibition seemed to extend to sixth cousins. Then the tide turned: so extensive a taboo could not be enforced; few are those in any age or society who are confident they can name any of their sixth cousins, let alone all; the kings and princes of Europe rapidly exhausted the families into which they could marry. The prohibited degrees were pruned and a regular system of papal dispensations introduced to allow those within the prohibited degrees to marry.

These extraordinary rules were first established in the fifth and sixth centuries and were part of the accepted order long before the period which we are studying. Their origin is very obscure. The reasons advanced for them vary from a religious horror of incest at one extreme to social and economic pressure at the other. The most valuable discussion of recent years is in Jack Goody's *The Development of the Family and Marriage in Europe*, a book in which an eminent anthropologist looks at medieval marriage with all the experience of his own studies and his own science at command.[39] It is an immensely helpful book, which blows away many cobwebs, for the social historians over recent generations have seen the relevance of anthropology but not sufficiently understood its message. Goody enters the mind of medieval theologians in one respect admirably: he shares their zeal for the peculiar

---

[38] For all this see Dauvillier 1933, pp. 146–52; and esp. Goody 1983.
[39] Goody 1983.

arithmetic of kin, and his explanation of the various systems for counting degrees of kinship is exemplary. His account of the grounds for their zeal is less satisfactory. He points out that the prohibitions tended to make inheritance within a kinship group—a natural device in many early societies for keeping an inheritance intact within a family—more difficult; he sees its advantage to the Church in its search for large landed endowments. Such calculations may have entered the minds of some theologians, especially in the early centuries when the rules were first devised. But they do little to solve the deepest puzzle, which is their extravagant extension to third and fourth or sixth cousins. We enter a region both deep and obscure, and simple or single explanations will not do; the whole question needs much fuller examination. But for us the crucial moment comes when St Peter Damian in the early 1060s, writing to interpret the rules for his colleagues among the papal reformers, who included Pope Alexander II and Hildebrand, the future Pope Gregory VII, revised the system of counting so as greatly to extend the area of prohibition.[40] The date is significant: we are in the world of the papal reform, when the Church was coming to vindicate its legal rights in this area; in the next century it had to face the consequences of all its earlier pronouncements—it had actually to handle hundreds of marriage cases—and to sound a retreat. The extension proposed by Damian had taken the prohibitions out of the world of possible enforcement, or of reasonable sense.

The man also is significant, for Peter Damian had a quite exceptional horror of human sexuality, and even among the great ascetics of his age stood out for his reluctance to accept the married state as within God's providence. He viewed marriage as a doubtful legal cover

[40] Goody 1983, pp. 136–43.

to sin, and rejoiced in any device which discouraged men on whom the divine image had been stamped from engaging in anything so degrading. It was an extraordinary chance that placed so near the centre of the Church's government in the 1060s a man with so virulent a hatred of sexual union, and so powerful a sense that avoidance of incest—a taboo which in more moderate forms had a much longer history behind it and some precedent in the Bible, but was an incurably ambiguous concept since the word incest can be applied to the marriage of any couple related by blood or marriage or godparenthood[41]—should and must be extended to include every person conceivably connected by any human tie.

These ties included affinity as well as kinship: marriage created bonds and taboos as well as birth; and not only affinity, but spiritual relationship, of godparents and godchildren, the result of baptism. In this respect as in so many, the *Concordia discordantium canonum* or *Decretum* of Gratian of Bologna of *c.*1140 marked the fulcrum and turning point. At the heart of the arguments of his predecessor Bishop Ivo of Chartres (d. 1115) on the marriage of King Philip I of France lay an agonized concern to avoid incest, a concern as absorbing as adultery.[42] After Gratian the issue receded; the list of prohibitions was severely pruned. In Gratian himself the matter is ground fine in the most absurd of Gratian's *Causae*—the imaginary cases round which he wove the structure of his book. *Causa* 30 supposes the case that in a crowded baptistery (such as must have been common in Italy in his day) a father by mistake takes his own son from the font, that is,

---

[41] Cf. Goody 1983, pp. 49 ff., 56 ff. The Old Testament text most pondered in this context in the Middle Ages was Lev. 18: 6–18, which prohibits incestuous marriages—but the list is much less tightly drawn than in the Middle Ages. The sentiment against incest grew in the Middle Ages until it could reach the pitch of feeling represented in *Hamlet*.

[42] For the date of Ivo's death see Poole, 1934, p. 226.

acts godfather to the boy, thus establishing a forbidden relationship with the boy's mother, who is his own wife. The question is: does it in some degree or sense break their marriage? And the wife, who intended to do just this, gets someone else's son by mistake. The ingenuity of these preposterous suppositions underlines the historical interest of Gratian, whose absurdities helped many generations of students to discover what canon law was really about. But if we are interested in marriage as an institution, it is a relief to hurry from the speculations of Gratian to the practical wisdom of the papal court. Yet if we want to unearth the mentality, to use the legal evidence for what it is—we must struggle with Gratian as well as with the case law.

The central issue in Gratian, as in all the canonists of the eleventh and twelfth centuries, was: what constituted a legally valid, a legally binding, marriage? This was the issue which was brought into the open and settled in the papal court.[43] The long inheritance of Roman law dictated that *consensus* should lie at its heart; and the tradition of the papal court had long ago confined this to meaning consent between the partners themselves. Working on ancient and traditional foundations, the popes and the canonists hammered out a definition something like this: when a man and woman freely and legitimately promised to marry—when they made no conditions, but said in the presence of witnesses that they took each other as husband and wife—then there could be no turning back; only annulment could part them. There were plenty of ramifications: freely and legitimately meant that they had to be of the age of consent, they had to be free to marry. The age of consent was reckoned to be about twelve for a woman, fourteen for a man—surprising as it seems to us; and

---

[43] For what follows, see esp. Moule 1983, correcting in detail Dauvillier 1933, chaps. 1–2. For doctrine in the decretists, see Weigand 1981; Brundage 1987, chaps. 7–8.

many marriages were made in fact much earlier.[44] But the law defined that no marriage made before the partners were seven could be upheld, and then only those which the partners freely confirmed in their maturity. And who was free to marry? Most parents thought this a matter for them not their offspring; but the popes slowly enforced the idea that in the eyes of God and the Church only the partners' consent mattered—here we see most visibly the effect of Christian theology, of the notion of marriage as a sacrament between the partners, forcing its way into the law courts. More striking still is the definition of freedom: the English Pope Adrian IV (1154–9) made so bold as to declare that even the marriage of slaves depended on their own consent alone for their validity; and though it took many long years for Western society to believe its ears— his ruling won the day in the end.[45] All sorts of problems remained: above all, the emphasis on consent left many puzzles as to its relation to sexual union, to the necessity and effect of consummation; few doubted that consummation was of the essence of marriage; but the pope firmly insisted that it was the promises which first bound the couple. If the man said 'I promise to take you to wife in the future' they were engaged, as we should say, but not married; if he said 'I promise to take you to wife here and now' by *verba de praesenti* he was tied; perhaps not fully married till they went to bed, yet bound in a way he could not escape. The definition first appears in a papal ruling or *decretal* of about 1140; it was elaborated by Peter the Lombard in his *Sentences* in the 1150s; it was firmly established by Pope Alexander III (1159–81) in a series of decretals of the 1160s.[46]

---

[44] Medieval canon law inherited the rules of Roman law, that no betrothal might be undertaken under seven, and that the age of consent was the age of puberty, deemed to be twelve for a girl, fourteen for a boy (Dauvillier 1933, pp. 43–8; Corbett 1930, pp. 51–2). See below, n. 51.

[45] Landau 1967.

[46] See below, pp. 150–6; Peter the Lombard, *Sententiae*, iv, Dist. 28, c. 1.

In later centuries it had a curious fortune. The Church had always wished it to be marked by some ecclesiastical ceremony; and in the late eleventh and early twelfth centuries we first meet fully integrated marriage rituals, in which all the elements, the exchange of gifts, the exchange of promises, the blessing of a priest, the nuptial mass, the benediction of the marriage chamber, were gathered in a single compass.[47] These rituals spread slowly all over the Western Church and constant efforts were made to urge the partners to celebrate their marriage *in facie ecclesiae*, publicly in the Church's view: from the twelfth century or so on, most frequently, with a ceremony at the church's door.[48] Not till the sixteenth century did marriage in church become a legal necessity—and then by edict of the Council of Trent, which was mandatory for Roman Catholics, ignored by the Protestant churches. In England the twelfth-century formula survived until the eighteenth century—the phrase *verba de praesenti* trips surprisingly from the lips of Webster's *Duchess of Malfi* early in the seventeenth; and it was only by Lord Hardwicke's Marriage Act of 1753 that marriage in church was enforced, and only in 1836 that civil marriage became a part of English law.[49] From the twelfth to the nineteenth century marriage and its laws lay in the courts of the Church.

Duby's account of the lay model of medieval marriage, and its evasion of the Church's rules, began with the French kings of the eleventh and twelfth centuries; and the changes enforced by the Church in and before the twelfth century can be illustrated most forcefully by two examples from the career of the most powerful French magnate of the mid and late twelfth century, Henry II,

---

[47] Molin and Mutembe 1974; cf. pp. 248–50.

[48] See p. 249. Dauvillier 1933, pp. 23–8, tried to argue that Alexander III, for a time, tried to enforce marriage *in facie ecclesiae*; this is refuted by Moule 1983, pp. 318–20.

[49] Winnett 1958, esp. pp. 131–2; for the effects of the 1836 Act see Anderson 1975.

king of the English indeed—but also duke of Normandy and Aquitaine and count of Anjou. In his quarrel with Thomas Becket he and his legal advisers put down in writing the vital points at issue between them in the Constitutions of Clarendon of 1164; and jurisdiction over marriage—as such—was not among them. I say 'as such' since the Church's marriage jurisdiction was in theory checked by the control of appeals to Rome—which was quite ineffective—and in practice very much hampered by the objection to excommunicating barons or tenants-in-chief.[50] But the absence of any clause relating to marriage is a thunderous silence. In 1175 Henry and his son, who like most of Henry's children had been married in babyhood, were present at the Council of Westminster in which it was propounded, in words which echoed a decretal in Gratian's *Decretum*—'where there is no consent of both parties there is no marriage; and so those who give girls to boys in their cradles achieve nothing [*nichil faciunt*]—unless both the children give consent after they have come to the age of discretion'—and Gratian himself had observed that no betrothals should be contracted before the age of seven which has sometimes led commentators to think that seven was the age of discretion in the Middle Ages.[51] But the council of 1175 went on to add—in deference doubtless to its royal visitors—that the rules could be bent 'when there is the most urgent necessity for the sake of peace [*pro bono pacis*]'. Now some modern commentators read this as yet another sign of the Church bending before the naked power of the ruler. It can be taken in the opposite sense: the whole decree, with its firm assurance that marriage jurisdiction

[50] For Clarendon see *Councils*, i. 2. 852–93; the prohibition of the excommunication of tenants-in-chief etc. is c. 7, p. 880: see below, p. 155.

[51] *Councils*, i. 2. 991; cf. Brooke 1978, pp. 15–18; Brooke 1980, p. 337 and n. 9. The draft agenda for the council (p. 981, no. 33 (35)) had spelt out that princes and great men needed special consideration; the young King Henry present in 1175 had been 'married' aged three and a half.

lay in the Church's hands, is a bold statement of the Church's authority; and the essence of what it says is: marriage is based on consent. The French kings went on having their divorces—even one Angevin (King John) joined them; then as always the practice of the courts was full of shifts and ambiguities. But the effective assertion of the Church's authority was made; for the first time in the history of the Church, a single definition of what constituted a valid marriage was devised. It was wrapped up in lawyer's language, and was as full of holes as a colander. But at least it was a definition. And with it went a development in the theology of marriage which established two points: that marriage was a sacrament, one of the seven, and that it was made—albeit with priestly blessing if at all possible—by the partners themselves.[52] What is most astonishing is the degree of acceptance that it received from the lay aristocracy and ordinary folk of Europe. We are hampered by an ignorance of stupendous proportions: there are areas of ground of which we have no knowledge at all, stretches of time and space where our knowledge is sketchy indeed. But in the long run for most of western Europe it was a definitive acceptance; and that is to me immensely surprising—much more surprising than all the tensions we can find between Duby's two models, which are part of the ordinary give and take of human variety.

No doubt the explanation is complex. The Church had been dropping water on the stone for a thousand years; the ideal of Christian marriage is by no means unattractive; there is a natural allurement about much of what the Church taught, at least to many folk. Human nature played a crucial role. Moreover there is a very obvious and central point in which the aims of the nobility and the aims of the Church coincided; and

---

[52] See esp. Le Bras 1926; Leclercq 1982.

this seems to me of the essence of the story, and to be obscured by the approach through Duby's two models. The aristocratic societies of western Europe were increasingly concerned with the effective passage of landed estates and kingdoms by hereditary succession. A succession of clearly defined heirs was needed, and in an ideal world would be created by every lord producing a son. This was the starry-eyed doctrine of the Capetian kings, and they engaged in endless divorces in order to try and ensure it. In that one particular—male succession—they succeeded, though at considerable cost in other ways.[53] But most of the dynasties realized well enough that human affairs cannot normally be conducted on this basis: a married couple may produce no children or only girls; and the boys may die as Henry I's only legitimate son died in the wreck of the White Ship, leaving the Empress Matilda as his sole legitimate child and heiress. But in the long run his inheritance, so far from suffering, was greatly enhanced by this misadventure—for it opened the succession to his daughter, who married the count of Anjou; and that marriage and the union of their son, the future Henry II, made Henry II lord of an immense region of France. If you take the rough with the smooth—if you take a wider view of the nature of inheritance than just the production of a ceaseless flow of male heirs—the doctrine of legitimate monogamy may produce very satisfactory results. In any case you cannot work a hereditary system at all unless the nature of inheritance is tolerably clear; and as in any sport or any mart, the presence of an umpire is of the essence of successful competition and play. In the marriage market and the marriage games of medieval catholic Europe the Church

[53] The Capetian kings did not fail to produce a male heir between 1000 and the early fourteenth century (there are convenient summaries in Mas Latrie 1889, cols. 1521–3; Hallam 1980, esp. pp. 113, 249).

1   Bathsheba, by Rembrandt, in the Musée du Louvre.
See pp. ix–xi.

2 The Lady Margaret Beaufort, bronze effigy by Torrigiani, on her tomb in the Henry VII Chapel, Westminster Abbey (photo by Wim Swaan). See pp. 36–7.

3 and 4 Two Porches: see pp. 255–6.

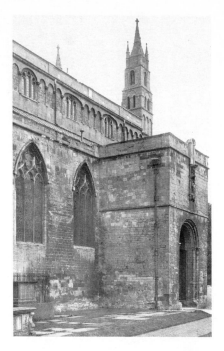

3 (*Right*) The porch to the abbey church at Tewkesbury, twelfth century.

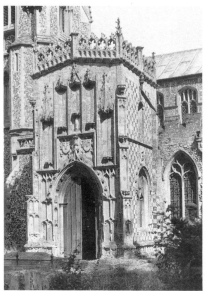

4 (*Left*) The parish church at Woolpit (Suffolk), *c*.1430–55, has a richly ornate porch with a room over it.

5 Detail of the mirror, showing the two witnesses, and the roundels of the passion and resurrection of Jesus. See p. 281.

6   The Arnolfini Marriage. See pp. 280–6.

Tuc rex furo?c rcplcrus ca cedi scorpionibz iubet er
obscurum in carcerem mitti ibiqz.xij.diebz sac
auctari ad quam unsitandam regina nimio eius
amore suscensa cum principe militum accedit

7   St Catherine bound to a column, by Paul(?) Limbourg, 1408–
9, one of the illustrations to the Life of St Catherine in the *Belles
Heures* of the Duc de Berry. The Metropolitan Museum of Art,
New York, The Cloisters Collection, Purchase, 1954 (54.1.1, fo.
17 recto: see M. Meiss and E. H. Beatson, *Les Belles Heures*,
London, 1974, fo. 17; and below, p. 284).

he right hand panel of the Portinari Altarpiece by Hugo
er Goes, mid or late 1470s, in the Uffizi Gallery, Florence.
panel shows St Margaret and St Mary Magdalene (see
34), with the donor's wife and daughter kneeling below.

9 St Eligius, by Petrus Christus, 1449, The Metropolitan Museum of Art, New York, Robert Lehmann Collection, 1975 (1975.1.110). The saint, who was a goldsmith, and so the patron of goldsmiths, weighs a wedding ring for a young couple. This is another symbolic picture of marriage by a painter who was a disciple of Jan van Eyck.

and the papacy acted as umpires, and were blessed and cursed accordingly.

Case-Studies

So far we have dwelt in a region of generalization. But if the legal evidence is to come alive, to yield its fruit, we must try to see marriage law in action in the lives of a group of well recorded families or communities. By good fortune three of the best recorded cases of the twelfth century give us an exceptional insight into the problems and assumptions with which the popes had to grapple to establish and enforce the law; and two of them are actually *causes célèbres* which influenced Alexander III in the search for definitive answers to the fundamental questions. But this is to put the cart before the horse: the central point about the formation of marriage law is that the popes did not set out to provide watertight legislation: they handled actual cases that came before them and sought to give them as fair, humane, and consistent solutions as they could.[54] By way of coda I append two other case histories: the special kind of evidence the inquisition courts could produce, in the celebrated, even notorious case of Montaillou in the early fourteenth century; and the tragic farce of the marriages of Henry VIII—a fitting epilogue to our story and an inescapable one, for it is perhaps the most richly documented, and the most deeply studied, case in the history of marriage.

---

[54] For these qualities see esp. below, pp. 156–7. The humanity of Alexander III's outlook has been stressed in a series of recent studies: Duggan 1981 (esp. p. 72); Donahue 1976; Brundage 1986; Brooke 1980, 1981.

6. Marriage in Law and Practice

Christina of Markyate

The Life of Christina of Markyate is far from being a legal record; it is the life of a saint who was never actually canonized, one of the most vivid and perplexing of medieval biographies.[55] Christina was born in Huntingdon just before 1100 and died about 1160, nun and prioress of a small community at Markyate near St Albans.[56] Most of the story is palpably—can only be—a faithful transcript of reminiscences given to the author by Christina herself. It is marvellously vivid and immediate; and as the whole story took place within two small regions not very far apart—in Huntingdon and round St Albans—there must have been plenty of living witnesses to check the general veracity of the account. But amid stories which only Christina herself could have told—and in some cases only she could have known—our scepticism is sometimes aroused. These are of two kinds. It is claimed that she was very attractive to men, and that two men—one of them no less than Ranulf Flambard, the celebrated or notorious bishop of Durham, the other the cleric into whose charge the young Christina was put after the hermit who instructed her had died—made strenuous efforts to seduce her.[57] The other kind of story comprises her visions. Some of these are visions of Jesus and of the devil, of a kind not at all unusual—though she appears as exceptionally given to visionary experience. But peculiar to her was the gift of keeping an eye on her friend Abbot Geoffrey of St Albans, so that she always knew what he was at wherever he went—a gift which evidently made the abbot uncomfortable, especially when he knew she would not approve of what he did. Of these stories of Flambard, the hermit, and Abbot Geoffrey I can only say

---

[55] Talbot 1987 (repr. in OMT of 1959 edition, with corrigenda and index).
[56] Details in Talbot 1987, esp. pp. 14–15; cf. Holdsworth 1978; *Heads*, p. 215.
[57] Talbot 1987, pp. 40–3, 112–19.

that they have a quality of fantasy about them which can
be met in the modern world—and where it would be met
with simple scepticism. I have little doubt that she was a
remarkable woman of exceptional spiritual gifts; she
inspired not only her biography but the St Albans Psalter,
one of the notable artistic creations of her day. But it
would be credulous to believe all she tells us. Yet when
the circumstances are such that the story reflects what
many must have known, we can readily believe it.

Thus it may well be true that her maternal aunt Alveva
had been concubine to Ranulf Flambard and born him
children—even if the account of his efforts to seduce
Christina herself has an element of fantasy in it.[58] We may
equally believe that as a young girl she felt a call to
the life of celibacy, like the young St Catherine; and
it was very natural that her parents, well-to-do citizens of
Huntingdon, should think (like Catherine's mother) that
this was childish nonsense.[59] In due course (perhaps
with the aid of Flambard himself), they found a noble
youth called Burthred, and a marriage was arranged.[60]
According to the *Life* she continued to resist; but her
parents and friends thought this unreasonable: a young
girl's destiny was for her parents to decide. In the end,
'some time later, when they were all gathered together to
go to church [*ad ecclesiam*] they made a concerted and
sudden attack on her. To be brief how it happened I
cannot tell. All I know is that by God's permission, with
so many exerting pressure on her from all sides, she
yielded (at least in word), and at that very hour Burthred
and she were married [*Burthredus illam in coniugem sibi
desponsavit*].'[61] *Desponsavit* is often translated 'betrothed',
but it was the common, indeed the normal, word for the

[58] I accept the doubts expressed in Offler 1971, p. 12; cf. Offler 1968, p. 105.
For Alveva, see Talbot 1987, pp. 40–1.
[59] Talbot 1987, pp. 36–9; cf. above, p. 25.
[60] Talbot 1987, pp. 44–5.
[61] Talbot 1987, pp. 44–7 (slightly adapted).

exchange of promises which formed the core of matrimonial consent. It is clear that what is described here is a marriage 'at church door'.

It was not yet, however, a complete marriage, not *perfectum*. As may have commonly happened, she returned to her parents until the couple were ready to set up house together: Burthred meanwhile was building a new matrimonial home.[62] But Christina stoutly maintained that she would never consummate her marriage. Her parents tried to interest her in worldly amusements and separate her from devout counsel.

> See finally how she acted, how she behaved herself at what is called the Gild merchant, which is one of the merchants' greatest and best-known festivals.[63] One day when a great throng of nobles were gathered together there, Autti and Beatrix [Christina's parents] held the place of honour, as being the most important amongst them. It was their pleasure that Christina, their eldest and most worthy daughter, should act as cup-bearer to such an honourable gathering. Wherefore they commanded her to get up and lay aside the mantle which she was wearing, so that, with her garments fastened to her sides with bands and her sleeves rolled up her arms, she should courteously offer drinks to the nobility. They hoped that the compliments paid to her by the onlookers and the accumulation of little sips of wine would break her resolution and prepare her body for the deed of corruption. Carrying out their wishes, she prepared a suitable defence against both attacks. . . .[64]

Her parents were not yet foiled. They arranged for her husband-to-be to be let secretly into her room at night. But she sat up all night, explaining to him why she

---

[62] Talbot 1987, pp. 46–7.   [63] Cf. Brooke and Keir 1975, p. 280.
[64] Talbot 1987, pp. 48–9; and for what follows, pp. 50–5. These stories also seem a little far-fetched.

wished to remain unmarried. The young man tried again, but in vain. Her parents brought her before the prior of Huntingdon, who read her a little homily on marriage. 'We know that you have been married [*desponsatam*] according to the Church's custom [*ecclesiastico more*]'—a clear indication that the marriage was *in facie ecclesie*.[65] 'We know that the sacrament of marriage, which has been sanctioned by divine law [*institucione*], cannot be dissolved, because those whom God has joined man may not put asunder'—and we are treated to familiar texts from the Gospels and St Paul. To this Christina answered: the sacrament was forced on me; I never thought of becoming a wife; I chose chastity in my infancy and vowed to remain a virgin in the presence of witnesses. The author has repeated the standard marriage homily, evidently, of his period; none the worse for that. The legal issue seems tolerably clear; and it is not at all surprising that the bishop of Lincoln, after initially looking with favour at Christina's plea, listened to the parents and the aggrieved husband, and refused to release her. The *Life* asserts that he was bribed, and we may believe that money changed hands; it is also true that there was sound authority in canon law for preferring a vow of chastity to a later betrothal, and against marriage by force.[66] But to defend the romantic wish of a young girl—even if supported by the witness of a local canon who had befriended her—against the authority of her family and the unquestioned promises she had made at the door of the church: that was quite another matter.

In the sequel Christina escaped from home and went into hiding; and in the end she was successful in gaining

[65] Talbot 1987, pp. 58–61.

[66] Talbot 1987, pp. 64–73. For the force of a vow of virginity against subsequent marriage, see Gratian, *Decretum*, C. 27 q. 1 c. 9; for condemnation of marriage by parental compulsion, ibid., C. 31 q. 2 cc. 1–2; cf. Dauvillier 1933, pp. 90–2 for later authorities against forced marriage; and Peter the Lombard, *Sentences*, iv, Dist. 29, cc. 1–2.

an 'annulment of her marriage, the confirmation of her vow, and papal permission for her husband to marry another woman' with the aid of Thurstan, archbishop of York.[67] Thurstan's intervention is perhaps the most puzzling part of the story, for at first sight nothing seems more improbable, or less likely to win approval from the pope or the bishop of Lincoln, than the intervention of Thurstan of York at the height of his quarrel with the archbishop of Canterbury.[68] Most emphatically, his writ did not run in these regions. But some truth there must be in the story; by some means she won release, and the account later in her Life of how Thurstan tried to make her prioress of his own foundation at York or transfer her to Marcigny or Fontevrault suggests some real knowledge of his interests.[69] He was certainly a sympathetic and fearless man; he was in frequent touch with the pope in the mid and late 1120s; he may well have delighted to intervene in the affairs of the see of Lincoln. He may even have had some personal knowledge of the family, for his own family and Flambard's had rubbed shoulders in St Paul's.[70] In any case Christina's escape to the life of a recluse and a nun touches two worlds of ideas: the honour paid to virginity, the cult of celibacy on the one hand— and the attempt to balance proper parental authority and the free exercise of consent in marriage on the other.

Mabel de Francheville and Richard of Anstey

The letters of Heloise and Abelard revealed a moment in the history of marriage when a deep personal tragedy

---

[67] Talbot 1987, pp. 112–13.

[68] For York's pretensions to the see of Lincoln, see Hugh the Chanter, new edn., ed. M. Brett, C. N. L. Brooke, and M. Winterbottom (1990), pp. 14–17.

[69] Talbot 1987, pp. 126–7. Cf. Nicholl 1964, pp. 192–212; for St Clement, York, see Dobson and Donaghey 1984; Burton 1979, p. 6; for Marcigny, cf. Hugh the Chanter (1990), pp. 154–5.

[70] See above, p. 85.

deflected the course of the history of ideas and of the theology of marriage. The legal definitions of the twelfth century, and especially of Pope Alexander III (1159–81), reflect a struggle to find a simple, intelligible formula which was at once strict and legally sound, fought out in a series of *causes célèbres*.[71] Here are two of them. Both began on English soil—not a surprising fact in itself, for so did many of the cases which went to the papal curia on appeal in the twelfth century. But it is very significant that marriage law was advanced by the pope setting the legal frontiers of marriages made a thousand miles away. There is a local flavour to them—both concerned families which lived and flourished in Suffolk and Essex; but both had estates across the Channel too, and they were argued out and solved in Christendom at large.

Richard of Anstey was an Essex squire who in the late 1150s had the unchivalrous idea of ousting his cousin Mabel de Francheville from her inheritance by claiming that she was illegitimate, and that he, as her father's legitimate nephew, ought to inherit. We know about his adventures from two famous documents: his diary of expenses in the suit from beginning to end which reveals the whole process and all his travels and costs—and the precise and fascinating description of the pleading in the ecclesiastical courts which survives in a letter John of Salisbury wrote for Theobald, archbishop of Canterbury, when the case went on appeal from Canterbury to Rome.[72] We also know that Richard won: that the pope found in the end in his favour and the king gave him the inheritance.[73]

'Richard of Anstey's diary is a monument to the law's delays: delay in the king's court, delay in the archbishop's; an innumerable succession of hearings; appeal to Rome, delegation to judges in England; expenses

---

[71] See n. 54.   [72] Barnes 1962; John of Salisbury, *Letters*, i, no. 131.
[73] Barnes 1962, pp. 13–14, 22–3. For the family and estates, see p. 312: Brand 1983.

in travel, tips and bribes, the heavy cost of transporting advocates and witnesses to Rome.'[74] It arose like this.

There was a man called William de Sackville who had a fine estate centred in Essex. He entered a marriage contract with one Aubrey de Tresgoz, exchanged oaths with her, and then sent her home till the time came to consummate the marriage. Meanwhile William's roving eye, or landed ambition, had induced him to marry Alice the daughter of Amfrid the sheriff, and this marriage was duly solemnized with the Church's rites and a great crowd of wedding guests. Aubrey tried to challenge the marriage, but 'she failed to make herself heard by reason of the crowd and the frowardness of her husband'.[75] William and Alice lived together and reared a family of children, including Mabel. In due course Henry I died in 1135, and, according to Mabel's counsel, 'justice was banished from the realm, and as the madness of those who rejoiced in overturning the old order grew ever stronger, every man was provoked to all manner of evil'.[76] For William the old order meant his wife; he had her ejected from his house and secured a judgement from Geoffrey the archdeacon of Colchester annulling the marriage. Alice sought justice from successive papal legates, so it seems; and the case was seriously tried by Henry of Blois, King Stephen's brother, bishop of Winchester and papal legate, while he was acting vicar of the bishopric of London, in which the parties lived, during a vacancy in the see.[77] The case then paid its first visit to the papal Curia and Pope Innocent II about 1140

[74] Brooke in John of Salisbury, *Letters*, i, p. xxxiii.
[75] John of Salisbury, *Letters*, i, no. 131, pp. 227–8.   [76] Ibid., pp. 230–1.
[77] For Geoffrey, archdeacon of Colchester from after 1132 to before 1142, see Greenway 1968, p. 18; the legates were Alberic of Ostia, 1138–9, and Henry of Blois, bishop of Winchester, 1139–43 (*Councils*, i. 2. 766–7, 780; Tillmann 1926, pp. 38–41, 41–50; Voss 1932, pp. 22 ff., 38, 41–53). The London vacancy probably ended in July 1141, and one of the leading witnesses died in 1140 (Greenway 1968, p. 2; John of Salisbury, *Letters*, i. 233 and n. 17), so we may date the trial before Henry of Blois to 1139–40.

issued the decretal which first firmly stated the doctrine that consent *de praesenti* was binding. The first marriage of William, to Aubrey, 'was not a promise for the future, but a present arrangement with immediate effect'.[78] And the second marriage and all that came of it was roundly denounced. It is not clear how much of the true circumstances the pope really knew, and good testimony could be found that William de Sackville on his deathbed had admitted that he had acquiesced in a fraud in allowing the archdeacon to declare his second marriage null.[79] Clearly William had a short way with his wives, but hoped at his life's end to make all well for Mabel, his surviving daughter and heiress. She succeeded, held the fief for some years in peace, married, and began to rear a family—one of the reasons why the case took so long was because she was always having another child when the hearings were due.[80] In any case, come the accession of Henry II and a new force and vigour in the courts, Richard thought he would have a shot at claiming her inheritance as his own—on the ground that she was illegitimate. Long and complex procedural delays followed. He had to chase Henry II to the gates of Toulouse on his famous campaign of 1159 to get the necessary writs for the case to be heard at all; then it was transferred to the church courts to settle the issue of marriage and legitimacy, and it rapidly passed into the archbishop's court, where there were eighteen fruitless hearings:[81] no

[78] John of Salisbury, *Letters*, i. 228–9: '*Non enim futurum promittebatur, sed praesens firmabatur.*' This decretal of Innocent II is known also from a fuller text of Henry of Blois's letter (Voss 1932, pp. 166–7) and numerous decretal collections: it seems quite likely that the decretal survived in Henry of Blois's letter, and was copied from it by John of Salisbury, by Richard of Anstey's advocates, and the first collectors of decretal collections (see *Letters*, i. 268–9 n.). The phrase '*de futuro*' occurs in Peter the Lombard, *Sentences*, iv, Dist. 28, c. 1.

[79] John of Salisbury, *Letters*, i. 233: William's deathbed confession was made in the presence of Gilbert, abbot of Colchester (1117–40, *Heads*, p. 40) and many other religious, who witnessed to this effect.

[80] John of Salisbury, *Letters*, i. 237.

[81] Barnes 1962; John of Salisbury, *Letters*, i, pp. xxxiii–xxxiv.

doubt there was force in Richard's complaint that Mabel's advocates did everything to delay his progress, since she was in possession. While the case was getting under way Peter the Lombard, the great Italian theologian in Paris, was propounding the doctrine of putative marriage—that children born to a marriage which had every reasonable appearance at the time of being valid and legal—might be considered legitimate; and this was one of many grounds propounded by Mabel's advocates.[82] But once the case was in Rome the pope was confronted with his predecessor's decision, and no doubt Alexander had already some predisposition in favour of the doctrine of consent *de praesenti*; and William and his two wives were dead, so his decision could not break a living marriage. Even so, he referred it back to judges delegate who allowed one further appeal; and eventually the pope confirmed that she was illegitimate and the curia regis granted Richard the inheritance, five years after he had opened his case. To us it may seem a deplorable decision; but it ushered in a line of clear decisions which greatly humanized the law of marriage, and in that sense did good. We seem to be very close in this case to a major decision in canon law; to the adoption of consent by *verba de praesenti* as the basis of marriage.[83]

The Countess Agnes

Not many years later Alexander was confronted with another English suit whose edges were even harsher than that of Mabel and Richard. This was the extraordinary case of the marriage of Agnes, countess of Oxford, from whom the longest continuous line of English earls was to

---

[82] *Sentences*, iv, Dist. 41, q. 3: see Brooke in John of Salisbury, *Letters*, i. 270.
[83] See n. 37.

descend.[84] Aubrey de Vere first earl of Oxford (in the mid twelfth century) married two wives and had no children; so he was well stricken in years—that is to say well into his forties—and still without an heir. Some sort of marriage plan seems to have been made between his brother, Geoffrey de Vere, and Henry of Essex, a great royal official and landholder under Henry II of England, for a marriage with his tiny daughter Agnes. At the age of three her father had made an agreement for her marriage to the earl's brother Geoffrey and she was handed over to the earl as a hostage for the arrangement; at the mature age of six she was moved to Geoffrey's household and (so Geoffrey alleged) treated with all the honour due to his future wife. It was later claimed that she had agreed to a betrothal with Geoffrey; but the girl herself steadfastly denied this; and we may believe her statement. In 1162 or 1163, when she was eleven or twelve—on the verge of the age of consent herself—the earl betrothed himself to her, evidently by *verba de praesenti*. Then in 1163 her father, Henry of Essex, fell into disgrace and forfeited his lands. Agnes's value in the marriage market evaporated. According to the rules of aristocratic society, great men married for the benefit of their estates—good breeding stock, bringing heirs, dowries, and desirable family alliances. Agnes was no longer desirable and the Veres might reasonably expect to set her aside. But the law of marriage was administered by the Church and subject to the Church's doctrines. This did not necessarily and always make much difference: the fact that it made all

---

[84] The essential documents in the case are in *GFL*, nos. 162–4, pp. 214–18; cf. *GF*, pp. 236–7; *CP*, x. 205 ff.; Brooke 1980, pp. 338–9, partly corrected in Brooke 1981, pp. 31–2. There is an excellent family tree, containing additional details, in Barrow 1987, pp. 188–9—but Aubrey the second earl must have been born later than 'post 1165' since his parents' marriage was evidently not consummated before 1172. *Handbook*, 3rd edn., p. 476, gives *c*.?1172. Since the earl was apparently over sixty and without an heir, we may presume that the marriage was consummated fairly rapidly after the end of the case in early 1172—*c*.1173 seems most likely for the birth of the first child.

the difference in Agnes's case reveals something quite fundamental about the history of marriage. There had come to be so deep a bond of common interest between landlords seeking an orderly system of inheritance and the Church trying to enforce Christian monogamy, that the aristocracy was prepared for most purposes to be subject to the jurisdiction of the Church—not only in fits of penitence, but actually when making marriage treaties affecting their inheritances and standing in the world. This was largely because legitimate monogamy had come to be the heart of the system of inheritance, as it was the heart of the Church's idea of marriage as an institution. Doubtless the two affected each other, perhaps quite profoundly—but they would hardly have done so if there had not been a bond of common interest. It also had important effects for the future, since it made each partner in this curious alliance more open to understanding and compromise with the other. But what concerns us most immediately in the case of the Countess Agnes is that the alliance was full of strain and stress and tension, as we should expect; and this case brings out the tension with remarkable clarity. When Henry of Essex fell into disgrace and his daughter's market value plummeted, the Veres naturally thought they would get rid of her. She was about twelve and they thought little enough, quite naturally, of her interest in the matter. But the girl was not so easily disposed of. She must have had friends to help her—we do not know who they were—and she clearly had courage and determination in an unusual degree; and was prepared to put up with almost anything to save her own and her family's name. She won a hearing in the court of the bishop of London, and the Veres were forced to put up an effective case.[85]

---

[85] It is intriguing to observe that the earl's brother William de Vere was a canon of St Paul's in the early 1160s and left to become a canon regular at

The Church was coming to insist on *consent*. The
earl, his brother Geoffrey, and the girl's father had all
supposed that marriage in high society was a treaty made
by the parents; handing over the girl was for them the
crucial act—a similar (and to us horrifying) treatment of
brides-to-be as hostages occurred for example in the royal
families of the day, so that two little French princesses
were brought up under the wing of the English court to be
brides to English princes.[86] What *could* consent mean
under these circumstances?

The disgrace of Henry of Essex occurred in 1163, the
year Richard of Anstey won his inheritance. But it was not
till 1166 that Agnes's case came seriously to court.
The bishop of London, Gilbert Foliot, was the chief
opponent of Thomas Becket in the great dispute between
Archbishop Thomas and King Henry II, and thus high in
royal favour. But even he trod very warily in handling
the matrimonial entanglements of great lords. He had
recently agreed to the Constitutions of Clarendon under
which he was not permitted to excommunicate a tenant-
in-chief without royal consent, hardly likely in such a
case.[87] He was in no hurry. Agnes and her advocates had
little trust in the fair dealing to be expected in an English
court, and she appealed to Rome. That was in 1166,[88] and
though there were rumblings, little happened for the next
five or six years. The earl shut her up in a tower and
treated her with every contumely, it seems, in the hope
that she would give way.[89] But she was very determined,
and evidently had some talent in melting the hearts of

St Osyth in or not long after 1163. But there is no evidence of his involvement in
the case (Barrow 1987, esp. pp. 176–7; *GF*, pp. 208–9, 284; Greenway 1968, p. 64).

[86] John of Salisbury, *Letters*, ii. 6–9 (no. 136) and 7 n. 17; Warren 1973, pp. 72,
77, 90, 611.

[87] *Councils*, i. 2. 864–5, 880; *GF*, chap. 9.

[88] For the date of her appeal, 9 May 1166, see *GFL*, p. 215; the document has
since been calendared in Hodgett 1971, p. 191, no. 969.

[89] *GFL*, no. 164, p. 218—also for what follows.

those far away. The pope was no more in a hurry than the bishop; but in the end he appears to have been deeply moved by the account of her plight which he received. While the Becket dispute lasted he could do (or anyway did) very little. But after Becket had been murdered and the preliminary demarches made towards reconciliation, one of his first acts—we are now, in all probability, in 1172—even before reconciliation was complete, was to send a peremptory mandate to the bishop: the earl is to take her back as his wife, to treat her with due respect, to share his table and his bed with her as husband and wife; and he is to do this within twenty days of the arrival of the Pope's mandate, or else the bishop is to lay an interdict on his lands and excommunicate the earl himself. Dated at Tuscolo on 30 January 1172.[90] The bishop obeyed, the earl complied; and the marriage of Aubrey and Agnes was consummated.[91] The heroic vigil of the young girl had a successful ending. Whether it had a happy ending we shall never know. He was now about sixty, she not far past twenty.[92] He lived till 1194, and they reared a family of at least five children from whom the later Veres were descended. One can hardly imagine a more inauspicious beginning to a marriage; it shows us some of the harshest edges of contemporary custom, and it shows us custom in conflict with the Church. It is not the case that the Church always won; but it modified the harsher customs; and the pope of this case, Alexander III, may be

[90] The year is a probable deduction: see *GFL* no. 164, p. 217. The pope was not in Tuscolo in January between 1172 and 1179, save possibly in 1173.

[91] The documents speak throughout of Agnes as his wife, *uxor*, so that it is possible that it had been consummated already in 1162–3. But this seems almost impossible since she could hardly have been more than twelve in 1163. It is much more likely that there was a betrothal by *verba de praesenti*—possibly *in facie ecclesiae*.

[92] He is supposed to have been born *c*.1110, and she was evidently born *c*.1151–2 (*CP* x, 199 n., 205 ff. and app., pp. 116–17; additional evidence and family tree in Barrow 1987, pp. 188–9). For the children see Barrow 1987, pp. 188–9; *CP* x, 208–13 and app., pp. 116–17.

reckoned to have had a deeply beneficent influence on the history of marriage.[93] But over the private lives of the participants social custom and papal mandate had a limited influence. Could it have been a happy marriage?—stranger things have happened; but it is hard to believe it was so.

We now press forward from the twelfth to the fourteenth century.

Epilogue 1. *Montaillou*

Our case histories so far have been based on pleading in the twelfth-century courts, and on papal decretals. The formation of the Inquisition in the thirteenth century brought forth a new type of document of astonishing, and sometimes horrifying, intimacy, the inquisitors' records.

Jacques Fournier was bishop of Pamiers in the south of France, on the edge of the Pyrenees, in the early fourteenth century, and later, as Pope Benedict XII, patron of the first and more austere surviving chambers of the Palais des Papes at Avignon; an ascetic, dedicated, intolerant Cistercian. His Register as inquisitor at Pamiers is now world famous as the source and inspiration of Professor Le Roy Ladurie's *Montaillou*.[94] Ladurie's book is a vividly evocative work of social history; and I admire profoundly the skill with which he portrays and analyses the society and attitudes and culture, spiritual and material, of this small community of peasants, priests, goodmen, and shepherds in the Pyrenees, in which the faith of the Cathar, dualist heretics made one of its last stands. But its method and details have been severely criticized; and it puzzles me that there is so little discussion of the validity or diplomatic—the scientific

[93] See n. 54.
[94] For what follows see Ladurie 1978 (I have also used Ladurie 1975 which is more fully annotated). The basis is the Register, Duvernoy 1965.

investigation of the form and context and historical value—of the record.[95] A brilliant inquisitor, aided by loyal and well-trained friars and clerks, sat for some 370 days in the years 1318 to 1325; and the result is a record at once incredibly vivid yet tragic and depressing. But is it true?—or rather, in what sense and in what measure is it true? It is all most precisely and vividly recorded; and one need not doubt that the bishop's aim was to elicit the truth. But it would be unwise for us to assume that he succeeded in too precise a sense; or that conversations which are recorded in dialogue form years after they occurred precisely represent what the parties said. It is important for our purpose to bear this in mind, for *Montaillou* and the Register on which it is based carry unique evidence for the attitude of a Cathar community to marriage. It can only be used as evidence if we consider the way it was made; the audience it was composed for; the diplomatic of its record—very much as if it were a piece of literature, which in a sense some of it is.

A brief word on two of the main characters which emerge from the Register will make my point clear. One of the most engaging and attractive is the wandering shepherd Pierre Maury; and it is probable that the account of his way of life, of his manner of earning his living, of his friendships, is authentic enough.[96] There is a great deal of picturesque detail, and entertaining conversation, in his own evidence and the evidence about him which we do not have to believe literally—but this does not affect the substance of the picture. There is one moment which arouses my scepticism: his friend Guillaume Bélibaste was a Cathar *perfectus*—that is to say, was supposed to lead the ascetic, celibate life of the *perfectus*. Bélibaste tricks Pierre Maury into a brief marriage with

[95] See esp. the penetrating criticism in Boyle 1981; for what follows cf. Brooke and Brooke 1984, pp. 125–6.
[96] Ladurie 1978, pp. 77–88; for other refs., ibid. pp. 375–6.

his mistress so as to hide the fact that Bélibaste has made her pregnant; or so it is alleged.[97] It is, however, a notable feature of the record that it succeeds in some considerable measure in discrediting the *perfecti*: either the Cathars of Montaillou were a fairly decadent lot, or else (one cannot help suspecting) the Inquisitor has succeeded in making them appear so: not by lying, but by playing on the village gossip which is the stuff of his record.[98]

The most remarkable portrait in *Montaillou* is that of the parish priest, Pierre Clergue, who emerges as a monster of treachery and lust.[99] He is represented as a Cathar by conviction, who none the less went through the motions of the Catholic liturgy conscientiously enough; but was also a double agent. In 1308 he had arranged a round up of heretics by the Inquisition of Carcassonne; and in 1320 his enemies (who not unnaturally were numerous) gave Bishop Fournier information on which he had the priest himself arrested.[100] One of the main accusations against him was that he was sexually promiscuous: a number of women claimed to have slept with him; yet we do not hear of any bastard children, and one of his mistresses even described (in very implausible detail) a method of contraception to explain this.[101] Pierre Clergue made many enemies, and was evidently a rascal; but he was just the kind of man to inspire the most unreliable gossip; and this is unfortunate, since the evidence of his conversation is important.

The original Cathar doctrine was that all matter was evil, and therefore that the procreation of human bodies

---

[97] Ladurie 1978, pp. 99–100.
[98] Ladurie 1978, p. 364 for references: every effort seems to have been made to discredit Bélibaste, and he was eventually burnt (p. 218).
[99] Ladurie 1978, pp. 154–68.
[100] Ladurie 1978, pp. 14, 65–6; but cf. Boyle 1981, pp. 134–5.
[101] Ladurie 1978, pp. 172–4: Clergue talked of making his mistress pregnant (p. 174), while claiming that it was his herb which prevented it (pp. 172–3). On Clergue's evidence, cf. Boyle 1981, p. 121.

was inherently sinful, for it imprisoned potentially good spirit in bad matter. Their enemies from early days alleged that this made the Cathar missionaries highly critical of marriage; if men and women must sleep together, better to do it irregularly than in the organized, quasi-legal frame of marriage. But it is exceedingly difficult to find any confirmation of such teaching; and those who have studied the Cathars most closely and sympathetically have tended to emphasize the high moral tone of their teaching, the lofty asceticism to which they aspired, and the evidence that when they assumed responsibility for whole communities, they encouraged the preservation of established social standards and institutions.[102] There is evidence in Fournier's Register of both attitudes. The general impression, if one takes the evidence at face value, is that standards were extremely lax; that it was a permissive society, in which none the less there was a very strong sense of family and house-hold, the *domus* or *ostal* on which Professor Ladurie so strongly insists.[103] He argues, or intuits, that the honour paid to marriage in Montaillou, and its essential stability in spite of the number of unofficial liaisons and bastard children, was a feature of its Pyrenean inheritance and tradition not fundamentally affected by the tensions between Cathar and Catholic teaching.[104] I personally suspect that the Register may exaggerate the permissive nature of Montaillou society, and Ladurie even more; but fundamentally this view may be correct. What are we to make, however, of the suggestion that some of the convinced Cathars actually spoke against marriage, and

[102] The *locus classicus* for the doctrine that marriage is worse than adultery is in Alan of Lille: see Thouzellier 1969, pp. 91–2. See also Moore 1977, p. 180. Cf. Ladurie 1978, p. 179 for the grudging support of marriage by the Cathar *perfectus*.

[103] Ladurie 1978, chap. 2.

[104] Ladurie 1978, chap. 11, esp. p. 179.

for informal unions?[105] Unfortunately the key figure in this is the priest, Pierre Clergue: if we could believe everything he is alleged to have said, he would establish the point that a convinced Cathar could hold such views, anyway in the early fourteenth century. But even if there is substance in the charges, it may be no more than a lively dialectical excuse for his amorous adventures; and I am afraid my own scepticism bites deeper than that.

There are more authentic things in *Montaillou* than this: the incidental references which show young brides having husbands found for them, while others entered love-matches; the stories of how even the most devoted couples quarrelled violently from time to time; the rough treatment some husbands regularly meted out; the dominance of some wives, mothers, and grandmothers— much of this comes quite incidentally out of the evidence and offers an entirely convincing portrait of a society.[106] We do not have to take every word literally to accept that the picture itself is true. There is a famous account of how Samuel Johnson composed the Parliamentary debates for the *Gentleman's Magazine* without actually visiting the House of Commons, 'but once'. The friend to whom he told the story commended him for dealing out 'reason and eloquence with an equal hand to both parties. "That is not quite true", said Johnson; "I saved appearances tolerably well, but I took care that the Whig Dogs should not have the best of it." '[107] Fournier and his scribes sought truth according to their lights; but they made sure the Cathar dogs did not have the best of it. I came upon the passage on Johnson most recently when reading Professor Lionel Stones's and Dr Grant Simpson's study of the Great Cause

[105] Ladurie 1978, p. 171. But on pp. 171–2 n., from Duvernoy 1965, i. 224–5, he cites only Pierre Clergue; on p. 179 he quotes the preference for marriage expressed by the Cathar *perfectus*.

[106] Ladurie 1978, chaps. 11 , 12.

[107] Quoted in Stones and Simpson 1978, i. 35 from Arthur Murphy's *Life of Johnson*, printed in *Boswell's Life of Johnson*, Hill and Powell 1934–50, i. 504.

on the succession to the Scottish throne in the 1290s, *Edward I and the Throne of Scotland,* another recent classic of the historian's art.[108] I was struck immediately by the contrast: in *Montaillou* the diplomatic—the form and nature of the document—is taken for granted; the description of the Register and its makers is pungent, but exceedingly brief. *Edward I and the Throne of Scotland* is essentially an edition of the main texts of the Great Cause, a very different kind of book in character and purpose; even so, it is full of good historical interpretation. Yet its heart and core are an enquiry into how the records were made, and what relation they are likely to have to the celebrated debates which they claim to record. Nor is the answer simple. Like Fournier, Edward and his aides were seeking the truth, as they saw it; but great issues were at stake—the ancient and splendid inheritance of the throne of Scotland, all the legal issues involved in inheritances, and the rights of the English king. All these subtly affect the form of the record—an area the historian must always explore. How much more is this true of my last example.

Epilogue 2. The Marriages of Henry VIII

With the marriages of Henry VIII we are suddenly transported into a kind of parody of the *causes célèbres* of the eleventh and twelfth centuries, first to the predicament of the French kings who had thought that the rules of marriage should be devised to provide them with legitimate male heirs, and second to the precise definitions of the canon lawyers. It is an extremely confused, confusing, and sordid story. But much of it is compulsive reading none the less; and the familiarity and unfamiliarity

[108] Stones and Simpson 1978.

of the story makes it an essential epilogue to my gallery of case histories.[109]

The story is familiar in two senses. First of all, everyone knows the tragic story of the six women who had the misfortune or the folly to marry the king. To Catherine of Aragon he was married for over twenty years, and it took him six years to divorce her; but thereafter he grew impatient and his servants more compliant: his marriage to Anne Boleyn rapidly ended in annulment and execution; and four wives shared Henry's eleven declining years. When Catherine of Aragon died in January 1536, it might have been taken as a stroke of good fortune for Anne Boleyn, who reigned thereafter without a rival. But in fact it had the opposite effect, of helping to sow in the fertile minds of Thomas Cromwell and the king the notion of how much more swiftly and effectively divorce could be compassed by the axe on Tower Green than by subtle and ceaseless argument in church courts. Henry's matrimonial adventures thus became a tragic farce.

It is also familiar in another sense. The king's mind was a maze and a morass which we shall never properly understand. Somewhere in his complex and contradictory ego his conscience told him that—to the simple lay mind—Leviticus 18: 16 was only too plain: marriage to a brother's wife was among the prohibited and incestuous unions there listed. It is hard for a modern audience to take this taboo seriously; and Henry changed his mind about Catherine and the precise grounds of his divorce so often it is hard for anyone to take his scruples seriously at all. Yet there was a genuine element here—even if good learned opinion was mostly against him.[110] The only

---

[109] What follows is based on Kelly 1976, amplified and corrected in exemplary fashion by Murphy 1984. See now also Surtz and Murphy 1988. Scarisbrick 1968, chaps. 7–8, is still extremely useful; and for Anne Boleyn, Ives 1986. But I have set my own interpretation on the events, which sometimes differs from Kelly's.

[110] Kelly 1976, pp. 33–7; Murphy 1984, esp. pp. 67–80, 262–3.

consistent thread running through all his adventures was the search for male heirs to secure his dynasty. The Tudors came in after a century of dynastic strife; they never slept easy in their beds. Henry's first concern must be a strong secure succession; his father had only achieved it by having two sons who survived into their teens, and that must be his first and principal aim, which he never achieved. When Catherine of Aragon was past child-bearing—after giving birth to a number of children only one of whom survived, the future Queen Mary— Henry VIII was exactly in the position of the French kings of the eleventh and twelfth centuries. He needed sons; and he collected new wives for the purpose. It may well be that he felt his lack of boys as a judgement and was kept awake at night by the text of Leviticus. It may well be that he was a little bewitched by Anne Boleyn. But he shifted his ground so often on what precisely was wrong with his first marriage, and waited over five years before making Anne pregnant—so that these motives, though they may have been powerful, were not primary.[111] Holbein has canonized the picture of Henry as a massive renaissance prince. But to me he is rather the caricature of a medieval dynast, whose pleasure lay chiefly in hunting and jousting, and whose sense of duty extended as far—and not much further for most of his life—as an urgent desire for legitimate sons.

For legitimate they had to be: like Henry I he may have toyed with the idea of making an illegitimate son king; he certainly made arrangements for his daughters to succeed if necessary.[112] But like Henry I he was heir to an upstart dynasty, still very insecure; and legitimate heirs were crucial to its survival. Henry VIII had made Anne's sister his mistress for a time; and we are often told that Anne herself avoided a like fate by insisting she would only be

[111] Cf. Ives 1986, chap. 9, esp. pp. 212–14.
[112] Cf. Scarisbrick 1968, pp. 350–2, 508, etc.

his queen; that may be.[113] But the most powerful motive for delay was Henry's: her children must be his heirs. When he was free to choose an archbishop of Canterbury whose arm could be twisted he slept with her; when he thought she was pregnant he secretly married her; when Elizabeth was securely on the way he had his marriage publicly confirmed—and it was a very nasty shock for both of them when the child turned out to be a girl. Catherine of Aragon was queen for over twenty years; Anne for only three—but even so her stay on the throne lasted longer than that of any of her three successors, and her reign was only exceeded by Catherine Parr's by a few months. Henry annulled his marriage to Anne Boleyn and had her executed; Jane Seymour (most short-lived of all) died after giving birth to Edward VI; Anne of Cleves was so fortunate as to have her marriage annulled before it was well begun; Catherine Howard was executed; and Catherine Parr—after a very narrow shave—outlived the king. It is a fearful story.

It is in this longer perspective that we have to view the sad saga of the fall of Catherine of Aragon, if we are to understand it. She had come to England as a young girl of fifteen or so in 1501 to be married to Arthur, Henry's elder brother; they were married by *verba de praesenti*, and lived together; they seem for a time to have shared a bed.[114] That the marriage was consummated she steadfastly denied, and as she and her chief supporter St John Fisher are about the only people in the story whose word can reasonably be trusted, we may believe her.[115] In 1533 Henry admitted to Cranmer that he had to break her

---

[113] e.g. 'when full sexual relations began, they were initiated by calculation—and the calculation was very probably Anne's': Ives 1986, p. 214.

[114] Kelly 1976, pp. 150–3. Catherine was probably born on 15 Dec. 1485 (Rumen de Armas 1974, p. 136, a reference kindly given me by Dr J. R. L. Highfield), and so was still fifteen in November 1501.

[115] Kelly 1976, pp. 276–8, tries to believe Henry's word on certain points. It is a heroic failure. For what follows, ibid., pp. 233–4; cf. pp. 225–6, 235–6.

hymen on their wedding night—but he added that he was sure that Arthur had consummated his marriage to her, for legally consummation simply involved the deposit of his semen—a view which was indeed held by some canonists. Henry had previously maintained for years that she had consummated her marriage to Arthur *tout court*, and his witness is exceedingly suspect; but for what it is worth it seems to us to confirm Catherine's stand.

Equally in her favour is the fact that it did her no good in law. She and Henry both took what we may call the layman's view, that it was physical union that really made a marriage, and so she denied and he asserted, the consummation of her first union. 'Thou shalt not uncover the nakedness of thy brother's wife: because it is the nakedness of thy brother', quoth Leviticus (18: 16) and it seemed to speak plainly of physical union. But for two reasons it was found not to be so in law.

When Henry began to worry deeply about his lack of an heir in the mid 1520s, Cardinal Wolsey at first seems to have supposed, as anyone might, that it would be an easy matter to arrange an annulment. But he rapidly found that there were too many witnesses, too much information, and too much politics at Rome—especially owing to the influence of Catherine's nephew the Emperor Charles V. In due course Wolsey (who for all his faults had a conscience, and was an academic by origin) came to understand the legal tangle and to have serious doubts.[116] We cannot enter every avenue of this extraordinary story, but roughly speaking, the doubt was this.

When Arthur died Henry VII immediately started a plan for Henry VIII to succeed to his wife: he tried various others plans (including perhaps the idea of marrying her himself) before the marriage was firmly established—and

[116] Kelly 1976, pp. 56–7; Murphy 1984, pp. 11–17.

the extraordinary prevarications of Henry VII may well have given his young and impressionable son the idea that royal marriages could be arranged and disposed of at will. Marriage to a brother-in-law raised an impediment which could only be set aside by papal dispensation. Henry VIII was later to claim that it was contrary to divine law; but his arguments were weak in theology and law as currently understood in the late fifteenth and early sixteenth centuries. It is very significant that John Fisher, already a leading spiritual counsellor in the royal court in the years when their marriage was being arranged, immediately sided with Catherine when Henry began to have doubts, and became her stoutest supporter.[117] He had been a close witness of the original marriage and seen that it was sound in theology and law (as he understood these things).

What had happened at the time was this. The hard-bitten royal lawyers who applied for the dispensation which enabled Henry and Catherine to marry simply took it for granted that if a couple went to bed together, their marriage had been consummated. So they asked for dispensation from ground of affinity—that is, one which assumed consummation—not from what was called 'public honesty', which was the impediment raised by the marriage contract if it had not been consummated. If the marriage was not consummated this ought to have been the ground stated in the dispensation, and wasn't. This was a chink in Catherine's case, but a mighty little one.[118]

In canon law as then interpreted Catherine's case ought to have been quite straightforward, and appeared so to

---

[117] Kelly 1976, esp. pp. 81–8; Murphy 1984, pp. 11–13, 51–5, 101–27, etc. Fisher claimed that Lev. possibly referred to marrying a sister-in-law while the brother lived (cf. Murphy 1984, pp. 117, 120); but this would not have commanded general assent. It has always been apparent that it was in conflict with the positive encouragement to marry a sister-in-law in Deut. 25: 5 (cf. e.g. Murphy 1984, pp. 17, 117–20).

[118] Scarisbrick 1968, pp. 192–4; Kelly 1976, pp. 30–1, 151–6; Murphy 1984, pp. 5–7.

Fisher. She had a papal dispensation, and had been properly married. The only secure answer Henry could produce, in the end, was to deny the basis of the papal dispensation by denying the authority of Rome itself, and securing an annulment from a new archbishop, Thomas Cranmer, and a pliant Parliament. But even so, Henry obscured the issue by endless argument on consummation: his case had really to depend on the marriage contract, the only thing certain, and the weakness of the papal dispensation against it.

For there was a flaw in Catherine's case, though not one which would be likely to prove fatal in a less exalted marriage. Because her dispensation was based on a consummated marriage not just on the contract, it was weakened by her denial of consummation.[119] It is a curious irony that her insistence on this point actually weakened her case, and that Henry's insistence against her obscured the clear lines of his. The strength of her case was that she had really been married to Henry, and that to undo that marriage brought the whole institution into disrepute. In seizing on this, Fisher acted as Alexander III acted in the case of the Countess Agnes.[120]

It is a fascinating case: almost to the last we are in the world of the French kings and the popes of the twelfth century—even though the panoply of papal dispensation belonged to a later age. Henry II of England, confronting Pope Alexander III in his dispute with Thomas Becket, threatened to go over to the anti-pope. But in the 1520s there was no anti-pope for Henry to turn to. Instead there was a rising Cambridge theologian called Thomas Cranmer who showed a learned sympathy for the king's predicament; and a charming lady of the court with

---

[119] Scarisbrick 1968, pp. 192–4; Kelly 1976, pp. 30–1, 151–6; Murphy 1984, pp. 5–7.
[120] See pp. 156–7.

strong and sincere Protestant sympathies, called Anne Boleyn, to listen to his troubles.

Royal marriages in the sixteenth century as in the eleventh and twelfth, had to face special problems and endure peculiar strains: here the public, external face of marriage is contorted so that its inward view, its sacramental quality, could at times have little say. Henry VIII's adventures reveal the limit of human experience in this region, not the normal course of things even among the aristocracy. But the law of marriage has to grasp the needs of great men as well as ordinary married folk.

Note: the Chronology of Alexander III's Marriage Decretals

Donahue 1982 comprises a heroic attempt to save something of Dauvillier's interesting suggestion that Alexander III's decretals on marriage could be made to show a coherent chronological development. Dauvillier (1933, pp. 17–32) had traced five stages: (1) Rolandus the canonist propounding a view in which both consent and consummation were needed for a binding marriage; Pope Alexander propounding (2) a purely consensual view, (3) then one in which consent *de praesenti* was needed to make the union binding; (4) a period in the mid-1170s when he placed marriage *in facie ecclesiae* on a pedestal; (5) and finally, at the end of his pontificate, a period in which consent *de praesenti* again formed a binding union, with consent *de futuro* and consummation as an alternative—the doctrine which was to prevail till the Council of Trent. We no longer believe that Rolandus the canonist and Alexander were the same man (Noonan 1977) and Donahue rightly doubts the evidence for stage 2; but by an elaborate redating of all available decretals he attempts to salvage something of the chronology of stages 3–5. It is evident that very little separates the doctrines of stages 3 and 5, though Donahue notices the many nuances in Alexander's decisions, e.g. on impotence, which could be related to changing opinions. But I am sceptical of the possibility of finding a coherent chronology at all, on the following grounds.

1. Great weight has to be given to the evidence for stage 4, which, however, essentially depends on a single decretal, in Holtzmann's numbering WH 439 = JL 14311; on its meaning see Dauvillier 1933, pp. 23–8, Donahue 1983, p. 84. But Moule 1983, pp. 318–30, shows strong grounds to doubt Dauvillier's interpretation. Alexander naturally supported marriage *in facie ecclesiae*, but there is no sound evidence that he ever made it override other criteria.

2. The texts of many of Alexander's decretals depend on inferior or careless manuscripts, and often, in the present state of knowledge, on inadequate editions. Only when we have really good texts in early decretal collections, edited e.g. in Chodorow and Duggan 1982, can we be confident of their precise wording; and the difficulty is frequently most acute in details of names etc. on which dating most depends.

3. A close examination of the dates assigned by Donahue shows that he has sometimes resorted to a circular argument—that one can only date many decretals at all closely by the supposed chronology of his doctrines. Good examples are the three decretals in which Donahue (p. 105) sees evidence of 'another important movement in Alexander's thought' in the period 4, the mid 1170s. But their dates are, critically viewed, as follows: WH 620 (JL 14091), 1159 × 81; WH 476 (JL 13787), 1159 × 79; WH 675 (JL 14153), 1159 × 71 or 1174 × 81 (Donahue 1982, pp. 78–9). There is no evidence to date any of these decretals to the 1170s.

Alexander's most important doctrine was that of consent *de praesenti*. This was revealed to him in the decretal of Innocent II quoted by Richard of Anstey's proctors, which came to the *curia* in October-December 1160 in John of Salisbury's *Letter* 131, that is, at the outset of his pontificate (see pp. 150–2). This Alexander accepted, and there is no evidence that he ever changed his view on *verba de praesenti*. It may be that his decision to accept consent *de futuro* with consummation as equally binding came later; but most of the decretals which specify it are quite undatable (see Donahue's table, pp. 100–1: only WH 973, JL 13,937, can be dated closely, to 1177). The most important qualifications relate to Alexander's various statements on the effects of impotence; but in these he observed that he was bending, now to the Roman, now to the Gallican custom; doubtless he preferred the Roman, but there is no evidence of developing doctrine in his statements (see pp. 132–4).

Alexander may not have been entirely consistent in his decisions. But even if our texts are imperfect, they may well be fuller than the materials he had himself to hand; and I have tried to outline his doctrines above in a way which brings out the fundamental consistency of his views. He was concerned to preserve his heritage, represented by Innocent II's decretal upholding consent *de praesenti*, by growing emphasis on the Church's role, and by the Gallican customs on impotence. Some elements evidently embarrassed him, especially the rules about prohibited degrees, in which he attempted to turn a blind eye to anything beyond the second degree of relationship unless it was 'public and notorious' (WH 827 = Chodorow and Duggan 1982, no. 32, p. 55, dated '1159–81'). His persistence, shrewdness, and caution—and the humanity which seems to have inspired him—ensured a lasting success for his work. Maitland unkindly said that the distinction of *de praesenti* and *de futuro* was 'no masterpiece of human wisdom' (Pollock and Maitland 1898, ii. 368). But at least it focused marriage litigation onto consent, on which witnesses may speak the truth, rather than on consummation, on which, perhaps, they rarely can or will.

7

THE USE OF LITERARY EVIDENCE FOR THE HISTORY OF MARRIAGE: WOLFRAM VON ESCHENBACH[1]

Prologue: Literary Evidence

There have been some social historians to whom imaginative literature has been the stuff of their subject; to others it is anathema. To some demographers drama and the novel are red herrings set across the track which leads to the actual history of human societies. Peter Laslett in a celebrated chapter entitled 'Misbeliefs about our ancestors' has castigated historians who incorporate titbits from their favourite reading into their picture of the social history of England and Europe.[2] His chosen example is the age of Juliet in Shakespeare's play, which led some Victorians and a few modern social historians to suppose that thirteen was a common age for girls to marry in sixteenth-century England—or fourteenth-century Verona. He brought a weight of learning to bear on this curious problem—and with a characteristic wave of the hand he dismissed much literary evidence as fiction. He reckons literary evidence on marriage useless until we have made advance in literary sociology.[3] Save the mark!—What a desperate

---

[1] In my approach to literature I have had invaluable help over many years from Nicholas Brooke, Hugh Sacker, and Marianne Wynn—but none is responsible for the use I have made of it.
[2] Laslett 1983, chap. 4: cf. Laslett 1976.
[3] Laslett 1976; cf. Laslett 1983, esp. pp. 81–6, 312.

notion. It is true that for really humdrum, run-of-the-mill ephemeral literature, quantifiable analysis may be helpful—in the kind of way that Neil McKendrick converts the common message of hundreds of eighteenth- and nineteeth-century pamphlets and novels into an overall picture of attitudes and mentalities to economic progress in the consumer age and the industrial revolution.[4] But for Shakespeare this will hardly do. Laslett made some show of consulting an eminent Shakespearean critic as to why Juliet was so young; but he hardly drew the moral of his own sensible action—for if we want to use literature as historical evidence, we must first of all treat it as literature, and become for a space at least literary critics. So too with art: I remember an eminent art historian telling me all works of art were for him historical documents: an inspiring thought for a historian—if a trifle daunting for those of us who wish to enjoy great pictures without pretending to any expertise. Yet the message is clear: if we wish to understand buildings or pictures as documents, we must study them with the same sceptical expertise we should bring to chronicles or charters—or at least we should try; and I make no more claim for the next three chapters than that I am trying.

In a general kind of way we may sympathize with Peter Laslett's grumble—and with the annoyance of demographers who find fireside readers deducing from *Northanger Abbey* and *Mansfield Park* that in Jane Austen's time young ladies were married at seventeen or eighteen or anyway nineteen; that by the early twenties they were coming to be regarded as old maids, by twenty-five given up for lost.[5] Miss Austen wrote fiction; the parish registers tell us the facts.

[4] McKendrick, forthcoming; see meanwhile McKendrick 1977, 1978.

[5] In point of fact Jane Austen's heroines married at ages not far removed from those of her own family: I hope to write on her novels as evidence for the history of marriage elsewhere.

An ecclesiastical historian is always inclined to smile when he hears that parish registers—or bishops' registers, or inquisitors' records—contain only facts. I have very friendly feelings for the Reverend J. A. Giles, in a sense my predecessor, for he edited Gilbert Foliot's and John of Salisbury's works, and countless others, in the 1840s and 1850s; he made a living out of editing medieval texts—no mean feat—in compensation for the living he lost; for he was deprived of his benefice in Oxford for the kindly misdemeanour of altering his parish register to save the reputation of a young lady parishioner.[6] I have often thought of Dr Giles when reading the works of modern demographers.

But nothing is further from my purpose than to denigrate the work of modern social historians and demographers; for their achievement I have the highest respect, and for their manner of work the kind of envy born of impatience and a failure in numeracy. My point is simply that parish registers and the novels of Jane Austen are alike historical evidence, and neither can be used with safety unless one has meditated a little on their nature and purpose, and studied what we might call their diplomatic—their status as documents and evidence. Jane Austen's picture of the age of marriage actually conformed fairly well to the practice of her own family and even if it were true that she had misrepresented any normal viewpoint—which is a matter of evidence in itself—we cannot suppose that so influential a novelist can have failed to impress many of her young female readers with the desirability of following in the footsteps of Elizabeth Bennet or Fanny Price—or alternatively of taking a warning from Lydia Bennet or Maria Bertram.[7] The use of imaginative literature as historical evidence is indeed full of booby-traps; and for no one more than for a

---

[6] On Giles see *DNB*; *GFL*, pp. 21–2.
[7] See n. 5.

medievalist. One has only to consider for a moment what truths of social history one might try to wrench from some version of the stories of Lancelot and Guinevere or Tristan and Isolde to take out an insurance policy against ever being wholly dependent on such stuff.

Yet in the history of marriage one cannot afford to ignore any kind of evidence. If one wishes to know anything of the inwardness of marriage—of how choices were made, of the true relations of marriage partners—the evidence is scattered and nearly always difficult; to ignore, or voluntarily renounce any use of literature, is an act of austerity or even blindness in the end. Not only so, but one of the convictions of my own scholarly life has been that the literary critics have much to teach the historian; that long hours spent with Shakespeare or Chaucer help to equip a man to interpret the records of the inquisition or the rare surviving correspondence between husband and wife; and if we wish to interpret the most famous of all medieval marriages, that of Heloise and Abelard, we must remember that their own letters are works of literature.[8]

There is a wealth of medieval literature which could be brought forth to help us, but I have deliberately chosen two of the most sophisticated of medieval poets to illustrate my theme: Wolfram von Eschenbach and Geoffrey Chaucer—with Shakespeare as epilogue to remind us of the significance and insignificance of the barriers in and around 1500. To Wolfram we, and Wagner, owe the supreme version of one of the great traditional international stories of the Middle Ages, the story of Sir Perceval the Welshman and the Holy Grail. It was a Celtic legend in German costume; it came at the end of two generations at least of romantic elaboration. The chief legendary centre of courtly romance in the twelfth century

---

[8] See p. 99. Nicholas Brooke has commented to me on his 'complementary conviction that the literary critic desperately needs to attend to the historian'.

was the court of King Arthur; its actual centre lay in France; and the first major poem on the Grail legend was *Li Contes del Graal* of Chrétien of Troyes, an extremely sophisticated romance poet of the late twelfth century.

Chrétien wrote poems which revolve round the fantastical conventions of courtly love—of the courtesy which makes capricious woman an object not only of adoration but of worship. There has been a ceaseless discussion as to the meaning of courtly love. Was it the origin of the romantic tradition? Was it romantic at all? Did it sanctify adultery, or marriage?[9]—and it is partly for this reason that I concentrate on specific texts. No one doubts that a chivalric code of some sort was characteristic of much twelfth-century vernacular literature; that one can discern in the French courtly romances, in a variety of forms, a code of chivalry; nor that it survived for many centuries. We may meet it elaborately enriched in the fifteenth century, fantastically fossilized in the sixteenth; it even survives in attenuated form in P. G. Wodehouse. *The Code of the Woosters* assumes that if a man wishes to be thought a *preux chevalier* he must treat a lady's whims with reverence and obey them—even to the point of accompanying her to the altar if she insists. Theft and blackmail are quite within the code—'Good old blackmail!' said Aunt Dahlia, 'you can't beat it'; but refusing a damsel's unreasonable requests is not.

There was always much tradition in it of a purely literary kind. Whatever we may wish to ascribe to Islamic

[9] I use the word 'romantic' here solely because it is a label widely used, like 'feudal'—not because it has any precise meaning. Both words are in essence concepts of the nineteenth and twentieth centuries. Lewis 1936, for all the justified criticism it has received, is still a stimulating introduction. Cf. the essays in Newman 1968. For recent appraisals of the literature on courtly love, see Boase 1977 and Liebertz-Grün 1977; for the relation of courtly love and marriage see Kelly (H.A.) 1975 and the extensive literature cited. For its place in twelfth-century culture, see Brooke 1969, chap. 6; Brooke 1971, chap. 1. On Chrétien, see Noble 1982.

influence from Spain on the early Provençal lyric, there is no doubt that Ovid was the master of many twelfth-century poets and lovers—and many of later epochs.[10] But the romance poets developed their own conventions too, appropriate—in the paradoxical sense in which literary conventions are appropriate to the societies which embrace them—to their own world. A cynic might say that the code of chivalry represented the opposite of the society in which it thrived: chivalry is about heroic knights who perform endless improbable feats of prowess and magic in a slavery of homage to their ladies; feudal society was in fact a man's world in which women were inferior creatures whose whims were disregarded. Human affairs do not operate in this simple fashion. Parzival and Gawan, the undefeated champions of the world of fiction, had their counterparts in men like William the Marshal, the Anglo-Norman baron whose sober life reads in many passages like a vernacular romance.[11] For he was a landless man—the younger son of a baron; bred to war and chivalry indeed, but with no hereditary prospect of high position. He was the victor in many a tournament, and the model of loyalty to his overlords; by good service he won one of the greatest heiresses in the Anglo-Norman empire, and rose to be regent of England. His wealth was mainly based on his wife's inheritance. Not entirely—for as he said on his deathbed (if his biographer may be believed): 'The clerks are too hard on us. They shave us too closely. I have captured 500 knights and have appropriated their arms, horses, and their entire equipment. If for this reason the kingdom of God is closed to

---

[10] There are helpful accounts of Ovid's influence in Kelly (H.A.) 1975, Leclercq 1979, pp. 64–85, and Martindale 1988; and an admirable summary of recent scholarship and literature on Ovid in *OCD* 1970, pp. 763–5 (E. J. Kenney). The old argument about Islamic influence on Provençal and courtly literature still goes on—but the notion of any precise Arabic sources for Provençal lyric seems out of fashion.

[11] Meyer 1891–1901; Painter 1933.

me, I can do nothing about it, for I cannot return my booty. . . . But their teaching is false—else no one could be saved.'[12] In the modern world an undefeated champion in a fairly brutal sport is sometimes made a hero; and this is bizarre enough. We should regard it as ludicrous to seek out such for a president or a premier. But in twelfth- or thirteenth-century Europe the ruling nobility were knights; and though the Marshal's promotion was unusual there was nothing incongruous in its causes. In a similar way the English King Edward I prepared for many years of hard-headed kingly rule by crusade and chivalry and tournament.[13]

The knightly adventures in the courtly romances dwell in a world of fantasy. They are commonly performed to do honour to a lady—and even when they are not, it is often implied that they ought to be, or that the audience will expect them to be.[14] The female dominance in the society portrayed by the poems seems at first only to add to the fantasy, however much we recognize the role in that world of many remarkable women. What possible use can such absurdities be to the historian of marriage? We shall not seek in them for realism, or for any simple transcript of human experience. We recognize that there is much of literary tradition and of fashion in them. Yet we cannot evade the power of the sentiments they express, or imagine them wholly without influence. Real life is full of paradox; and the romances reveal some of the paradoxes of medieval society with a good deal of force. But there is much more to it than that. For the romances were used by their authors—and especially by the more intelligent and reflective of the poets—to search out the paradoxes and the meaning of the strange world their characters inhabit.

[12] Trans. Painter 1933, pp. 285–6; Painter 1940, p. 89; quoted Brooke 1961, p. 243.
[13] Powicke 1947, ii. 606–17, esp. 613.
[14] A striking example is Wolfram's *Willehalm*, where heathen and Christian alike are expected to be inspired by their ladies.

7. Literary Evidence: Wolfram

Chrétien of Troyes

To do honour to a woman: but in what sense? Did the romances tend to idealize marriage, or adultery?—Or did they have a platonic tendency, leading to the worship of unattainable deities? Such questions have been frequently asked, and have received very various answers. Some critics have resorted to statistics and counted the number of successful marriages in this or that poet. But for our purpose the problems and the questions they posed are of more value than the answers: for it is in grappling with unanswerable questions that Chrétien of Troyes, foremost among the French poets of the late twelfth century, and Gottfried von Strassburg and Wolfram von Eschenbach, leading German poets of the early thirteenth, showed the depth of their understanding of the problems of which this book is composed.

Chrétien can describe with relish and panache a good conventional wedding. In *Erec et Enide* he fetches in the archbishop of Canterbury to bless them in the solemnity, and bishops and archbishops assemble to see them to bed.[15] When he gets home, Erec goes to church to give thanks: he kneels before the altar of the crucifix, his wife before the image of Our Lady. But even in this poem a major theme is the damage a happy marriage brings to a hero. Erec so much rejoices in his wife's company that he loses all incentive to knightly prowess—and so falls into a disgrace which Enide feels as acutely as he. He has to put her and himself through countless trials before his honour, or at least his self-respect, is restored. In his *Cligès* Chrétien seems indeed to be parodying the whole romance tradition. He sets the tone early in the poem by describing how a queen observes a young man and a

[15] *Erec*, 2025–2134 (Foerster 1884–99, iii. 75–9). On *Erec* cf. Leclercq 1979, pp. 129–32.

maiden rapidly changing colour on a sea voyage—which
she attributes to seasickness. This was a trick Chrétien
had learned from the *Ars amatoria* of Ovid,[16] and the
poem is an extraordinary mingling of Ovid's amorous
works and of the romance of Arthur and Alexander;
a kind of light-hearted ecumenical gathering of the
matter of Greece and the matter of Britain, in which
many improbable amatory problems are explored. The
conversion of Ovid into romance is indeed a common
event in this literary world; for Ovid himself had mingled
serious and comic, had explored the byways and the
paradoxes of human love, with just the mixture of
gravity and whimsical humour which delighted the
more sophisticated minds of the twelfth and thirteenth
centuries. A celebrated example is *The Treatise on Love* of
Andreas the Chaplain, which converts Ovid's and other
more contemporary situations into a solemn scholastic
tract analysing all the elements of love—how it is to be
conducted, how advanced, how men show their devotion,
how women their caprice, and a great deal more—for
there is in a section at the end a kind of *Remedium
amoris* after the *Ars*, that propounds clerical morality
condemning all manner of carnal delights.[17] Andreas
delighted the clerks of Paris, and this led to his being
taken too seriously by the bishop of Paris in 1277, who
caught him in the same net as St Thomas Aquinas when
trawling for errors.[18] But he remains an authentic witness

[16] *Cligès*, 541–74 (Foerster 1884–99, i. 22–3); cf. Ovid, *Ars am.* i. 723–34;
Brooke 1969, p. 176.
[17] For the *De amore*, sometimes called *Ars honeste amandi*, see Trojel 1892;
Parry 1969; above all, the new edition by P. G. Walsh (1982); for recent
commentary, Benton 1961, pp. 578–82; Benton 1962; Leclercq 1979, pp. 115–19;
Karnein 1981; Monson 1988; cf. Silvestre 1985, p. 193. An earlier generation of
critics was inclined to take it too seriously and date it too early; but for the
former offence they had good precedent in the act of the bishop of Paris in 1277.
It could be as late as the early thirteenth century, but a date at the end of the
twelfth seems more likely—for to the twelfth belong the characters he cites.
[18] Parry 1969, pp. 21–2.

of his world, in which clerical and lay tastes could often mingle. He also has many references to the leading ladies of his day, or of a previous generation.[19] Most intriguing is the celebrated text he gives of a judgement by Marie, countess of Champagne, which is in form a delectable parody of a papal decretal. 'We declare and we hold as firmly established that love cannot exert its powers between two people who are married to each other. For lovers give each other everything freely, under no compulsion of necessity, but married people are in duty bound to give in to each other's desires and deny themselves to each other in nothing.'[20]

The Countess Marie was daughter of Eleanor of Aquitaine, wife of both Louis VII of France and of Henry II of England, and herself wife of Henry the Liberal, count of Champagne (1152–81).[21] She evidently had some celebrity in these discussions, since Chrétien attributed to her the material of—and the instruction to write—his Lancelot, *Le Chevalier de la charette.* Queen Guinevere was captured, and an unnamed knight, later revealed to be Lancelot, sets off to rescue her. To find his way he must mount a cart: to travel thus will disgrace him in the eyes of fellow knights; not to leap instantly to any disgrace in her service must lower him in the eyes of his lady. He hesitates a moment, then leaps aboard. His hesitation somehow comes to the queen's ears, and he is duly punished for it. But otherwise all goes well, and after a series of improbable adventures, he receives his reward.

> He comes to the bed of the queen, whom he adores and before whom he kneels, for he has no such faith in any holy saint. All that night Lancelot's joy and pleasure were very great. But, to his sorrow, day comes when he

---

[19] It is not certain that the author was really a chaplain of the Countess Marie.
[20] Parry 1969, pp. 106–7; Trojel 1892, pp. 152–5.
[21] Benton 1961; for Count Henry see also John of Salisbury, *Letters*, ii. 314–15 n.

must leave his mistress' side. It cost him such pain to leave her that he suffered a real martyr's agony . . . When he leaves the room, he bows and acts precisely as if he were before an altar; then he goes with a heavy heart . . . .[22]

Perhaps some risk was involved in showing a knight committing adultery with a queen; Chrétien may have been prudent to attribute the message of his poem to an eminent patroness. But the story is told with the utmost panache—and the scene of adultery with gusto. We need not take Chrétien's excuses any more seriously than we do Wolfram's, when he attributes his version of the story of Parzival to Kyot the Provençal, who had it from the Arabic, or some such tongue.[23] The effect of Lancelot's adultery is clear: if love is carried to such extremes that it becomes a cult, then it parodies the cults of the saints; Lancelot suffers a martyr's agony. We cannot know what Chrétien himself thought, or wished us to think. But we can read the paradox and the problem: if the world is God's world, and good, there must be a place for human love within it; but its pursuit may lead us to blasphemy. We do not have to follow Peter Damian to see that.

The Grail and Tristan

Some writers sought an escape from this dilemma into a purer world in which knighthood and courtly love are separated: this made the fortune of the Grail legend, in which the quest is undertaken not solely, or primarily or

---

[22] Chrétien, *Lancelot* (in Foerster 1884–99, iv), 4668–4739; Chrétien 1914 (W. W. Comfort's translation, p. 329), slightly adapted.
[23] *Parzival*, 453. 11–14; 827. 3–6; Hatto 1980, pp. 232 ('heathenish'), 410; cf. Brooke in James, Brooke, and Mynors 1983, pp. xx–xxi, and esp. Wynn 1984, pp. 262–70.

at all, for a lady, but in pursuit of some spiritual goal. This was the theme of another of Chrétien's romances, and in its turn—by reinterpretation of Chrétien—of Wolfram's *Parzival*.[24] What Chrétien meant by the Grail we cannot tell, for his poem was unfinished, but it seems to be a container for the host—not as in other versions a chalice. Indeed, there is no more hopeless quest than for the Grail's origin, since it was by definition unattainable—as Wolfram was to say rather noisily in his conclusion.[25] It could be a cup, reminiscent of the Last Supper—it could be a stone, as Trevrizent describes it in *Parzival*; but it *must* be a mystery.

In sharp contrast, the story of Tristan and Isolde held a special fascination for those who wished to pursue the theme that the god of love was also a god of adultery—all the more clearly so since no issue of moral intent could be involved in the amours of Tristan and Isolde as their love was induced by a love potion. All this is made abundantly clear in the *Tristan* of Gottfried von Strassburg—written at much the same time as Wolfram's *Parzival*, for Wolfram and Gottfried were sworn antagonists—about the first decade of the thirteenth century.[26] Gottfried's analysis reminds a modern reader of the kind of biologist who attributes all human emotion to chemistry. But that is not to say that Gottfried himself held amoral opinions; what he believed himself, heaven knows.

It is a repellent story, brilliantly told. Never has a rich

[24] Chrétien, *Li Contes del Graal* in Hilka 1932; see also Linker 1952; for Wolfram's use of Chrétien, see Wynn 1984; for the Grail in general, Loomis 1959. But I am extremely sceptical of attempts to find a common origin for the Grail legends, for reasons given in the text. For Wolfram's version of the Grail as a stone, see Sacker 1963, pp. 121–2; *Parzival*, 469. 3–7, 28; Hatto 1980, pp. 239, 431–2.

[25] See below, p. 190.

[26] I use the edition of Gottfried by Weber 1967; and Hatto 1960, in which a translation of Gottfried and the surviving fragments of Gottfried's main source, the *Tristran* of Thomas, are included. For the issue of moral intent, see p. 186. On Gottfried cf. Von Ertzdorff 1981.

medieval costume been so lovingly, so lavishly described as in the rococo phrases with which Gottfried portrays the robes of Isolde.[27] Never has a medieval shrine been so vividly portrayed as in the description of the cave of lovers in which the pair secretly cohabit.[28] Yet, these are but the limbs and outer flourishes of a tale which is not at all, in any modern sense, romantic. Isolde is by nature a tigress. When she first encounters Tristan, she has an urge to murder him in his bath—with some reason, since he has killed her uncle.[29] But later, he and she seek refreshment while at sea on their way to her wedding with King Mark and accidentally drink the magic potion intended for Isolde and Mark—and from then on they are hopelessly, inescapably, bound by love. When she approaches her wedding-night she is no longer a virgin, so they arrange for her attendant Brangane to sleep first with Mark—an entirely satisfactory arrangement, for one woman is much like another to the besotted king. But it puts Isolde in Brangane's power and she plots to murder her too—though she is luckily prevented.[30] Tristan is not quite so bad—he is a decent cultivated prince, and a champion prize-fighter who would like to be loyal to his uncle King Mark if he could—but love is more powerful than loyalty. As for Mark, he is the type of the feeble cuckold. What will come to them in the end is not quite clear, since the poem is unfinished—and though we have the conclusion of its principal source, the *Tristran* of the Anglo-Norman Thomas, Thomas had given it a tragic ending which reminds a modern audience a little of *Romeo and Juliet*—and it is hard to see how Gottfried's characters had earned anything so moving.[31] Love is the

---

[27] Gottfried, 10885–10985; Weber 1967, pp. 303–6; Hatto 1960, pp. 185–6.

[28] Gottfried, 16679–17139; Weber 1967, pp. 464–77; Hatto 1960, pp. 261–6.

[29] Gottfried, 10080–10497, 11958–11963; Weber 1967, pp. 281–92, 333; Hatto 1960, pp. 174–9, 199.

[30] Gottfried, 11875–13096; Weber 1967, pp. 331–65; Hatto 1960, pp. 198–213.

[31] Hatto 1960, pp. 349–53; cf. Beroul's version, also fragmentary: Fedrick 1970.

moving force of the poem; but it is not the love of God, nor a human emotion capable of good and evil; but a tyrannical, arbitrary, murderous deity. Gottfried may have been a scoffer and a sceptic; his learning, however, strongly suggests he was a clerk; he could even, just possibly, have been a fervent ascetic enfolding the whole beastly world of courtly love in layers of critical irony. It is hard to imagine him so. We cannot tell what he himself believed; but we can feel the force of his poem.

Wolfram's Parzival

It is, however, a work of literature far removed from human problems as we experience them; and for our present purpose Wolfram has more to offer. He was a knight, proud of his order; he makes no secret that loyalty, *triuwe*—to God, one's fellow creatures, one's order and one's wife—a quality which is itself a spectrum of qualities, is the central pillar of his universe.[32] He was a fervent believer. But he also claims to be virtually illiterate, to know nothing of books; and he keeps the clergy well out of his world. There are chaplains to sing mass;[33] but no bishops or archbishops. The anchoress Sigune prays without ceasing and never hears mass; and the saintly figure who instructs Parzival in the truth of God's providence and of the grail is a lay hermit, his uncle Trevrizent. Yet the poem is shot through with theology, and he makes Trevrizent say 'Although I was a layman I could read and indite the message of the Scriptures';[34] the

[32] On *triuwe*, see Brooke 1971, p. 151; Sacker 1963, pp. 44, 50–1, 54–5—and for God's *triuwe*, pp. 96–9; Wynn 1984, pp. 215–31, who gives a searching analysis of this central concept.

[33] See e.g. below, p. 192. For his supposed illiteracy, see n. 73.

[34] *Parzival*, 462. 11–13; Hatto 1980, p. 236.

text has many hidden echoes of the Bible;[35] the names of people and places in his *Parzival* and *Willehalm* reflect a fantastic range of learning assuredly not all culled from hearsay. Above all, though he does not give the display of culture that glitters in the pages of Chrétien or Gottfried, he had a powerful and highly sophisticated sense of literature. The *Parzival* is far longer than any of Chrétien's surviving poems: it is comparable in length to the *Odyssey*. From summaries one may cull the impression that it is excessively long, and full of purely decorative detail. But it does not read so: the alternation of pace is marvellously controlled: it reads like the fast and slow movements of a symphony—perhaps even more like the alternation of recitative and aria in an oratorio. Equally striking is the alternation of explicit statement and controlled silence. A powerful theme running through it is heredity, inheritance: Parzival combines the qualities and looks of his devoted mother Herzeloyde and his wandering father Gahmuret; so, even more strikingly, and absurdly, does his half-brother Feirefiz who is striped black and white.[36] But the silence is most thunderous when it comes closest to the centre of his faith—when he expounds the inwardness of *triuwe* and of marriage, when he explores God's providence for Parzival.

Parzival's father, Gahmuret the Angevin, had been a knight errant for whom Christendom was far too small. On one occasion he found himself surrounded by Moors—by 'many dusky ladies . . . whose colour resembled the raven's'.[37] He served their Queen Belacane nobly and married her. But presently he was on the move

---

[35] e.g.below, n. 52. For the names in *Parzival*, see Schröder 1982.

[36] Feirefiz is not only striped black and white and equally happy to be a heathen and a Christian, his attitude to his wives is a striking counterpart to his father's—he performs great deeds to honour Secundille (who is certainly his queen if not his wife) but deserts her with only a slight qualm when enamoured of Repanse.

[37] *Parzival*, 20. 4–6; Hatto 1980, p. 23.

again; and in his travels found a new wife, Herzeloyde, who was to be Parzival's mother.

Professor Marianne Wynn, in her recent, distinguished study of *Wolfram's Parzival*, observes that in Chrétien of Troyes's *Li Contes del Graal* there are no betrothals and no marriages, while in Wolfram's poem, in certain respects closely based upon it, there are fourteen—to four of which 'he gives considerable prominence'.[38] She studies with particular care the two marriages of Parzival's father—first to the heathen Belacane, a marriage of love, but one which the husband freely abandons when caught in a trap by the Christian Herzeloyde, whose attitude is a kind of serious parody of Duby's secular model.[39] She is an heiress and must provide the territories she has inherited with an heir; so she stages a tournament whose prize shall be marriage with her—and Gahmuret inadvertently wins the prize. He briefly marries her—and the poet most delicately and ironically shows the marriage of convenience beginning to turn into a marriage of love—when the husband sets off on his travels again, never to return.[40] It is very evident that Wolfram portrays Gahmuret as deliberately casual. You may marry a black heathen if you love her: it seems clear that Wolfram expected his audience to be surprised, to think it something unnatural—the striped visage of their son enforces this when he appears later in the epic—as doubtless Shakespeare intended Desdemona's marriage to appear. But he makes us see it as a real marriage none the less, and poses the question whether Gahmuret was free to abandon it. Herzeloyde and her advisers brush this

[38] Wynn 1984, pp. 317–18.
[39] See above, p. 120.
[40] Wynn 1984, pp. 318–31, with a very subtle analysis especially of the relations between Herzeloyde and Gahmuret, and their influence on Parzival. It is interesting to note that the marriages of Gahmuret and Gawan are consummated on the first night, while Parzival, like Tobias, waits three nights before consummating his marriage with Condwiramurs (see p. 194).

Wolfram's Parzival

aside: she was a heathen; he is free to desert her—a nice point, as very probably was known to Wolfram, in contemporary canon law.[41] We have here, and in his treatment of Feirefiz much later, some adumbration of the theme of tolerance greatly enlarged in *Willehalm*.

Herzeloyde, the deserted wife, attributes her suffering to Gahmuret's chivalric code, and determines to rear Parzival in ignorance of his order and his destiny. But the call to wander comes; he meets an old knight, Gurnemanz, who gives him preliminary instruction in knightly ways, and tells him never to ask questions, and his daughter, Liaze, with whom he begins to fall in love.[42] Then he wanders further, rescues and marries Condwiramurs, and goes on to his first encounter with the palace of the Grail. This is a bald summary: but Wolfram takes us quite swiftly through these crucial stages in the story. In the Grail castle Parzival, true to Gurnemanz's advice, asks no questions, and so fails to fulfil his destiny, which is, by asking the ailing Grail king Anfortas 'Uncle what ails you', to cure him. For this failure and his other sins Parzival is condemned to five years of quest, deprived of the Grail, deprived of his wife.[43] He briefly visits Arthur's court, where he is bitterly denounced by the Grail messenger Cundrie, and wanders despairing away.

The space is filled, not with any prolonged account of Parzival's adventures, but with a long description of the adventures of another knight of the Round Table, Arthur's nephew Gawan—Gawain or Gauvains in French. Gawan's adventures form a sub-plot inherited from Chrétien; and some commentators write as if he formed a distracting, even tedious, interlude. I do not imagine that

[41] See Schumacher 1967, pp. 26–30, and the discussion below, p. 210 and n. 90.
[42] *Parzival*, 162–79; Hatto 1980, pp. 91–9.
[43] Parzival's sins are expounded and shriven in bk. 9 (esp. Hatto 1980, p. 253), his meeting with Trevrizent: see Sacker 1963, chaps. 4, 6. For the chronology of *Parzival*, see Hatto 1980, pp. 432–3.

this was how he struck Wolfram's contemporaries. For this part of the poem—punctuated only by a brief, climacteric return to Parzival, who is taken on his crucial visit to Trevrizent (book 9)—forms in itself one of the most exciting tales of knightly adventure, of war and rumour of war, among all the courtly epics. Gawan is successful in resuming his good name, in rescuing Arthur's mother, trapped by a sorcerer, in winning his wife, in returning to Arthur's court in time to meet Parzival again, as he prepares himself for his second visit to the Grail. After this long portrayal of chivalry at work among knights less exalted than Parzival the poem comes to a conclusion of a similar rapidity to that with which Parzival's adventures opened: after a fierce fight ending in mutual recognition between Parzival and Feirefiz, Parzival returns to the Grail castle, asks the question, cures Anfortas, succeeds him as king—and is now at last free to be reunited to Condwiramurs, his wife. She is indeed on her way to join him (books 15–16). So far the form is marvellously contrived and effective; but the coda which ends the poem—to balance the prologue describing Gahmuret's adventures at the outset— is curiously perfunctory. Parzival and Condwiramurs had two sons, and Loherangrin grows up a Grail knight. But his Grail kingdom remains a secret: he goes off to Brabant, marries a wife, begets children—but she must never ask him who he is. If she does, as in the end she must, a swan will come and carry him off home to his other kingdom. No one has ever made much sense of this epilogue; all that it seems to say is—ask me no more about the Grail kingdom, for it must for ever be mysterious. Chrétien got it wrong; with Kyot's help I have corrected him. And then the conclusion, tremendous in its understatement. 'When a life comes so to an end that God is not deprived of the soul through the body's guilt, and the man yet can keep the world's respect in a worthy manner, that is a useful work [*daz ist ein nütziu arbeit*].'[44]

It will be apparent that neither the visits to the Grail castle, nor Parzival's marriage nor his life with Condwiramurs, occupy any great space in the poem; but Wolfram contrives none the less, by delicate repetition, to enforce the point that both are central to its meaning. After Parzival's marriage five years of separation ensue, and most of the action of the poem, before they meet again; but we are frequently reminded that while other folk were inspired by a variety of ladies, Parzival never ceased to recall his wife: his *triuwe*, his loyalty to her, is more constant than his loyalty to God.[45]

The marriages of Gahmuret—fleeting, yet profound in their consequences for his deserted wives—form the backcloth to the most notable marriage scene in *Parzival*, the marriage of the hero himself with Condwiramurs. Wolfram is confusing to read, because he is at once extremely secular and thoroughly sophisticated, a deeply orthodox Christian and firmly anti-clerical—at least to the point of keeping clergy out of all important scenes including marriage rituals; and he is just as firm with the lawyers on this point—so that there are no legal arrangements and no nuptial blessing or nuptial mass; but his fourteen betrothals and marriages and numerous liaisons of less formality include every possible variety of union between man and woman; though their informality reminds us that the borderline between love and marriage could not appear so distinct to a layman as they appeared to the lawyer and the priest.[46] He is like Shakespeare in

[44] *Parzival*, 827. 19–24; my own translation (Hatto 1980, pp. 410–11). On Kyot see esp. *Parzival*, 453. 11–455. 24; Hatto 1980, pp. 232–3.
[45] For Parzival's doubt of God, see p. 199. For his recollections of his wife, see *Parzival*, 282. 23–293. 16; 333. 23–6; 441. 4–14; 460. 9–10; 467. 25–30; 474. 14–19; 619. 4–12; 732. 1–14; 734. 10–16; 743. 12–22; 781. 17–21 and 783. 4–10; 799. 1–11; Hatto 1980, pp. 148–53, 173, 226, 235, 239, 242, 310, 364, 366, 370, 387–8, 396—for their reunion, see below pp. 199–201.
[46] And in some contexts *minnen*, to love, in medieval German can mean 'marry'.

being at once utterly detached from and deeply involved in the official formulas of his age. Gahmuret, Parzival, and Gawan are 'married' to their wives by entry to the bridal chamber; but in Parzival's case this does not mean (as we shall see) immediate consummation. The anchoress Signune prays ceaselessly by the shrine of the man she loved: 'I am a virgin and unwed: yet before God he is my husband'— thus paradoxically focusing on a problem to which we frequently return.[47]

The wooing of Parzival and Condwiramurs is brief. Parzival, still very young and untried, but already in love with her cousin Liaze, comes riding to the court of Condwiramurs, which he finds besieged and in great straits. A warrior king is trying to seize her throne and marry her by force. After a dull evening in which he shows the same shyness to ask and to talk which is to be his undoing in his first visit to the Grail castle soon after, he retires to bed; and in the middle of the night the queen steals to his room to seek his help. The poet is emphatic that her purpose is conversation and not love;[48] and in an odd way the moving scene in which she weeps beside him and begs his help serves to emphasize that their relationship is one of total trust. Next morning 'he heard a great ringing of bells, calling to church and minster those whom Clamide [the enemy] had rendered joyless. From his couch the young man rose. The queen's chaplain sang mass to the honour of God and his lady. The guest could not choose but gaze at her' till the blessing[49]—and thus the mass serves a double function. It gives Parzival the

---

[47] See pp. 186, 262; *Parzival*, 440. 7–8; Hatto 1980, p. 225. For what follows, *Parzival*, bk. 4: Hatto 1980, pp. 100–19.

[48] In a similar scene Chrétien gives the opposite impression (*Li Contes del Graal*, 1952–2074, Hilka 1932, pp. 80–1; Linker 1960, pp. 88–93): Wolfram's purpose here may be partly to enforce on his hearers the difference between Condwiramurs and any character in Chrétien's poem.

[49] The quotations are from the translation in Richey 1935, pp. 62–71, here p. 68; *Parzival* 196. 12–19.

opportunity to realize how beautiful she is and that his promise to serve her, though entirely chivalrous in motive, may bring other rewards with it. And the mass itself sets off by contrast the ceremonies which follow. Priests and ecclesiastical ritual are rare in Parzival;[50] there seems to have been a layman's distaste for clergy somewhere in Wolfram's being—at least that tremendous sense of pride in his own knightly order which plays so large a part in his world of ideas. Yet the poem is deeply religious, and it is significant that at an even greater turning-point than his marriage, when he visits his uncle Trevrizent many books and four years later, it is in confession to a layman—albeit a knight turned hermit— that the true revelation of God's purposes comes to him.[51]

Meanwhile the enemy's champion rides to battle and Parzival duly defeats him; and he offers him instead of the death which the champion himself had so often dealt to others, service to this or that of his former enemies. The champion reckons his chances of survival minimal, and eventually accepts Parzival's final punishment—to go to Britain. Then the hero is led before the queen, thrilled to be released from the champion of her enemy, Clamide, her would-be husband. 'She embraced [Parzival], hugged him close and said: "I will wed no man on earth save him, whom I have just embraced". Then she helped unarm him, gave him the best of her service. After his great exertions, he broke his fast on whatever lean fare they had. And now the burghers came and swore homage to him, saying he should be their lord; and the queen, replying, said he should be her lover, after so fair a victory as he had won.' Then relief comes in the shape of ships laden with food, and the rest of the day is spent in feasting. In the evening 'the question was asked: Should the bridal bed be got ready? He and the queen said "Yes."'

---

[50] See p. 186.
[51] Bk. 9, esp. 501. 15–18; Hatto 1980, p. 254.

—and he lay with her. But Parzival showed his courtesy and piety and forbearance, in contrast to Gahmuret and most of Wolfram's men, by not making love to her at once.[52]

> So he whom they called the Red Knight left the queen a maid. She, however, thought she was now his wife, and in token of his love bound her hair matronwise next day, with a fillet. The virgin bride then openly bestowed both land and castles on him, who was the beloved of her heart. So they remained, glad in their love for each other, two days and a third night. Often he thought of embracing, and recalled his mother's advice, and how Gurnemanz, too, had said that man and woman were one. And now I may tell you, he soon discovered the old and ever new custom of love, and found it pleasant.

Wolfram, deeply pious man though he was, shows no sympathy for the ascetic idea that celibacy was a better way of life.

Wolfram makes sure we know that their day began with mass, as in all the best Christian royal households of the day;[53] and that the height of Parzival's reward for his success in pursuit of the Grail was the love of his wife. All this makes the marriage ceremony, if such it can be called, the more astonishing. There is no formal betrothal, no exchange of oaths, no priestly blessing at church door or anywhere else, no nuptial mass; and the poet emphasizes

---

[52] *Parzival*, 199. 24–200. 5; 201. 19–20; 202–3; for what follows 202. 21–203. 10; Richey, pp. 69–71. Parzival was following the precedent, much admired by medieval moralists, of Tobias, in the Latin version of Tob. 8: 4–5: Tobias and Sara passed three nights in prayer, in which '*Deo iungimur; tertia autem transacta nocte in nostro erimus coniugio. Filii quippe sanctorum sumus, et non possunt ita coniungi, sicut gentes quae ignorant Deum*'. The precedent was not followed by Gahmuret or Gawan. Wolfram may well have Tobias in mind; we cannot be sure; but there are a number of hints that he knew the Bible well, like Trevrizent—e.g. in the way he puts biblical echoes into his characters' mouths, thus attributing Gen. 2: 24 ('*erunt duo in carne una*') to Gurnemanz (see below).

[53] A monarch of exceptional piety might hear three masses a day, as was alleged of Henry III of England: Brooke and Brooke 1984, p. 164.

that the virgin queen regarded herself as fully his wife none the less, and proceeded to endow him with a dowry. There are many strands here, and books have been written on the theme.[54] There is a deliberate oddity about the marriage, for to emphasize Parzival's tendency to dumbness at this stage of his career the queen makes all the first advances and proposes to him. But it is a perfect marriage none the less; and the effect of the way the poet describes it is to make us see that all the legal forms and ceremonies, even the religious blessing, even consummation, are secondary—to a deep inner consent and union. In Wolfram's own language, *triuwe*, loyalty, is the supreme virtue—and *triuwe* to one's wife the supreme virtue in marriage. What happens here is the mutual giving by husband and wife of *triuwe* to each other. Later theologians propounded the doctrine that marriage as a sacrament is not made by priests or by outside witnesses, but by the partners themselves, first as an oath (*sacramentum* in one of its original senses) then by mutual self-giving.[55] There were doubtless hints of this in some twelfth-century theologians, and it is very clearly implied in the letters of Heloise and Abelard, which are unlikely to have been known to Wolfram—though their story may well have been. But the force of the passage seems to me quite clear: marriage is an inner consent and bond made by the queen and Parzival; they needed no ceremonies or legal forms.

Wolfram thus shows us what a thinking layman, without formal theological training, but a deep knowledge of the trends and tendencies of twelfth-century theological speculation, could believe. The similarity between Wolfram and Shakespeare is that they both present to us a vision of

[54] Schumacher 1967; Wiegand 1972.
[55] See p. 274: and for what follows—there are no MSS of the letters of Heloise and Abelard earlier than the late thirteenth century, but it has recently been argued that they were known to Chrétien of Troyes (Laurie 1986).

marriage as it appeared to a highly intelligent, deeply reflective layman.[56] Both had a considerable range of knowledge of the laws and ceremonies surrounding marriage (so far as we can tell); and Parzival's marriage indeed is not intelligible without some understanding of canon law. For it seems deliberately to avoid all the crucial points—the formal promises, consummation (which follows indeed but after an interval), a priestly blessing. Wolfram was interested in all these things, and avoided them; presumably to emphasize the inward nature of the sacrament—that a true inner assent, the private, personal union of husband and wife, was to him of the essence. It is a union based on trust, *triuwe*, however obscure to us may be the root and origin of that trust. It is much more doubtful if Shakespeare was so interested in law or theology; but he was deeply interested in the exploration of human experience and of human attitudes at all sorts of levels. In both cases the literary evidence gives us a precious glimpse of the range of human enquiry and human interest: the exceptionally intelligent layman's view perhaps—but it is the range of experience which we could not hope otherwise to explore.

Wolfram's lasting interest for our enquiry is evidently for the statement of the doctrine of marriage which he gives, and its bearing on both the secular and the religious values of his age. First of all, the contrast he draws between the perfect marriage of Parzival and Condwiramurs—as it is meant to be—and the inadequacy or shallowness or folly of other relationships, be they the more superficial union of Gawan[57] or the informal affairs through which Wolfram shows his contempt for courtly love as commonly understood. The difference is deliciously expounded in the attitude of Feirefiz to his queens. When he entered the scene he was inspired (like his father before him) by a

---

[56] See chap. 9.
[57] *Parzival*, 643; Hatto 1980, p. 322; see also above, p. 192.

heathen queen, Secundille.[58] After his arrival at the Grail castle he falls head over heels in love with Repanse de Schoye, the lady who carried the Grail and is Parzival's aunt—his maternal aunt, so not related to Feirefiz. Meanwhile the princes of the Grail discover that Feirefiz cannot see the Grail because he is a heathen—and urge him to be baptized. But Feirefiz asks if baptism will help him 'to win love'; and Parzival answers that it would at least enable him to woo her. So Feirefiz has it firmly in mind that baptism and wooing are closely linked—and both with doing service for one's lady—'If one gets baptism by fighting, send me there at once', he eagerly cries out.[59] Next day Parzival and an aged priest try to instruct him in the Christian faith and to explain how he must renounce his heathen gods and receive the water of baptism.

'If it will soothe my anguish, I shall believe all you tell me [he says to the priest] . . . If her love rewards me, I shall gladly fulfil God's commandments. [And to Parzival:] Brother, if your aunt has God, I believe in Him and her . . . In the name of your aunt's God, baptize me!'[60] And so he was baptized and received his reward—the poet does not pause to consult Repanse on her view of the matter—and poor Secundille is renounced along with Jupiter and the devil. This is almost the last incident in the poem, and so it ends as it began by touching the question: can a Christian marry a heathen; can such a marriage be valid?—Or if a heathen spouse renounces his faith, is he tied to his heathen mate?[61] In *Parzival* Wolfram brushes the edge of the question—and with it the wider issue of God's destiny for the unbeliever; in his *Willehalm* it comes

---

[58] *Parzival*, 740. 7–12; 757. 6–14; 768. 10–771. 22; 811. 8–14; 822. 19–20 and 823. 6–7; Hatto 1980, pp. 369, 376, 381–3, 402, 408 (for Secundille's death). Secundille is queen of Tribalibot in 'India'.

[59] *Parzival*, 814. 25–7; Hatto 1980, p. 404; for what follows, pp. 404–8.

[60] *Parzival*, 818. 2–12; Hatto 1980, p. 406.

[61] See p. 210 and n. 90.

much nearer the heart of the poem. For the moment he resolves it by sending messengers who greet Feirefiz and his new wife, as they prepare to set off for Feirefiz's kingdom, with the news that Secundille has conveniently passed away.[62]

There is an element here of comic relief, but a serious message too. Feirefiz urges Anfortas to sail away with him and his new wife to his kingdom; but Anfortas refuses. He had earned his suffering by breaking the rules of the Grail. He had jousted in women's honour: but the knights of the Grail are sworn to chastity, and even their king may only be a husband, not a lover.[63] Henceforth Anfortas will joust again—but for the Grail, not for the ladies.

The Grail offered an inspiration for a knight on his quest alternative to service for a lady. Wolfram profoundly modified this by introducing Condwiramurs as Parzival's wife. In Wolfram's presentation of the Grail ethic, as expounded by Trevrizent, the king can marry, and he alone—though other servants of the Grail, like Repanse, were evidently allowed to leave the castle on marriage. But the marriage of Parzival is not just a concession; it is central to the meaning of the poem and the life and inspiration of the hero. The main theme of the poem, then, is the quest of the Grail: at the human level the story of how Parzival, owing to his early failures, loses all faith in himself, and yet by dogged loyalty, by *triuwe*, the knight's supreme virtue, wins God's approbation and providential help.

It is a poem profoundly theological in intent. In his agony after Cundrie, the Grail messenger, had denounced

---

[62] *Parzival*, 822. 18–20; 823. 4–7; Hatto 1980, p. 408. Her removal seems perfunctory—but she may be intended, like Belacane, to die of grief owing to Feirefiz's departure.

[63] *Parzival*, 819–20; Hatto 1980, pp. 406–7; cf. Trevrizent's explanation of the chastity of the Grail knights: 'Those knights who are resolved on serving the Grail must forego women's love. Only the king may have a spouse in wedlock, and those others whom God has sent to be lords in lordless lands' (495. 7–12; Hatto 1980, p. 251).

him, Parzival cried 'Alas, what is God? . . . Were he all-powerful—were God active in his all-mightiness—he would not have brought us to such shame! Ever since I knew of Grace I have been his humble servitor. But now I will quit his service.'[64] God's *triuwe* has failed him: he makes his act of *diffidatio*, of knightly defiance. But this cannot be truly so, and in the end Parzival comes to acknowledge it. In the meeting with Trevrizent it is emphasized that Parzival is under God's providence: it is his dogged *triuwe* in spite of that moment of total despair which has won God's aid. Or is it? May it not be that as the heir to the Grail he was under God's predestined fate? Wolfram leaves this question in silence.[65] But the final sentence of the poem shows clearly where his sympathies lie: with those who see in a man's striving to do good in this world a way of earning God's election in the next. Knightly *triuwe* sums up all that is best in the world of chivalry in Wolfram's eyes; and he searches out every aspect of it with great subtlety and gusto, and at length. The significance of Parzival's marriage is that it enables him to show one of the highest forms of *triuwe* possible in knightly circles, *triuwe* to one's wife. The marriage we have witnessed had to survive five years of separation; yet it was never strained; the moment of real happiness and triumph for Parzival is his reunion with wife and children. For children there were already; Wolfram would have accepted that they were part of marriage, inseparable from its nature and purposes. But it is the union of husband and wife, at bed and board, their pleasure in one another, pleasure in each other's company, pleasure in sleeping together, which makes marriage so joyous a thing in Wolfram's eyes.

---

[64] *Parzival*, 332. 1–7; Hatto 1980, p. 172.
[65] Sacker 1963, pp. 166–71, esp. 170–1, and refs. Cf. esp. *Parzival*, 798. 2–5; Hatto 1980, p. 396. For what follows, see pp. 190–1 and n. 44.

Parzival rode through the night, for the Forest was well-known to his companions. When it dawned, he was approaching a place where many tents had been pitched, a find that pleased him greatly . . . They were the Princes of his own country who were encamped there. Parzival inquired where the Queen herself was quartered, and if she had her own separate ring, and they showed him where she lay surrounded by tents in a sumptuous ring.

Now Duke Kyot . . . had risen early. Parzival and his men were riding up. The ray of dawn was still silver-grey, yet Kyot at once recognized the Grail escutcheon worn by the company, for they were displaying nothing but Turtle-doves. . . .

Kyot went up to Parzival and received him and his people kindly. He sent a page to the Queen's Marshal to ask him to provide good lodgment for whatever knights he saw had reined in there. Parzival himself he led by the hand to where the Queen's wardrobe stood, a small tent of buckram. There they unarmed him completely.

Of this the Queen as yet knew nothing. In a tall and spacious pavilion in which numerous fair ladies were lying, here, there, and everywhere, Parzival found Loherangrin and Kardeiz [their children] beside her, and—joy perforce overwhelmed him!—Kyot rapped on the coverlet and told the Queen to wake up and laugh for sheer happiness. She opened her eyes and saw her husband. She had nothing on her but her shift, so she swung the coverlet round her and sprang from the bed on to the carpet, radiant Condwiramurs! As to Parzival, he took her into his arms, and I am told they kissed.

'Welcome! Fortune has sent you to me, my heart's joy', she said. 'Now I ought to scold you, but I cannot. All honour to this day and hour that have brought me this embrace, banishing all my sadness! I have my heart's desire. Care will get nothing from me!'

The boys Kardeiz and Loherangrin, who lay there naked in the bed, now woke up. Parzival, nothing loth, kissed them affectionately. Tactful Kyot then had the boys carried out. He also hinted to those ladies that they should leave the pavilion, and this they did after welcoming their lord back from his long journey. Kyot then courteously commended the Queen's husband to her and led the young ladies away. It was still very early. The chamberlain closed the flaps.

If ever on a past occasion the company of his wits had been snatched away from him by blood and snow . . ., Condwiramurs now made amends for such torment. . . . He had never received Love's aid for Love's distress elsewhere, though many fine women had offered him their love.[66]

If *Parzival* is a theological poem, the theology is a layman's; the ascetic clergy have been put outside the tent. Yet not perhaps very far outside, for it is equally clear that many basic doctrines of Christian marriage are taken for granted—it is implicit that it is a sacrament between the partners, monogamous, consecrated; that though it cannot be in Wolfram's world the only relationship between the sexes which is acceptable or tolerated, it is a unique ideal. It opens our eyes to a world which would be unimaginable if we read only the theologians; but let us give the theologians their due. If we could never read Hugh of St Victor, or Abelard's *Ethics*, or Peter the Lombard, or St Bernard on God's love, or St Aelred on friendship, we would not be able to interpret Wolfram[67]—neither could we see where his

---

[66] *Parzival*, 799. 14–802. 8; Hatto, pp. 396–8.
[67] See pp. 267, 278–9.

more sophisticated notions came from, nor the world of ideas which he was so original in revising.

Wolfram's Willehalm

Parzival is a courtly romance: although high politics and yet higher spiritual adventures are essential to its themes, much of it is taken up with the solitary journeys of knights adventuring in honour of their ladies. Love, marriage, and knightly prowess provide the inspiration for many of its numerous pages. Some years later—perhaps in the late 1210s—Wolfram wrote his other major epic, the *Willehalm*.[68] This is, on the surface at least, a throw back to the older tradition of *chansons de geste*, of military adventures not necessarily inspired by ladies—still less by the Grail—in which large armies were involved, whose centre was the court of Charlemagne rather than the court of Arthur, whose tendency was to idealize the crusade. Such was the Song of Roland in its earliest surviving form of the late eleventh century; such the *Rolandslied*, of the second half of the twelfth.[69] Such too the songs of William of Orange, culminating in the late twelfth-century *La Bataille d'Aliscans*.[70] The *Willehalm* derives its story from *Aliscans*, with many additions, and its themes from both *Aliscans* and the *Rolandslied*. When Wolfram asks 'Is it a sin to slaughter like cattle those who have never received baptism?' he is challenging a central principle of the *chansons*, explicit in both his sources, and especially in the *Rolandslied*: the heathen are on their way to hell and it is a good work to speed them; they are cattle

[68] Ed. K. Lachmann, 6th edn. by E. Hartl, Berlin, 1926; trans. M. E. Gibbs and S. M. Johnson 1984—there is another useful translation in Passage 1977. I owe my own first introduction to the poem to Hugh Sacker, with whom I had many conversations on it in the 1950s: see Brooke 1971, p. 10.

[69] Kartschoke 1971; Urbanek 1971; Brooke 1987, pp. 110–11, 163–9.

[70] Gibbs and Johnson 1984, pp. 230–7; Bacon 1910.

for the slaughter.[71] The popes who launched the crusades did not believe this, nor did Wolfram; but it had been a deeply held belief among popular crusaders and had inspired them to many sadistic acts. We do not know indeed if Wolfram was at all involved in the crusades.[72] Perhaps not: he was too young in all probability for the Third, launched in 1189, too old for the Fifth of the late 1210s or the Sixth of the 1220s; and the Fourth of 1204 never got near the Saracens. But *Willehalm* is in some sense a crusading epic none the less—for it is a most powerful attempt to portray religious warfare in all its horror.

It opens with a stately prayer—

> Thou Purity immaculate,
> Thou Three yet One,
> Creator over all Creation

—which develops into Wolfram's Credo, claiming kinship with Christ's humanity, sonship from the Lord's prayer, the 'Our Father'.

> Likewise does Holy Baptism give me an assurance
>   that has freed me from despair, for I have the
>   certainty that I am thy namesake;
> Wisdom above all knowledge,
> Thou art Christ,
> Thus I am a Christian. . . .
> Thy Spirit has informed the sound and the words of
>   Holy Scriptures.
> My mind feels the force of thy presence.

---

[71] *Willehalm*, 450. 15–17; Gibbs and Johnson 1984, p. 218; Brooke 1984, pp. 57–60, and literature cited p. 160. Cf. Kartschoke 1971, pp. 8–9, 42–3, 372–3 (Rolandslied 59–64, 870–2, 8579–8594).

[72] For brief accounts of what we know of Wolfram, see Sacker 1963, pp. xiv–xvi; Gibbs and Johnson, pp. 227–30. We are almost entirely dependent on what he himself tells us in his poems and the little which contemporary rivals added (see p. 184). For the background, see esp. Wynn 1984, pp. 10–83.

> I have remained ignorant of what is written in books
> and I am tutored in this way alone: if I have any
> skill, it comes from my mind.[73]

William of Orange had had a strange destiny. He
had been a leading count of the southern marches of
Charlemagne's empire and in his later years had retired to
become a monk: his tomb at Saint-Guilhem-le-Désert in
the Languedoc, in a remote place west of Montpellier,
became a modest centre of pilgrimage and he himself
was venerated as a saint.[74] He also became the hero of one
of the most blood-curdling cycles of the *chansons de geste*.
So Wolfram gives us a prayer to St William to help us on
our way. But after these leisurely preliminaries we are
launched with the minimum of warning into the first
battle of Aliscans. Willehalm was one of the sons of Count
Heimrich of Narbonne, all of whom had to make their
own way in the world. But 'you have surely heard
before . . .'—you know the story: 'Willehalm won the love
of Arabel, and because of this innocent people died. She
who gave him her love and pledged herself to him in
marriage was baptized and took the name of Giburc.
What host of men paid for that with their lives! Her
husband, King Tibalt, lamented the loss of her love.'[75]
And so he inspired the great heathen overlord, Terramer,
Arabel-Giburc's father, to gather all the forces of heathendom for revenge against Willehalm and to recapture
Giburc. It is the story of Helen and the siege of Troy, and
doubtless Wolfram knew as much. He may have had a
little Latin and no Greek; it is certain that he never
enjoyed Shakespeare's experience of opening Chapman's

---

[73] *Willehalm*, 1. 1–2. 22; Gibbs and Johnson 1984, pp. 17–18. On the much-
debated question of how ignorant Wolfram really was, see Wynn 1984, pp. 74–
80, and refs., esp. nn. 94, 95; Sacker 1963, pp. xv–xvi. Most scholars think he
much exaggerated his ignorance of books.

[74] Brooke and Swaan 1974, p. 49 and plates 65–7. For the growth of the legend
of St William, see Orderic, iii. 218–27 and pp. 217 n. 4, 218–19 nn. 3, 4.

[75] *Willehalm*, 7. 23–8. 3; Gibbs and Johnson 1984, pp. 20–1.

or anyone's Homer. But he had a deep knowledge of the byways of mythology and the story of Helen was widely known.[76] In any case, Giburc figures in *Aliscans*. But Wolfram presents her in new guise. Unlike Helen, she had a religious justification: she was a convert to the Christian God and she was baptized. Wolfram usually puts baptism first among her motives—though not always;[77] for it is constantly emphasized in the *Willehalm*, in the romance tradition, that love is the major force behind all that happens: the heathen themselves may come to the west to avenge Tibalt's wrongs and support their own gods—but they also do it to honour their ladies at home. However this may be, Giburc's infatuation with Willehalm, and her conversion and baptism, unleash a fearful slaughter of noble Christians and heathen. The portrait of Giburc is wholly sympathetic: at one point Wolfram treats her almost as a saint and prays to her.[78] She is brave and steadfast and heroic. She mourns bitterly for the destruction of her old family as well as her new. But all this serves to sharpen the edge of the basic paradox which Wolfram labours ceaselessly to unfold. The baptism of Giburc has caused the medieval equivalent of a world war.

It is normal in the *chansons* for the armies to be large. But Wolfram has used all his skills to portray armies of immense proportions—especially on the heathen side—in a fashion scarcely comparable to the cavalier efforts of

---

[76] He characteristically introduces (out of context) one Ekuba (Hecuba) in *Parzival* and Ektor (Hector) in *Willehalm*. Chapman's Homer was published in Shakespeare's lifetime, but not till 1611–15, some years after the completion of *Troilus and Cressida*; but his first extract from it (1598) probably had a share in drawing Shakespeare's attention to the *Iliad*.

[77] Baptism is put first at 215–18; 298. 20–3; 310. 17–20; Gibbs and Johnson 1984, pp. 114–15, 151–2 ('more on account of baptism than through any worth of mine'—but this is Willehalm speaking), 157; love first at 7. 23–8. 3; and perhaps 30. 21–31. 7; Gibbs and Johnson 1984, pp. 20–1, 30. The heathen viewpoint—that Willehalm had stolen her love—is given at 44. 13–16; 75. 3–20; 107. 13–108. 22; 342. 7–30; 354–356; Gibbs and Johnson 1984, pp. 36, 50–1, 65–6, 171, 176.

[78] *Willehalm*, 403. 1–10, 'heilic vrouwe'; Gibbs and Johnson 1984, p. 199.

earlier poets to deploy casts of thousands. In the first battle Willehalm's army—which is not so large, but contains many noble heroes—is annihilated: seven are captured, he alone escapes; the rest are killed. The heathen suffer much greater losses, but their main forces are intact. Willehalm flees north—pausing only to put heart into Giburc at Orange and gain comfort from her embraces—and seeks aid from the emperor, Charlemagne's son Louis the Pious, here presented as Willehalm's brother-in-law. The horror of the battle scenes and the tender pathos of the dialogues with Giburc are set off, or relieved, by some extraordinary ham comedy in which Willehalm and his queenly sister behave with extreme discourtesy, and we are introduced to Rennewart, the mysterious scullion-hero—equally mysterious in *Aliscans* —who plays a crucial part in the second battle.[79] Willehalm returns to Orange with a large army, chiefly consisting of his family and their forces, but supported by imperial troops as well, though not by the emperor in person. They find Orange in flames but Giburc's castle intact; the enemy have withdrawn to regroup further south, near the sea. There is a pause here, in which Willehalm and Giburc entertain their guests and supporters, and prepare for battle. Giburc, deeply conscious that she has brought upon both armies this fearful conflict—and for herself the bitter tragedy of destructive war between her two families —makes her celebrated address to the Frankish lords, culminating in a plea for the heathen. If you defeat them, you will be increasing God's honour; 'you will find them formidable fighters. And if you defeat the heathens you should act so that your salvation will be assured'.[80] But this did not mean destroying them, for in the unforgettable words which form the climax of her speech

[79] See esp. *Willehalm*, 145–53, 189–202; Gibbs and Johnson 1984, pp. 81–5, 101–7.
[80] *Willehalm*, 306. 24–6; Gibbs and Johnson 1984, p. 155.

> hoert eins tumben wîbes rât,
> schônt der gotes hantgetât.

'Hear the counsel of a simple woman, and spare God's handiwork.'[81]

For a moment we are transported onto a higher plane: amid all the blood and thunder one eloquent word from the converted heathen queen—and a little later, one from the poet himself [82]—remind us that the heathen are under God's providence; or perhaps we should rather say, having regard to Wolfram's audience in thirteenth-century Germany in the age of the crusades, two brief sentences shock us into tolerance all the more violently because the bulk of the poem unrolls so ruthlessly the slaughter launched by a single woman's love and baptism.

In the final battle the Christians are victorious, Terramer puts out to sea with the shattered fragments of his army, and one of his subject kings is released by the chivalrous Willehalm with a group of helpers to carry the noble dead to the ships.[83] Meanwhile Willehalm searches for Rennewart, whose prowess had played a critical part in the victory. Rennewart, single-handed, had met the imperial forces slipping away in the face of battle and turned them back (not without some casualties); he had led them to the ships and released the Frankish prisoners; he had been an army in himself. But at the end he had mysteriously disappeared and Willehalm was full of anxiety. In *Aliscans* Rennewart's model, Renouart, likewise a buffoon turned noble soldier, a good boy who turns out to be of heathen origin and Giburc's brother, was

---

[81] *Willehalm*, 306. 27–8: translation from Brooke 1969, p. 157; Gibbs and Johnson 1984, p. 155.

[82] See p. 202 (*Willehalm*, 450. 15–17).

[83] *Willehalm*, 460. 27–467. 8; Gibbs and Johnson 1984, pp. 222–5. For what follows see *Willehalm*, 324. 8–328. 5; 415–16; 452. 15–459; Gibbs and Johnson 1984, pp. 163–6, 204, 219–22.

baptized and married the Frankish princess Alize; and there are hints and indications that Rennewart is destined for a like happy end.[84] But there are other hints too: he has steadfastly refused baptism;[85] the battle ends with no sign or sight of him. Notoriously, the poem is unfinished: the end of *Willehalm* is for medieval Germanists what the ending of St Mark is for the synoptic scholars.[86] It seems evident that Wolfram intended to complete his epic in satisfying fashion, and if Rennewart does not become a Christian and marry Alize, there will be too many loose ends untied. But to some that has seemed a tame ending, unworthy of the deeply tragic tone of much of the poem. To others its present jagged edge seems peculiarly appropriate: for a major theme of the poem is baptism and the baptized, and yet we have been squarely faced with the proposition that the good heathen are under God's providence too.[87] No more obvious ending could have been devised which left us with the question so piquantly, so eloquently posed: what difference will Rennewart's baptism make? I hardly think it likely that Wolfram—any more than St Mark—intended so incomplete an end, but there is no doubt that there is a kind of artistry in both; and maybe Wolfram paused at this point to ponder his ending more deeply, and paused too long.

But baptism is not the only theme of *Willehalm*. Unlike *Parzival* it contains no weddings: Giburc's two weddings lay in the past, Rennewart's in the future, if anywhere at all. But the two marriages of Giburc dominate the whole

[84] *Willehalm*, 190. 25–194. 8; 284–5; 330. 27–331. 20; Gibbs and Johnson 1984, pp. 102–3, 145, 166–esp. 145: 'the love of Alize will protect him' (285. 18).

[85] *Willehalm*, 193; Gibbs and Johnson 1984, p. 103.

[86] For the ending of *Willehalm*, see the résumé of the discussion in Gibbs and Johnson 1984, pp. 248–52, 268–73. The classic defence of Mark 16: 8a as the end of the Gospel is by Lightfoot 1950, pp. 80–97; most scholars probably disagree— cf. e.g. the brief statement in Moule 1965, pp. 132–3.

[87] The end of Parzival confirms that Wolfram found it difficult to conclude his major works (see p. 190).

action: to put it bluntly, the tragedy occurs because she left Tibalt and married Willehalm: and if the heathen are under God's providence, may not their marriages be also? Can we be sure that she was justified by the excuse of baptism? The only answer which is wholly apparent in the text of the poem is that if she had given way to Tibalt and gone back to him, she would have had to abandon her Christian faith. But did that justify her original departure? May she not have been Helen after all? There are various hard sayings in the Gospels which may seem to justify a Christian in leaving home for Jesus' sake, of which the kindliest is perhaps Luke 18: 28–30. 'There is no man that hath left house, or parents, or brethren, *or wife*,[88] or children, for the Kingdom of God's sake, who shall not receive manifold more in this present time and in the world to come everlasting life'—and so surely too for women. But would that justify a broken marriage in the eyes of a devout thirteenth-century layman? Ought he not rather to consider St Paul's instruction to the spouse of a non-Christian to stay with his partner in the hope of doing good—1 Corinthians 7: 14—'For the heathen husband now belongs to God through his Christian wife'.[89] Doubtless Jesus and Paul had no such situation as Giburc's in mind, in which she was surrounded by heathendom if she stayed—yet cosmic terror would be unleashed by her going; nor can we tell what Wolfram himself thought. There is certainly no clear condemnation of divorce and remarriage in his writings: only an implicit and fervent commendation of Parzival's fidelity and a quick contempt for the fugitive quality of Gahmuret's marriages—and Gahmuret had excused his rapid departure from Belacane precisely on the ground that she had not been baptized, a ground his readers were presumably

[88] For the variant texts, and the omission of this word from the original Greek of Matthew and Mark, see pp. 44–5.

[89] See p. 49.

expected to see as conceivably correct in law, despicable in a worthy husband. As to whether the marriage of heathens was in any sense valid, the lawyers and theologians were not agreed; but Pope Innocent III had recently, and firmly, declared that they were, quoting 1 Corinthians.[90]

Willehalm was a saint in heaven, and Giburc a tragic heroine. But we have no reason to think that Wolfram meant us entirely to overlook the point of view of Tibalt—that Willehalm had seduced his wife from his hearth and his faith.

[90] Ivo of Chartres and Gratian were clear that heathen marriages were valid; and Gratian would have regarded even Giburc's marriages—one before and one after baptism—as bigamy: C. 28 qq. 2–3. But the matter was settled by Innocent III in a decretal of 1199 (*Decretals of Gregory IX*, iv. 19. 7; cf. c. 8) in the contrary sense. He took St Paul's statement in 1 Cor. 7: 12–15 to be permissive in the case of mixed marriages. If a Christian could encourage a non-Christian spouse one day to become Christian, let them stay together—but if that was impossible, a Christian could not be tied to a non-Christian. This could be used to justify Giburc's marriage to Willehalm; but it hardly met Gahmuret's case, for the marriage of a Christian to a heathen was generally reckoned illegal (Brundage 1982, p. 263 n. 27).

8

THE WITNESS OF CHAUCER[1]

Chaucer is perhaps the most difficult of the poets whose aid I have sought in this book. He was a man of letters, deeply steeped in the heritage of English, French, Italian, and Latin literature of his age: with Ovid, the *Roman de la rose*, Dante, and Boccaccio at his fingertips, constantly searching out new modes of expression, strange worlds of fantasy and symbol, new experiences in this immensely rich tradition. But he was also a man of the world, a vintner's son, a page in a ducal household, a royal valet and esquire to Edward III, a frequent traveller about the king's business, sometimes his secret business, husband of a lady-in-waiting to Queen Philippa and the duchess of Lancaster. Philippa Chaucer, his wife, was said in later tradition to have been sister to Catherine Swynford, mistress and wife to John of Gaunt, duke of Lancaster, and in later life Chaucer was a customs controller in London, a knight of the shire in Kent and a clerk of royal works in Somerset: an exceedingly successful civil servant. He knew the pageantry of court, the counting-houses and the slums of London; he had a wide

---

[1] The theme of this chapter has been much discussed, from Kittredge 1911 via Brewer 1954 to Kooper 1985, to which I am much indebted—as also to the books and articles cited below and many more which have helped me to understand other aspects of Chaucer. Kittredge 1911, on the 'marriage debate' in the *Canterbury Tales*, retains all its value, even if one cannot fully accept its romantic conclusion that the *Franklin's Tale* represents Chaucer's own views. Quotations are from F. N. Robinson's 2nd edn. (London, 1957); but *Troilus and Criseyde* is quoted from Windeatt 1984, to which I am also much indebted. The details of his life have been checked in Crow and Olson 1966: see esp. p. 69 for the sixteenth-century tradition that his wife was sister of Catherine Swynford—there is no earlier evidence.

experience of life. His poetry, like Shakespeare's, ranges from the bawdy to the refined.

Let us ponder the Wife of Bath in the *Canterbury Tales*.[2] Here we meet a coarser, more educated, anticipation of the Nurse in *Romeo and Juliet*: a well-to-do clothier, amiable, quick-tempered, self-important; a great gadabout who had been 'thries' to Jerusalem, and also to Rome, Bologna, Compostela, and Cologne.

> She was a worthy womman al hir lyve,
> Housbondes at chirche dore she hadde fyve,
> Withouten oother compaignye in youthe
>
> .   .   .   .
>
> In felaweschipe wel koude she laughe and carpe.
> Of remedies of love she knew per chaunce,
> For she koude of that art the olde daunce.
>
> (*Prologue*, 459–61, 474–6)

The Wife of Bath had had five husbands (as well as other company in youth) and so was an expert on marriage; and she drags us through all five of them—including the book which the fifth possessed, full of stories of wicked wives. Her view of marriage remained thoroughly earthy throughout, and her one contribution to human knowledge, if we may so express it, is the assertion of woman's superiority. A favourite topos of medieval literature, and of medieval satirical sculpture, is the domineering wife; beating her husband, or anyway scolding and nagging. This, says the Wife of Bath, is the woman's role. She opens with an incongruous display of theological learning: glossing Jesus and Paul on the doctrine of marriage; it is better to marry than to burn; virginity is a great perfection, but Christ did not preach perfection for all.

---

[2] *Prologue*, 445–76; *Wife of Bath's Prologue and Tale.*

8. The Witness of Chaucer

> I wol bistowe the flour of al myn age
> In the actes and in fruyt of mariage.[3]

As she begins, so she ends, with a lively little tale of how a thoroughly disreputable knight none the less won a life of *perfect* joy by as improbable a marriage as one could devise, *by submission to his wife*—who of course in her turn 'obeyed hym in every thyng' and 'Jhesu Crist us sende', concludes the Wife of Bath,

> Housbondes meeke, yonge, and fressh abedde,
> And grace t'overbyde [overcome] hem that we wedde.
>
> (*Tale*, 1258–60)

As so often with Chaucer's satire, the joke would be entirely flat if this were not at once a reversal of the normal role of husbands and wives in medieval society, and yet a plain reflection of obvious facts of human relationship within the experience of his hearers.

At the other extreme lie two idylls: the *Franklin's Tale*, and Chaucer's early poem, the *Book of the Duchess*, which is a fantasy written to console John of Gaunt on the death of his first wife, the Duchess Blanche.[4] Chaucer uses one of his favourite devices in telling the story through two narrators, each more simple and less subtle than the poet. The first narrator cannot sleep. He takes a book—the tragic tale of Queen Alcyone, who died of grief when she learned that her husband King Seys had lost his life at sea. Next he prays to Morpheus and Juno, and they answer his prayer and he falls asleep. As he sleeps he dreams that he is present at a great hunt, and as he wanders in the wood he meets a man in black—a knight in mourning for

---

[3] *Wife of Bath's Prologue*, 1–114, esp. 52, 113–14.

[4] For the *Franklin's Tale*, see below, pp. 219–20. In what follows I am much indebted to Kooper 1985. Blanche probably died in 1368: see refs. in Kooper 1985, pp. 258–9 n. 1. Kooper, ibid., p. 162 and p. 259 n. 2, discusses the date of the poem, suggesting a year as late as 1374 is possible. But the point of the poem would be lost if she were long dead, and the tact of it doubtful to say the least if he had already remarried—as he did in 1371 (*CP* vii. 413).

his lady, who has died. The heart of the poem lies in the Black Knight's lament, and slow unfolding of the story of his love, his wooing, and his ultimate acceptance—cut short by her sad death.

It is the complete converse of the story of the Wife of Bath, for although here too the lady dominates the scene, she is perhaps the most delicate and sublime of all Chaucer's creations: in a passage shot through with echoes of the Blessed Virgin, she is shown to have above all the quality of mercy, which makes the rough-hewn knight eventually acceptable to her. The many shades and subtleties of the *Book* have been brilliantly expounded in a recent study by Dr Erik Kooper of Utrecht.[5] Chaucer develops with remarkable skill and subtlety the story of the pure and spiritual and eternal love between White and the Black Knight. The knight and the narrator are crude and ignorant; but in the end the knight learns from his lady, though she dies before they can be married. In spite of various nuances it is clear that they are never even in their own eyes truly married; yet their love is eternal. Kooper shows the ethereal nature of loving friendship which this allows; but perhaps we can go further. In this case it is abundantly clear that Chaucer was not at all bothered with legal niceties but with a quite different range of problems such as we have scarcely found since the letters of Heloise. 'White' is a play on the name of the lamented Duchess Blanche; and the little tale is a delicately woven, fragrant consolation for the duke. Heloise had had to face the problem that though her love was eternal her marriage was not; it had been legally dissolved. In a rather similar way Chaucer had to face the problem that, however deeply afflicted the duke might be in 1368, he was likely to marry again—as he did in 1371, not for the last time.[6] His love might be eternal, but his

---

[5] Kooper 1985: for the echoes of Mary, see Kooper 1985, pp. 175–6, following Wimsatt 1967.   [6] Kooper 1985, pp. 258–9 n. 1; *CP* vii. 413.

marriage was not—at least in some senses, and in a very obvious visible sense. So there is a peculiar tact in avoiding the issue whether White and the Knight were married.

But if White and the Black Knight were not married, there are many marriages and innumerable married folk in Chaucer's other writings. It has often been observed that if Chaucer avoids matrimony in the *Book of the Duchess* or *Troilus and Criseyde*, it was not on account of any antipathy to the theme. Many of the *Canterbury Tales* in particular have problems of marriage at their heart. At the very start comes *The Knight's Tale*, a simple story of chivalry, and of a triangle of lovers: Palamon and Arcite, prisoners of Theseus, compete for the love of Theseus' sister-in-law, Emily. Arcite is the disciple of Mars, Palamon of Venus; when they fight for her Arcite wins, but is killed by a fall from his horse, and Palamon and Emily marry and live happily ever after—on this the poet is categorical. But is it so simple? It is certainly a conventional romance, more so than its principal source, the *Theseida* of Boccaccio: there are moments almost of light-hearted comedy, as in its rather trumpery conclusion. Yet there is quite another dimension. Half way through, the poet, almost casually, takes us to visit the temples of Venus, Mars, and Diana—and shows us, in Elizabeth Salter's words, a 'spectacle of violence and unhappiness inside the temples. Chaucer's intentions are now by no means comfortable, whatever he has led us to expect.'[7] First, in Venus' temple, we encounter

> Wroght on the wal, ful pitous to biholde,
> The broken slepes, and the sikes colde,
> The sacred teeris, and the waymentynge,
> The firy strokes of the desirynge
> That loves servantz in this lyf enduren . . .
>
> (1919–23)

[7] Salter 1962, p. 25.

These are enhanced by the enchantments of Medea and Circe. Glorious as the goddess Venus may be, there is no hiding the sorrows of her votaries. But Venus is presently overshadowed by the savage revelation of violence and suffering in the temple of Mars—perhaps the most terrifying passage in Chaucer's writings. There is here a revelation of a deeper, harsher world, quite apart from the world of chivalry—more alive, more terrifying, calling out a far deeper layer in the poet's inspiration.

But these are the temples of pagan gods, and we may feel a momentary relief: Venus and Mars have passed away—we live in the world of the Christian God. But do we? The horrors of Mars are the real horrors of Chaucer's world:

> Ther saugh I first the derke ymagining
> Of Felonye, and al the compassyng;
> The crueel Ire, reede as any gleede;
> The pykepurs, and eek the pale Drede;
> The smylere with the knyf under the cloke;

> (1995–9)

and so to the perpetrators of further violent and murderous crimes, in a passage reminiscent of the fiercest moments of Dante's *Inferno*. These are only the most dramatic of the passages which imply that we live in a world governed by dark forces. If Venus was a pagan deity long since rejected, the pains of love are as active as ever; and Mars is but the name for a violence and horror only too evidently a part of ordinary human experience.

All this is put in some sort of perspective by Theseus in the speech with which he brings the poem to its denouement.[8] It is an amazing statement out of Boethius

---

[8] Salter 1962, p. 25. I am much indebted to this fine study of *The Knight's Tale* and *The Clerk's Tale*, although I sometimes diverge from her findings.

(whose *Consolation* Chaucer himself had translated)[9] and
Aristotle of how we all live under the direction and
providence (one might almost say, predestination) of
'The First Moevere of the cause above' (2987)—who is
presently identified as Jupiter. Theseus comes to a
conclusion which is a remarkable mingling of philosophic
gravity and commonplace.

> Thanne is it wysdom, as it thynketh me,
> To maken vertu of necessitee . . .
>
> (3041–2)
>
> But after wo I rede us to be merye,
> And thanken Juppiter of al his grace.
>
> (3068–9)

But Boethius was a Christian, and Chaucer's audience
was Christian—and there are many Christian overtones
in the passage. What Chaucer himself made of it all, we
cannot tell. But we can admire, and shudder at, the harsh
consequences of the power of Mars and Venus, and
recognize a profoundly ambivalent view of the world.
Here, as in *Troilus*, and for all his deep knowledge
of pagan antiquity, Chaucer deliberately confuses the
frontier which separates pagan from Christian.

The variety of the marriage scenes in the *Canterbury
Tales* is well illustrated by another example of Chaucer in
ambivalent mood, *The Clerk's Tale*. This is the familiar
story of patient Griselda, of a good and loving wife who
was put to the test by her tyrannous husband, the
Marquis Walter, passed all her tests triumphantly, and
won even her husband's commendation in the end. She
did not however win the approval of all those who
studied her tale. Boccaccio advised his male readers not to
imitate the marquis. Petrarch made him 'more nearly an

---

[9] Chaucer, ed. Robinson, pp. 319–84; he also made much use of Boethius'
Consolation in *Troilus*. For Theseus' speech, cf. Salter 1962, pp. 35–6.

agent of divine purposes'; but a more human and emotional attitude to Griselda was added to the tale by *Le Livre Griseldis*.[10] Chaucer fashioned out of Petrarch and *Le Livre* a book which combines in an astonishing degree the harsh edges of the cruel story with a clear revelation of Griselda as a Christian saint. As with White in *The Book of the Duchess*, there are Marian overtones.[11] But the marquis is hardly presented as an instrument of divine justice: he is simply a cunning, suspicious, savage brute. The climax comes when he forges a papal bull dissolving his marriage to Griselda and makes pretence that he is preparing to marry a new wife, who has just attained the marriageable age of twelve (736–84). She is in fact his daughter, whom he has concealed with a son yet younger in Bologna. When Griselda, without a murmur, prepared their house for the wedding reception

> And with that worde she gan the hous to dighte,
> And tables for to sette, and beddes make

> (974–5)

and set everything into readiness for a splendid wedding feast—then at last Walter reckoned that she had passed her final test, kissed her fondly, and restored her to her place as his wife. Chaucer offers three epilogues. First, he tells us the story is told not to encourage wives to be as humble as Griselda, but as steadfast in adversity (1142–7). Then there is 'Lenvoy de Chaucer'

> Grisilde is deed, and eek hir pacience,
> And bothe atones buryed in Ytaille

> (1177–8)

and he strongly advises a husband not to follow Walter's example, since 'in certein he shal faille' (1182)—and there follows some fairly cynical advice for the wives. Finally

---

[10] Salter 1962, p. 37.   [11] Salter 1962, p. 42.

the host observes that he wishes his wife could have heard it (1212a–g, probably the original end). But in spite of all this light-hearted badinage, the tale itself has a serious aspect—or rather two: it tells a moral tale, of a sort; and it reveals some of the harsher sides of human relations; it makes no effort to hide the husband's cruelty—very much the reverse.

The *Canterbury Tales* contain an astonishing variety of marriage problems, of contributions to what is often called Chaucer's marriage debate. Let one more suffice. *The Parson's Tale* resumes standard church teaching on sin, including the sins of the flesh. This presentation of a very formal teaching by the character portrayed in the *Prologue* as the most admirable of all the pilgrims, has often puzzled the critics. It has been dismissed as an immature work, yet it clearly sits adjacent to Chaucer's retraction, at the very end of the *Tales*, and fits his mood of repentance for 'worldly vanitees'. There are passages in it which offer a very harsh view of sin—for example condemning as equivalent to adulterers married partners who make love 'oonly to hire flesshly delit' (903)—and present a savage view of the torments in store for sinners. All this was conventional teaching from an austere celibate; yet perhaps here too there is an ambivalent intent, for the harsher edges of the sermon sit oddly with the vision of divine mercy with which it opens and closes. But we tread here in a dangerous path; Chaucer's own views will always evade us.

It has been widely held, since G. L. Kittredge's classic study of the 'marriage debate' in the *Canterbury Tales*, that the *Franklin's Tale* portrays Chaucer's ideal.[12] It can be read as an idyll in which the bride promises obedience which her husband pledges himself not to exploit—in which mutual love and courtesy, gentility, 'gentillesse' are

---

[12] Kittredge 1911, pp. 460–7. For recent criticism of *The Franklin's Tale*, see esp. Minnis 1986, pp. 218–37.

the foundation of marriage. But this view can only be sustained if we wholly ignore the harsh (as some have thought, cynical) edges of the poem.

> Love is a thing as any spirit free;
> Wommen of kinde desiren libertee,
> And nat to ben constreyned as a thral;
> And so don men, if I soth seyen shal.
>
> (767–70)

Dorigen, the heroine, is trapped into promising her love to Aurelius if the impossible happens; magically, it seems to happen, and her husband Arveragus—whom she dotes on—insists that she yields to Aurelius. It is the chivalry of Aurelius which saves her; but the ambivalence of the moral, the puzzles it may engender, are all the more sharply revealed because of the relatively mild treatment Chaucer metes out to all the main characters—though Dorigen herself explores some murky paths to suicide when she finds herself trapped. We may be enchanted; we may be a little shocked; we must be puzzled too.

> Lordinges [said the Franklin] this question wolde I aske
>   now,
> Which was the moste free, as thinketh yow?
>
> (1622)

Far and away Chaucer's most elaborate exposition of human relations and human love is to be found in *Troilus and Criseyde*. The poem opens with an invocation of the goddess of torment, the fury Thesiphone (i. 6–8), by one 'that gode of loues seruantz serue' (i. 15)—*servus servorum Dei*, the pope of love, yet not himself (so he asserts) daring to be a lover. He goes on to pray that those who suffer as Troilus suffered shall receive the solace of heaven. Here we meet at once a number of the puzzles in the poem. It is firmly set in a pagan context, yet the poet is Christian. It is a charming romantic story with a sad end—yet the love whom Troilus serves is a fury, indicating a much darker interpretation of the poem than has been fashionable.

It was the twelfth-century poet Benoît de Saint-Maure who made Troilus son of Priam a central figure in the story of Troy; but Chaucer's chief source was the version of Boccaccio. In Chaucer himself (as in Boccaccio) Hector and all the other heroes take a back seat—from which they are rescued in ironic fashion in Shakespeare's *Troilus and Cressida*, a cynical amalgam of Chaucer and Homer. Troilus catches sight of Criseyde, a beautiful widow (not a maid), and her uncle Pandarus arranges for them to meet. Pandarus blossoms exceedingly in Chaucer's hands: the portrayal of a jovial, friendly, generous, kindly pimp deserved its reward in adding a word to the language. For Chaucer's Pandar, unlike Shakespeare's, has a jovial side to him, even a touch of the language of Christianity. When he finds Troilus in the dumps—not yet knowing the reason—he thinks the Greeks have reduced him to prayer: 'God saue hem . . . that bringe our lusty folk to holynesse!' (i. 558–60)—and when he undertakes to bring them together, he swears that he'll be bound to Cerberus in hell for ever, but he'll do it (i. 859–61)—a memory, one may suppose, of Dante's *Inferno*.[13] In Boccaccio the problem Pandaro faced was that Criseyde was *onesta*; for Chaucer's Pandarus it worked the other way: she is virtuous, and so has the virtue of pity (i. 897–903), a type of argument one frequently encounters in the poem; Pandarus hopes to find some 'grace' in her (i. 980). All goes well. After an uncomfortable night, he approaches Criseyde's palace, and enters with a prayer to Janus—the two-faced—the 'god of entree' (ii. 77); his arguments even once echo Heloise's 'I speke of good entencioun' (ii. 295). Criseyde has her struggles. She relishes freedom

[13] But see Windeatt 1984, p. 137, n. to 859, for other sources. For what follows see Windeatt 1984, p. 141.

8. The Witness of Chaucer

I am myn owene womman, wel at ese
I thank it god, as after myn estate,

.   .   .   .

Shall noon housboonde seyn to me 'cheke mate'.

(ii. 750–4)

Yet as she wanders in her garden with her maidens, one of them sings a song in which she observes that love banishes 'alle manere vice and synne' (ii. 852).

Criseyde agreed to be Troilus' lover so long as her reputation was respected; and so a clandestine affair is arranged, and after much persuasion by Pandarus on both sides, many nights were spent happily together. They exchange rings, and oaths, and Criseyde affirms with fine rhetorical flourishes, that their love is eternal: 'ffor I am thyn, by god and by my trouthe' (iii. 1512). But not for long, for Criseyde's father, Calchas, who has foretold the doom of Troy, has fled to the Greeks and plans for his daughter to join him.[14] A Trojan captive, Antenor, is offered in exchange for her, and she is bound by her father's will and the decision of Priam's 'parliament' to go. Pandarus tries to comfort Troilus, first by offering to find him another woman (iv, 400–6), then by assuring him that she will not go. When it is clear that she will, Troilus seeks comfort in Chaucer's favourite *Consolation of Philosophy* by Boethius, while Criseyde assures him that—though she must go—she will return. Calchas has misunderstood the oracle of Apollo: 'ffor goddes speken in amphibologies' (Chaucer seems to have coined the word for the occasion)[15] 'And for a soth they tellen

---

[14] In Greek legend Calchas was a Greek seer who insisted that Chryseis, a captive of Agamemnon, be restored to her father, the Trojan priest of Apollo. In medieval legend the two were amalgamated, and Calchas became a Trojan who had fled to the Greeks since he had interpreted the oracle of Apollo to foretell the destruction of Troy.

[15] Cf. Windeatt 1984, p. 427: 'the only instance recorded by *MED*'.

222

twenty lyes' (iv. 1406–7). Chaucer proceeds to the central ambiguity of the poem.

> And trewelich, as writen wel I fynde,
> That al this thyng was seyd of good entente;
> And that hire herte trewe was and kynde
> Towardes hym and spak right as she mente,
> And that she starf [died] for wo neigh whan she wente,
> And was in purpos euere to be trewe:
> Thus writen they that of hire werkes knewe.
>
> (iv. 1415–21)

Perhaps; and Criseyde swears a mighty oath to be true to him. But once she is in the hands of the Greeks, she begins to think it may be more prudent to accept the addresses of the Greek hero Diomed. She promised to return on the tenth day, and Chaucer evokes with vivid imagination Troilus anxiously waiting by the gate: for a moment he thinks he sees her, then knows he is mistaken (v. 1158–62). Criseyde, meanwhile, with some dispatch, puts off the old love—denies it indeed, for she tells Diomed that she had had a husband, but no other lover since he died, 'as help me now Pallas' (v. 975). She still tried to deceive Troilus in an exchange of letters; but he soon despaired of her love, yet fought bravely on to meet his death at the hands of Achilles (v. 1800–6). Meanwhile Chaucer begs the ladies of his audience, though they find Criseyde untrue, not to blame her—'gladlier I wil write, if you leste, Penelopes trouthe and good Alceste' (v. 1772–8)—a likely story after 8,000 lines on Criseyde. Chaucer ends the poem with a fine rhetorical contrast between Christian and pagan times, and an address to the Trinity.

When Chaucer claims that Criseyde meant to be true to Troilus, he invokes written authority—'as writen wel I fynde', 'Thus writen they that of hire werkes knewe'. In a writer of Chaucer's subtlety and ambivalence, such

223

statements could be an invitation to believe, to be credulous, or they could be the reverse: a shuffling off of responsibility on his authorities. It is fairly evident that he intends it to be taken both ways. The poem is exceedingly long partly because he labours endlessly to convince us that Criseyde is a good creature as well as an unfaithful mistress. The portrait of a beautiful concubine who changes partners under very excusable circumstances would not have shocked Chaucer's, any more than a modern, audience. It is the great panache with which her vows and promises are presented to us and her kindness and affection brought home to us that puts a sharp edge on her infidelity. The ultimate effect—the rapid and shattering change of the fifth book—is profoundly cynical. Shakespeare made Criseyde a courtesan, Pandarus a low-grade pimp, and idiots or rogues out of most of the heroes: his play is a deeply disturbing amalgam of Chaucer and Homer, in a mood of mordant scepticism. There are moments indeed in *Troilus and Criseyde* when it is hard not to say that Shakespeare wrote the best commentary on the poem; there are many other passages where he seems to have offered the crudest of parodies. There is no need to choose between these views: Chaucer offers us both.

In 1975 Professor H. A. Kelly published an enchanting book, full of intriguing insights and helpful material, intended to illuminate Chaucer in general and *Troilus and Criseyde* in particular. Its special aim was to present the case for believing that Chaucer meant Troilus and Criseyde to be married: clandestinely, perhaps, but in medieval eyes validly and honestly.[16] He began with the old tradition that in medieval literature love and marriage were incompatible, tracing its rise and fall through the

[16] Kelly (H.A.) 1975. In fairness, Kelly himself points out passages in which Chaucer has added to the ambiguity of his source, and emphasizes the nuances of Chaucer's purpose (Kelly 1975, pp. 230–1, 238–40).

classic statement in C. S. Lewis, *The Allegory of Love*, to more recent critics who have found married love in every corner of medieval literature, and especially in Chaucer; and to these he adheres, adding a weight of figures to show how even in the twelfth century most lovers were married in the end, and how in Chaucer unmarried lovers are very much in the minority. His statistics and his examples have lasting value; and he is particularly good on Ovid—both in his classical setting and in medieval dress, attempting to show that the poet was not so immoral as perhaps Augustus thought, and as many moderns have supposed, and how readily he was adapted to a variety of purposes, some of them highly moral, in medieval love poetry.[17] Kelly's suggestion that Troilus and Criseyde may have been married has not found favour;[18] but he has revealed a very intriguing element in the poem. He observes that clandestine marriages could be valid in fourteenth-century England, however much the law frowned on them; an explicit exchange of vows followed by consummation might make a marriage. And he can point to many hints of a matrimonial character in the poem. Pandarus quite early looks forward to a time 'whan ye ben oon' (ii. 1740); Troilus invokes Imeneus, Hymen, the god of marriage, as well as Venus (iii. 1254–60); he calls Criseyde a 'wommanliche wif' (a word ambiguous, however, in Middle English, meaning woman as well as wife, like *femme* in French) who will find truth and diligence in him 'al my lif' (iii. 1296–8); they exchange rings (iii. 1368);[19] Criseyde presently asserts that 'I am thyn, by God and by my trouthe' (iii. 1512); Troilus emphasizes to Pandarus his lifelong pledge of service to her (iv. 445–8), and Pandarus repeats that 'ye two ben al on' (iv. 592); even when about to depart

---

[17] For Ovid see chap. 7 n. 10.   [18] See esp. Brewer 1977.

[19] Cf. Windeatt 1984, p. 317 n. to 1368, for discussion of this scene and other references, esp. to J. B. Maguire in *Chaucer Review*, viii (1973–4), 262–78.

Criseyde swears a mighty oath not to be false to him
(iv. 1534 ff.); and as they get ready to say farewell Troilus
calls God to witness that he has never been and will never
be false to her 'til that I dye' (iv. 1654–7)—till death us do
part. The God Troilus invokes is omniscient. Chaucer is
quite capable of making Venus or Cupid omniscient if he
wished; but this is one of many deliberate ambiguities,
many places where pagan and Christian gods are juxta-
posed. The claim at the end of the poem that it belongs to
a lost pagan world is both profoundly true and very
misleading, for the poem shows us, time and again, a
mirror of human life, or at least of human relations,
affectionately and satirically portrayed. If this seems a
strange combination, it is peculiarly characteristic of
Chaucer: the *Prologue* to the *Canterbury Tales* bears
witness that he is at his most satirical when he appears
(and very likely is) most charitable. The prioress, for
example, kindly, sentimental, decorous, yet ostentatious,
a little vain of her appearance—

> Ful fetys was hir cloke, as I was war.
> Of smal coral aboute hir arm she bar
> A peire of bedes, gauded al with grene;
> And theron heng a brooch of gold ful sheene,
> On which there was first write a crowned A,
> And after, *Amor vincit omnia.*
>
> (*Prologue*, 157–62)

Affection and satire are similarly combined in *Troilus
and Criseyde*, and the same quizzical regard is evident in
the analogy occasionally hinted between the relationship
of the lovers and marriage. The echoes of married union
are clear, but they are echoes merely. It is evident that in
no public sense are they married; if 'marriage existed
between them', Derek Brewer says, 'Troilus could have
proclaimed it and saved Criseyde going to the Greeks'.[20]

---

[20] Brewer 1977, p. 197.

It is not indeed made clear why they cannot marry—
perhaps it is implied that a Trojan prince could not marry
a priest's daughter. But in any case their clandestine
union has many of the elements of marriage, and these are
drawn out. The reader may reckon that their tragedy was
brought on by the secret nature of their union; open
marriage would have saved them. Or he may wonder if
the ties of married folk are really stronger or deeper than
those of these Trojan lovers. Or he may reflect that
married and unmarried lovers alike are subjects of
Thesiphone, goddess of torment (i. 6–8).

These are suggestions merely, for Chaucer is profoundly
elusive. What is clear is that he had a capacious view of
love and sexuality, broad enough to comprehend the
sublime vision of *The Book of the Duchess* and the bawdy
humour of the Wife of Bath. In this he was truly a
forerunner of Shakespeare.

9

LOVE AND MARRIAGE IN SHAKESPEARE[1]

To discourse on love and marriage in Shakespeare is a bold, perhaps a desperate venture. It is not only that the material is so rich and complex and the voices of the interpreters so numerous and conflicting; it begins and ends in a simple fact: Shakespeare was cleverer than any of his critics. The famous encomium by Ben Jonson

[1] My approach to Shakespeare has been moulded over many years by my brother, Professor Nicholas Brooke. He is not to be held responsible for the existence or form of this chapter, but I am greatly in his debt; and my account of *Romeo and Juliet* depends much on his *Shakespeare's Early Tragedies*, Brooke 1968, pp. 80–106. References to *Hamlet, A Midsummer Night's Dream*, and *Romeo and Juliet* are to the New Cambridge Shakespeare (ed. P. Edwards, R. A. Foakes, G. Blakemore Evans, respectively, Cambridge, 1984–5); for *As You Like It* and *The Merchant of Venice* to the Arden edition (ed. A. Latham and J. R. Brown, edns. of London, 1955, 1955). Of the copious literature, I have found a special interest in Dusinberre 1975, though it is marred by unsupported assumptions about St Paul, the medieval cult of chastity, and other matters. Thus she writes on p. 308: 'Feminism nevertheless sounds a strange bedfellow for poetry, more like a joke in Aristophanes than a serious statement in Shakespeare. Shakespeare was not concerned to register in his plays his own presence as defender of women. . . . But Virginia Woolf was deceived by the poet's own unobtrusiveness when she declared that "it would be impossible to say what Shakespeare thought of women". Shakespeare saw men and women as equal in a world which declared them unequal. He did not divide human nature into the masculine and the feminine, but observed in the individual woman or man an infinite variety of union between opposing impulses. To talk about Shakespeare's women is to talk about his men, because he refused to separate their worlds physically, intellectually, or spiritually.' N. S. Brooke comments 'It's a brave statement, even if I immediately have doubts; but it isn't simply wrong.'

This chapter is essentially an epilogue to my study of medieval literature—for it is evident that poets like Wolfram, Chaucer, and Shakespeare can illuminate each other in their handling of these common themes. I have chosen a fairly close-knit group of plays—hence my omission of the deeply interesting *Measure for Measure* and *The Winter's Tale*.

attached to the First Folio of Shakespeare's works betokens the admiration of one who knew him well—not just for a dramatist, not just for a poet, not just for a friend, but for a mind of wonderful range and power. Shakespeare makes rings round us all.

Yet he is a very crucial witness in the history of marriage because he observed and recorded areas of experience beyond the normal reach of ordinary writers, and because modern interpretation has been exceptionally sophisticated. We must never for a moment forget that he wrote plays which live only on the stage; that he wrote for a living, not for our private entertainment or instruction; that his plays are not slices of ordinary life. Two words need to be eradicated from the vocabulary and the minds of everyone who would understand great literature: 'naturalism' and 'realism'. Shakespeare's plays are not transcripts of nature, thank the Lord: human nature is indeed infinitely various and the depth of human wickedness unfathomable, as Shakespeare well knew; but we do not have to live our lives in daily expectation of meeting Lady Macbeth or the villains of *Titus Andronicus*. By the same token the most powerful of the dramatic situations he evoked are not realistic in any conceivable sense of the term: one has only to think of Iago tormenting Othello or of Lear in the thunderstorm to know that this is so. Yet there is nothing here totally alien to human experience; and it is his capacity to explore every region of man's experience and make his characters, or their predicaments, comment on it, that gives Shakespeare his unique interest for us. He had seen human beings in many postures and human character under many aspects; he had read wide and deep; he was a walking encyclopaedia of tales and examples. But he was not in the formal sense a highly educated man; he was not an academic; he never embarked on the formal study of theology; he was—fully as much as Wolfram von

Eschenbach—a layman. In this most magical and extra-ordinary of mirrors we can see reflected the images of a thousand ordinary minds. What his characters expressed —however obscurely to us—must have been more or less intelligible to his audience, and not calculated to invoke the censor's lash. I say more or less since he evidently made rings round his audiences as he does round us; they need not have understood all the implications of every-thing his characters say.

On love and marriage he notoriously ranges from the bawdy to the sublime. To put the matter crudely there is probably more bawdy in Shakespeare than in any other of the world's great artists. This used to cause grave discomposure among his admirers, and he was only fully accepted in many households when Dr Thomas Bowdler, an eighteenth-century physician with an extensive if erratic knowledge of obscene language, at the end of his life published his *Family Shakespeare* in 1818.[2] In my schooldays something of this attitude still lingered, and I was made to study *Hamlet* in what we should call an O level form, in a version from which the word incest had been removed—a procedure which renders one of Shakespeare's most difficult plays unintelligible. In the last thirty years this aspect of the bard has become so fashionable that it is in danger of swamping his more delicate thoughts. But if one simply reads the text, the juxtaposition of the crude and the romantic underlines the effect of his loftier utterance, while never leaving us for a moment in doubt that man—though he may be only a little lower than the angels—is also one of the lower animals.

---

[2] Bowdler 1818; on Dr Bowdler, see *DNB*. He failed however, e.g., to cut the opening dialogue of *Romeo and Juliet*.

A Midsummer Night's Dream

A Midsummer Night's Dream

I have chosen a group of his early plays in which the role of marriage is obvious and central. What more obvious than its role in *A Midsummer Night's Dream*, which is widely assumed (on slender grounds) to have been an epithalamium to celebrate an actual wedding?[3] Perhaps it was; but I am glad it was not my wedding it celebrated, for it proceeds by showing us the lowest view of human marriage we have so far encountered. Like the shots from a light machine gun, it presents a series of deplorable visions of human relations of the most cynical character. The play opens with Theseus and Hippolyta looking forward to their wedding—

> Now fair Hippolyta, our nuptial hour
> Draws on apace; four happy days bring in
> Another moon—but O, methinks, how slow
> This old moon wanes! She lingers my desires,
> Like to a step-dame or a dowager
> Long withering out a young man's revenue . . .

making the entry to marriage a path to lust elegantly disguised; and just in case the audience has forgotten the story of how Theseus wooed her on horseback and subdued her by force—

> Hippolyta, I woo'd thee with my sword,
> And won thy love doing thee injuries;

---

[3] See discussion in Foakes 1984, pp. 1–4; and cf. Olson 1957. There is no real evidence to support the notion that it was written for a specific marriage. For the plays discussed below the following approximate dates seem now acceptable and are offered in Wells and Taylor 1986: *Romeo*, c.1594–5 (cf. Brooke 1968, p. 80; c.1596 in Blakemore Evans 1984, pp. 1–6); *Dream*, c.1594–5 (cf. Foakes 1984, pp. 1–4 who offers 1595–6—but there seems little specific evidence); *Merchant*, c.1596–7 (shortly before July 1598, Brown 1955, pp. xxi–xxvii); *As You Like It*, c.1598–1600 (Latham 1975, pp. xxvi–xxvii); *Hamlet*, c.1600, revised later (cf. Edwards 1985, pp. 7–8).

> But I will wed thee in another key,
> With pomp, with triumph, and with revelling.

Instantly Egeus enters, claiming total parental right over his daughter, and invoking the irrevocable law of civilized Athens,

> I beg the ancient privilege of Athens;
> As she is mine, I may dispose of her;
> Which shall be either to this gentleman
> [Demetrius, that is, whom Egeus has chosen for her]
> Or to her death, according to our law
> Immediately provided in that case.[4]

He can have her killed; but before he does so, the lovers—four of them, for good measure—flee to the woods where they can indulge their sweet romantic fancies. Or can they? What we actually see are the lovers chasing one another through a series of mistakes and misadventures, and we rapidly discover that love is a matter of potions and magic and unbelievable silliness. In another part of the wood we find Quince and his crew engaged in their rustic parody of romantic love—

'Marry, our play is "The most lamentable comedy, and most cruel death of Pyramus and Thisbe"' . . .

'Let the audience look to their eyes' says Bottom: 'I will move storms, I will condole in some measure'—but in his heart he thinks this sorry stuff—'my chief humour is for a tyrant'.[5]

Finally, there are fairies in the wood, and any hope that we may find among them a happier vision of matrimonial felicity is rapidly dispelled: 'Ill met by moonlight, proud Titania'—thus Oberon opens the exchange which sets in perspective the significance of all we have heard. First, Titania taunts him with having come from the farthest step of India because

---

[4] *Dream*, I. i. 1–6, 16–19, 41–5.   [5] *Dream*, I. ii. 9–10, 20–2.

> forsooth, the bouncing Amazon
> Your buskined mistress and your warrior love,
> To Theseus must be wedded, and you come
> To give their bed joy and prosperity.

To which Oberon's response is

> How canst thou thus, for shame, Titania,
> Glance at my credit with Hippolyta,
> Knowing I know thy love to Theseus?
> Didst not thou lead him through the glimmering night
> From Perigenia, whom he ravished;
> And make him with fair Aegles break his faith,
> With Ariadne, and Antiopa?[6]

which inspires Titania's retort that his quarrels with her have led to total disorder in nature, natural disaster of every kind, and confusion of one season with another. Shakespeare characteristically seizes on pagan myth for his purposes and makes incisive and cynical use of it. But there is another layer of meaning here, which is much more seriously meant—here he makes Titania apply to harmony in marriage the same theme Ulysses harps on in *Troilus and Cressida* in his famous analogy of disharmony in nature with disharmony in state and society.

> Take but degree away, untune that string
> And, hark! what discord follows.[7]

Titania's message seems to be: at the heart of marriage lies a union of harmony; break it and all about the married couple will fall apart. Amid all the cynical talk of the *Dream* this strikes a note of solid conservative orderliness and high morality. It is very noticeable that the note of order in marriage, like the note of order in the world and in society, is heard only in the

[6] *Dream*, II. i. 60, 70–80.
[7] *Troilus*, I. iii. 109–10. The whole speech is a collection of commonplaces eloquently and cynically expounded: for our purpose, none the worse for that.

young Shakespeare: the Shakespeare (already cynical) who created Ulysses and the patriotic trumpetings of Henry V. Even then, it was never unquestioned; even Henry V cries on the eve of Agincourt:

> We must bear *all*. O hard condition!
>
> . . . What infinite hearts' ease
> Must kings neglect that private men enjoy!—

while his wife-to-be prepares for his wooing in a scene of charming bawdy.[8] But this is nothing to the world of his later plays: the world is disordered in its very nature in Lear, and here are no happy marriages; in the great tragedies only between Macbeth and Lady Macbeth is there any sort of married intimacy; and even in the last of the *early* tragedies Hamlet can say

> We will have no more marriages

in the play of all Shakespeare's plays which unfolds the evil, unclean side of married bliss.[9] Among the later plays a kinder note is struck in *The Winter's Tale* or *The Tempest*, but the tragedies do not throw a kindly light on our theme. It is a relief to return to the early plays, even to the *Dream*. For one of the most obvious points of the play is that all the discord revealed in the first two acts and Titania's declamation can and do turn to happiness. The last act opens with Theseus' famous speech which ensures we do not take any of it too seriously—it shows us the poet laughing at himself, and in what Theseus says about the lover, he is remarkably unflattering to his bride.

> The lunatic, the lover, and the poet
> Are of imagination all compact:

---

[8] *Henry V*, IV. i. 253, 256–7; III. iv.
[9] *Hamlet*, III. i. 141 ('no mo marriages', Edwards, from Second Quarto). For the intimacy of the Macbeths see Brooke (N. S.), 1987, pp. 16–17.

A Midsummer Night's Dream

One sees more devils than vast hell can hold;
That is the madman. The lover, all as frantic,
Sees Helen's beauty in a brow of Egypt:
The poet's eye, in a fine frenzy rolling,
Doth glance from heaven to earth, from earth to heaven;
And as imagination bodies forth
The forms of things unknown, the poet's pen
Turns them to shapes, and gives to airy nothing
A local habitation and a name.
Such tricks hath strong imagination,
That if it would but apprehend some joy,
It comprehends some bringer of that joy;
Or, in the night, imagining some fear,
How easy is a bush suppos'd a bear!

Yet Hippolyta retorts:

> But all the story of the night told over,
> And all their minds transfigur'd so together,
> More witnesseth than fancy's images,
> And grows to something of great constancy;
> But howsoever, strange and admirable.[10]

Finally, in a jolly happy ending, the fairies bless the mortal couples. Thus Oberon:

> Now until the break of day,
> Through this house each fairy stray.
> To the best bride-bed will we,
> Which by us shall blessed be;
> And the issue there create
> Ever shall be fortunate.
> So shall all the couples three
> Ever true in loving be,
> And the blots of Nature's hand
> Shall not in their issue stand.

[10] *Dream*, v. i. 7–27.

Never mole, harelip, nor scar,
Nor mark prodigious, such as are
Despised in nativity,
Shall upon their children be.
With this field-dew consecrate,
Every fairy take his gait,
And each several chamber bless
Through this palace with sweet peace;
And the owner of it blessed
Ever shall in safety rest.
Trip away, make no stay;
Meet me all by break of day.[11]

I am sure I am not the only playgoer to have gone away from the *Dream* feeling that it is rather a faint hope that any of these marriages will turn out more harmonious than that of Titania and Oberon.

As You Like It

But on reflection I could not imitate Shakespeare's own claim in the prologue to *Henry V*, to be

Turning the accomplishment of many years
Into an hour-glass.[12]

So I shall say a word *As You Like It*, and on the *Merchant*; and then sail into harbour with Romeo under the secure guidance of my brother, Nicholas Brooke, who is an eminent Shakespearean from whom I derive such understanding of the bard as I have—but like a ship's pilot he is only on board for a relatively short period and cannot be held responsible for my erratic navigation out at sea. My selection, however, has the merit that it confines us to the plays of the 1590s, and especially of the mid-1590s (the

[11] *Dream*, v. i. 397–400. [12] *Henry V*, prol. 30–1.

probable era of the *Dream* and *Romeo*, and perhaps the *Merchant* too) when explicit searching out of the problem of marriage formed a central theme of all his plays; one theme and not the only one, as anyone who contemplates Shylock or Mercutio well knows.

As You Like It is one of his lightest comedies, though this does not prevent him from some searching comment on contemporary marriage practices. Here is Touchstone preparing for marriage. Jaques, Touchstone, and Audrey stand before Sir Oliver Martext under a tree.

JAQUES. And will you, being a man of your breeding, be married under a bush like a beggar? Get you to church, and have a good priest that can tell you what marriage is. This fellow will but join you together as they join wainscot; then one of you will prove a shrunk panel, and like green timber, warp, warp.

TOUCHSTONE [*aside*]. I am not in the mind but I were better to be married of him than of another, for he is not like to marry me well; and not being well married, it will be a good excuse for me hereafter to leave my wife.

JAQUES. Go thou with me, and let me counsel thee.

TOUCHSTONE. Come sweet Audrey.

We must be married or we must live in bawdry.[13]

But mainly the play is parody-romance, and by putting it in the Forest of Arden Shakespeare can switch from romance to parody and back at his whim. Orlando may nail on every tree rather halting romantic verses to Rosalind—and many a true romantic touch may melt the playgoer in the end and remind him to treat his wife or his lover with more devotion. But in the serious business of love-making it is Rosalind who has to do the work. Here she is, disguised as a boy, pretending to cure—and yet in a manner seducing—Orlando.

---

[13] *As You Like It*, III. iii. 74–88.

ROSALIND. But are you so much in love as your rhymes speak?

ORLANDO. Neither rhyme nor reason can express how much.

ROSALIND. Love is merely a madness, and I tell you, deserves as well a dark house and a whip as madmen do; and the reason why they are not so punished and cured is that the lunacy is so ordinary that the whippers are in love too. Yet I profess curing it by counsel.

ORLANDO. Did you ever cure any so?

ROSALIND. Yes, one, and in this manner. He was to imagine me his love, his mistress; and I set him every day to woo me. At which time would I, being but a moonish youth, grieve, be effeminate, changeable, longing and liking, proud, fantastical, apish, shallow, inconstant, full of tears, full of smiles, for every passion something and for no passion truly anything, as boys and women are for the most part cattle of this colour; would now like him, now loathe him; then entertain him, then forswear him; now weep for him, then spit at him; that I drave my suitor from his mad humour of love to a living humour of madness, which was, to forswear the full stream of the world and to live in a nook merely monastic. And thus I cured him, and this way will I take upon me to wash your liver as clean as a sound sheep's heart, that there shall not be one spot of love in't.

ORLANDO. I would not be cured, youth.

ROSALIND. I would cure you, if you would but call me Rosalind and come every day to my cote and woo me.

ORLANDO. Now by the faith of my love, I will. Tell me where it is.

ROSALIND. Go with me to it, and I'll show it you; and by the way, you shall tell me where in the forest you live. Will you go?

ORLANDO. With all my heart, good youth.

ROSALIND. Nay, you must call me Rosalind. Come sister, will you go?[14]

Shakespeare's women are commonly wittier and cleverer and more mature than his men; that was perhaps a touch of realism in his world of fantasy.

The Merchant of Venice

The *Merchant* is altogether more sombre. It is well known that Shakespeare took the theme from a tale of Boccaccio about the merchant who pledged himself to a Jew to furnish his godson for an expedition to win a fair heiress. The godson won his heiress but forgot the pledge until it was almost too late: he was only just able to ride back to Venice before the forfeit, the pound of flesh, was exacted. Meanwhile his wife came separately to Venice dressed as a young lawyer and by cunning pleas released the godfather and confounded the Jew. Yet the lawyer extracted his wife's ring from the godson and in her other role as his wife only restored it to him after reducing him to tears. Here is almost the whole story of *The Merchant of Venice* except for the theme of the three caskets, which comes from quite another tale.[15]

The *Merchant* has an element of anti-semitism in it—though it is by no means simple, and the satire on Christian attitudes has a cutting edge—which must be repugnant to us today; but the marriage theme is exceptionally interesting. The play starts with a scene in which the merchant Antonio confesses his melancholy, which his friends attribute to the fortunes and chances of a merchant's life—to his ships exposed to weather and the fates; and in which Bassanio makes his request for money to take him to make his suit to Portia. There follows the scene in

[14] *As You Like It*, III, ii. 386–423.   [15] Brown 1955, pp. xxxii, 140–53.

which Portia too pronounces her melancholy: 'By my troth Nerissa my little body is aweary of this great world' —as well it may be, for she is condemned to find a husband by the trumpery game of the caskets, of gold or silver or lead. Each suitor has to choose one casket—and the one who chooses the right casket wins the bride.

PORTIA. To choose me a husband,—O me the word 'choose'! I may neither choose who I would, nor refuse who I dislike, so is the will of a living daughter curb'd by the will of a dead father: is it not hard Nerissa, that I cannot choose one, nor refuse none?

NERISSA. Your father was ever virtuous, and holy men at their death have good inspirations,—therefore the lott'ry that he hath devised in these three chests of gold, silver, and lead, whereof who chooses his meaning chooses you, will no doubt never be chosen by any rightly, but one who you shall rightly love.[16]

A likely story! We are meant to feel how wrong and how hard the old father has been in not trusting his daughter to her own choice—and yet how wise to check thus the impetuous intrigues of the princes of this world. After all, would she have done better without the caskets? But is that the end of the story? No, for three further twists are offered in the tale of the marriages which make, at the bitter end, a happy ending.

1. By a mixture of pure chance and good sense, Bassanio wins his bride. His marriage to Portia is not won by mere romance or by mere calculation; they love before the caskets are open—and this forbidden love gives them a kind of hard preparation for their reward; but the reward comes by fate not by choice or effort. The history of marriage in high society had been for many centuries an argument between choice and love on the one hand,

---

[16] *Merchant*, I. ii. 1–2, 21–32.

and planning and arrangement on the other. Shakespeare puts in a new twist here: fate and good luck must have their place, and sometimes it is a higher place than choice or planning.

2. He has introduced a sub-plot, the love of Lorenzo and Jessica. It is for this that Shakespeare reserves the choicest, the most romantic poetry in the whole play.

> How sweet the moonlight sleeps upon this bank!
> Here will we sit, and let the sounds of music
> Creep in our ears—soft stillness and the night
> Become the touches of sweet harmony:
> Sit Jessica,—look how the floor of heaven
> Is thick inlaid with patens of bright gold,
> There's not the smallest orb which thou behold'st
> But in his motion like an angel sings,
> Still quiring to the young-ey'd cherubins;
> Such harmony is in immortal souls,
> But whilst this muddy vesture of decay
> Doth grossly close it in, we cannot hear it.[17]

Here as so often, Shakespeare is at his most dangerous when he appears most lyrical. He has just reminded us in the famous sequence of love stories—'In such a night as this'—in such a night did Troilus sigh for Cressida, Thisbe for Pyramus, Dido for Aeneas;

> In such a night
> Medea gathered the enchanted herbs
> That did renew old Æson.

[A reminder of one of the more beneficent acts of the most murderous heroine of classical mythology.]

> In such a night
> Did Jessica steal from the wealthy Jew,
> And with an unthrift love did run from Venice,
> As far as Belmont.[18]

[17] *Merchant*, v. i. 54–65.   [18] *Merchant*, v. i. 1–17.

To put the matter bluntly, she was stolen, along with many jewels and ducats, from her father: the jewels and the ducats are harped on in the famous scene of her abduction and Shylock's lament, to emphasize the fact. Neither has the least shame in the matter; yet in its own way the audience must feel this was as much a case of theft as Theseus' capture of Hippolyta in war. Nor do the lovers feel any compunction; anything goes in love and war; the romantic face of the coin, which is genuine enough, so far as it goes, hides another face, less attractively drawn.

3. Finally, even the most perfect devotion in the play, the love which had hazarded all in its pursuit—once it has achieved its purpose—proves as hollow as the chance infatuation. Bassanio is as unfaithful to his promise to Portia as Graziano—who falls almost casually for Nerissa and she for him; both are caught in the same trap. They hand over their wives' rings to the lawyer and his clerk, Portia and Nerissa. However much they are disguised, that is the fact. The play ends in joy and laughter, but the observant witness is left to wonder—if that is how Bassanio handles the first serious trial of his love—what is yet to come. Yet it is not too serious; we are not meant to despair of him. The story goes that a famous Shakespearian scholar of an earlier generation, at some kind of public quiz, was asked to which Shakespearian heroine he would like to be married; and he answered 'Portia—I like to be managed.' However that may be, Portia will manage him all right. She will keep him out of further mischief.

Romeo and Juliet

Meanwhile, in *Romeo*, perhaps a year or two earlier than *The Merchant of Venice*, a picture of marriage had been presented in its way fully as ambivalent as that of the *Dream* or the *Merchant*, unrelieved by their happy endings. For in *Romeo and Juliet* the most lyrical, the most romantic, and some of the most erotic of Shakespeare's poetry is set off in the most brilliant manner by the earthy, bawdy speech of Mercutio and the Nurse. Nor are these characters extraneous to the play. Mercutio reminds us that marriage is not the only theme in the play: it encompasses the crossing of faction in medieval Verona with personal friendship, the failure of Romeo to respond to the challenge and Mercutio's brave effort to stand in his place, the killing of Mercutio by Tybalt and of Tybalt by Romeo. The Nurse reminds us that *Romeo and Juliet* is not all about romantic love. The intrigue between the lovers which ends in their marriage and tragedy is brought on by two assistants—by the simple minded Friar Laurence who fondly imagines that by bringing the two young lovers together and marrying them he can help to heal the wounds of faction; and the Nurse. It is the crass folly of the Nurse—the fact that her mind equates marriage and bawdy, for all her deep affection for Juliet and her fond memories of her own husband—that misleads her into encouraging the disastrous intrigue. But the Nurse would be a failure if she were not at once a great comic creation, and entirely plausible. We first meet her expatiating on Juliet's age, burbling on to Lady Capulet's extreme impatience, and evidently for a purpose. Juliet is thirteen— she will be fourteen next birthday, which is quite soon; just so, says Lady Capulet: high time she was married. The point of the nurse's speech is to emphasize Juliet's age; and it needs emphasizing, evidently, because when we discover Lady Capulet's absurd haste to have her married, and her own remarkable sexual maturity when she falls in love with Romeo, we are meant to think she was a bit young. The point does not go undisputed, and has doubtless been exaggerated, especially by Victorian critics. One does not have to believe that the nurse's memory was quite so accurate as she believed—nor Lady Capulet's

> younger than you,
> Here in Verona, ladies of esteem,
> Are made already mothers. By my count,
> I was your mother much upon these years
> That you are now a maid—[19]

which somehow carries an implication she is exaggerating. But the whole tenor of the passage forces us to reflect, first that Juliet is very young indeed, and second that marriage at such an age is perfectly possible. For some mysterious reason, ages of puberty seem to vary from century to century as well as from person to person; but in medieval canon law twelve was regarded as the normal basic age of consent, and of puberty, for a girl;[20] and if recorded marriages at this age are not all that numerous, we may at least recall the marvellous effigy by Torrigiani in Westminster Abbey of the Lady Margaret (Pl. 2), married to Edmund Tudor when she was twelve, widowed at thirteen, beside the equally splendid portrayal of her only son, King Henry VII, thirteen years her junior.[21] It is improbable that Shakespeare knew Margaret's age, most probable that he did know the legal age of puberty and marriage. In a most effective way, Shakespeare holds together three quite different aspects of the relations of men and women, and of marriage, in this play. First, marriage is an indulgence to the lust represented by Mercutio's and the Nurse's bawdy speeches, commonly genial, though it may turn in Mercutio's agony to disease—'a *plague* a'both your houses'.[22] Second, it is a children's game: Romeo may be older, perhaps years

---

[19] *Romeo*, I. iii. 71–4.   [20] See pp. 36, 140.
[21] See p. 36 and pl. 2. For Shakespeare's knowledge of the law of marriage, cf. Schanzer 1960.   [22] *Romeo*, III. i. 97.

older than Juliet, but in love-making he seems somehow less mature than her.[23] Yet if Juliet seems at times remarkably mature, she is only thirteen; and this drives it home that there is an element both of pubic awakening and of childishness, childishness reflected in the parent's scheme to marry her off next Wednesday or Thursday, and in the equally preposterous secret wedding which Friar Laurence stages in the vain hope it will bring peace to the warring families. Shakespeare lays some emphasis on the fleeting nature of these schemes; it is a lightning before death, as N. S. Brooke has emphasized; there is not the slightest hint that they will live together in marriage or have children.[24] But neither the bawdy nor the childishness can obscure the impression of the love poetry, which is among the most moving and the most romantic in any literature. To the thoughtful witness of *Romeo and Juliet* it is revealed that marriage in human society is compact of three extremely diverse, not to say incongruous, elements—of family arrangement, animal instinct, and romantic love;[25] and yet which of us could go away from the play saying that any of them is false?

Two further points particularly engage my attention in this play. As in the *Dream*, Shakespeare seems fairly cynical about the entry to marriage—I say seems for we shall learn little from literature if we waste time arguing what the author really thought or wanted for *himself*. The play as we see it enforces the point: the Capulets' scheme for marrying Juliet, and her own scheme, are in terms of

[23] 'It is in fact common' as Nicholas Brooke has observed in his study of the play, 'for Shakespeare's heroines to appear more mature than their men—Portia, Rosalind, and Imogen all have this quality.' Brooke 1968, p. 93.

[24] Brooke 1968, pp. 99, 101–2.

[25] But we should take special note, perhaps, of the literary tradition. See Brooke 1968, p. 106: 'And the final sense we may have of a hot-house atmosphere, a slightly cloying over-sweetness, is no accident, for it is just that with which it is concerned: a highly perceptive exploring of the love-death embrace of the sonneteering tradition, which regards both its superiority and its inferiority to the world of common day.'

ordinary human experience, equally ridiculous; neither parental authority, nor the choice of love, looks likely to produce satisfactory results. The second point is that Juliet seems to have her own view as to how one actually enters marriage. At one level, it is a perfectly conventional progression: first they exchange kisses after the famous formal sonnet at the end of the first act, and vows on the balcony in the second act; then the Friar blesses them in 'holy church'; and finally they consummate the marriage. The circumstances are a little unusual, perhaps, but in medieval Verona a legal wedding, even if reprehensible in being clandestine.[26] But it has been observed that Shakespeare unrolls at length the betrothal and prepares elaborately for the consummation; but makes shift with the ceremony off-stage.[27] Furthermore, the betrothal is not quite according to the book. Thus Romeo—

What shall I swear by?

To which Juliet:

> Do not swear at all;
> Or, if thou wilt, swear by thy gracious self,
> Which is the god of my idolatry,
> And I'll believe thee.

and immediately after, 'Well, do not swear'.[28] It is implicit and explicit in this passage that they have exchanged vows, but there is no formal betrothal.

A similar emphasis is given here as in the marriage scene in the *Parzival* of Wolfram von Eschenbach. At its heart, marriage is mutual giving.

What in the end does all this add up to? The special value of Shakespeare in our enterprise lies in his love of having everything both ways—preferably all three or four ways. We are sauntering happily behind him along a romantic path and he will turn and shock us with a reminder of lust or violence or some other less attractive

---

[26] See p. 252 n.   [27] Brooke 1968, p. 98.
[28] *Romeo*, II. ii. 112–16.

face of marriage—or even, in *Measure for Measure*, of the ascetic ideal. If any historian jumps up and says 'Such and such a sentiment was impossible or rare in sixteenth-century England' we can answer that he has forgotten Shakespeare—he has forgotten the variety of human experience—that 'there are more things in heaven and earth . . . than are dreamed of in your philosophy', as Hamlet said to Horatio.

The historian is always balancing the theme of continuity and change in his hands; and in some respects the works of our most eminent social historians—of Ladurie himself and the great Braudel—have emphasized some changeless qualities in parts of our world; but yet it remains broadly true that the social and economic historians of our age have been fascinated by change to the point that they sometimes see nothing else. I do not at all want to say that nothing happened in these centuries: that attitudes in the eighteenth or twentieth centuries are the same as in the sixteenth. But to observe the differences one needs a much sharper focus on continuities; above all on the variety of human nature and human conduct which Shakespeare illustrates so well. A course in *A Midsummer Night's Dream* may be a poor prognostic for a happy marriage; but it is compulsory reading for the historian of marriage. For it reminds us how timeless are many of the elements inherent in our story—chance and human caprice, human plotting and heroism, and choice and love. But the timeless quality is enhanced by a vital fact: the setting is pagan; it is a fantastical history play. In the present, Christian doctrine had something to say—and we have seen that this made, in all sorts of ways—some inspiring, some singularly ambivalent—a profound difference to the interpretation of the eternal elements in marriage and human nature. This is why I have tried to draw Heloise and Shakespeare into my highly selective view of the history of marriage.

THE CHURCH PORCH:
MARRIAGE AND ARCHITECTURE

Where did marriages take place? The question seems seldom to have been asked and has received only faint answers. Students of medieval literature acquainted with the Wife of Bath—who took five husbands to the church door to marry them—have readily replied: at the door of the church. There is copious evidence that this was a normal practice in the late Middle Ages. But we know little of its origin and less of its popularity—of how common it was as compared with exchange of vows in other places.

In their fundamental study of marriage rituals, Molin and Mutembe showed how the various elements in the liturgies of marriage—legal preliminaries, the giving away of the bride, the formal grant of dowry by the bridegroom, the exchange of promises, the blessing of the ring and its placing on the bride's third finger, followed by nuptial mass and the blessing of the bridal chamber—how all these came together in the Anglo-Norman rites of the turn of the eleventh and twelfth centuries; to be more precise, in pontificals or missals deriving from Brittany, Normandy, and England.[1] Earlier books, so far as they knew, gave no indication of where the first steps took place. It is in a group of twelfth-century books that the church door seems first to be specifically mentioned. These were the pontifical of Lire in Normandy, and the

---

[1] Molin and Mutembe 1974.

missals of Rennes in Brittany and Bury St Edmunds in Suffolk.[2] The pontifical of Lire was said by Dom Martène to be of the early twelfth century; but it is now lost. The missal of Rennes can be securely dated to the twelfth century, perhaps to the first half; the missal of Bury is approximately of the period *c.*1125–35. In Rennes the *Ordo* opens: 'First let the priest come before the door of the church [*ante ostium ecclesiae*] robed in alb and stole, with holy water . . .'. In Lire, 'Before all else let those who are to be joined in the marriage bed come before the doors of the church [*ad januas ecclesiae*] before very many witnesses . . .'. Each partner is to rehearse his and her consent; the woman's dower is to be confirmed, and some pennies set aside to be distributed among the poor; the bride is to be given to the groom by her father or friends, and received by him 'in God's faith and his own, to be kept in health and sickness as long as she lives, and he is to take her by the right hand'; the ring is blessed and laid on three fingers of her right hand with the priest's assistance, in the name of the Father, the Son, and the Holy Ghost, and then the groom sets it on a finger of her left hand; prayers and blessing follow. They enter the church and prostrate themselves in the nave, and the priest recites more prayers over them. Then they enter the choir and stand on the right (in other rituals, each holding a candle), as mass is celebrated. After the *Sanctus* they prostrate themselves in prayer and four men hold a cloak or cloth over them, each taking a corner; at the *Pax* they rise, the groom receives the peace from the priest and gives it to his wife with a kiss, and the mass concludes with their communion—and the whole rite with the blessing of the bridal chamber at night. The details vary

---

[2] For this and what follows, see Molin and Mutembe 1974, pp. 34–7, 285–90; for the Rennes missal, ibid. pp. 284–6, for Lire, ibid. pp. 286–7, for Bury, ibid. pp. 289–91; for the Bury missal, cf. Ker 1964, p. 20; McLachlan 1978. I am very grateful for the help of Dr Rodney Thomson on this point.

greatly; the essence of the rite remained and was repeated through countless liturgical books.

In the rites of both Rennes and Lire, when the ceremonies at the door are over, they enter the church, and in the course of the mass—before the altar (Rennes) or in the choir (Lire) they are blessed by the priest. Similar rubrics adorn the Bury missal, in which the service starts *'ante hostium templi'*.[3] And similar words occur in legal texts of later date.[4] But the commonest phrase is ambiguous. *'In facie ecclesiae'*—in the church's presence— has been taken to refer to a church service, and doubtless it commonly involved one; but it has a wider significance—it means publicly, in the presence of the local community of the church or parish; not privately or secretly or clandestinely; it refers to the publication of banns or some similar attempt to bring a marriage into the view of the church at large.[5] But no one doubts that it was the church's consistent aim through the centuries from the twelfth to the sixteenth and beyond to bring weddings into church.

The Wife of Bath, if not a wholly admirable character, bears witness that the church succeeded: that many marriages took place at church door; that one could use the phrase in the late fourteenth century as part of the normal currency of social chit-chat. But the presence of the church or of a priest was not necessary to a valid marriage; and it is a very striking fact that the definition of marriage adopted by Pope Alexander III in the 1160s and preserved as the basic minimum for a valid marriage until the Council of Trent—in the Church of England till the eighteenth century—involved consent before

---

[3] Molin and Mutembe 1974, p. 289.
[4] For examples, see Molin and Mutembe 1974, p. 37 n. 48; Homans 1942, pp. 179–80; Smith 1986, p. 169.
[5] For examples of its use, see Sheehan 1978, p. 443. For what follows see above, pp. 138–9, 150–2, 169–72, 212.

witnesses; thus might a marriage be made strong, binding, without being *'in facie ecclesie'*.

Yet if we ask, where then did marriage take place, if not at church door?—we must proceed with caution. There may well have been—there probably was—a multiplicity of local custom. But we are exceedingly ill informed upon it. Nothing is so ill recorded as what everyone knows and takes for granted; it is the fundamental customs which are most difficult to trace.

The evidence from legal sources of the fourteenth and fifteenth centuries makes clear that in some parts of Europe at least it was a common practice for the marriage promises to be exchanged away from church. The evidence from the church courts at Ely and Canterbury and York analysed by Michael Sheehan and Richard Helmholz shows that in a large majority of instances in which a contract issued in a lawsuit the marriage had not been contracted in church: 89 out of 122 were clandestine in Sheehan's analysis of the Ely court books; and in a single Canterbury deposition book of 1411–20 Helmholz found that 38 out of 41 took place away from church, many of them at home.[6] He cites a charming case from York (1372):

> Here is an example which is by no means unusual:
> '[The witness says that] one year ago on the feast day of the apostles Philip and James just past, he was present in the house of William Burton, tanner of York, about the third hour past the ninth, when and where John Beke, saddler, sitting down on a bench of that house, called in English "le Sidebynke", called the said Marjory to him and said to her, "Sit with me". Acquiescing in this, she sat down. John said to her, "Marjory, do you wish to be my wife?" And she replied, "I will if you wish". And taking at once the said

---

[6] Sheehan 1971, pp. 249–50; Helmholz 1978, pp. 28–30.

Marjory's right hand, John said, "Marjory, here I take you as my wife, for better or worse, to have and to hold until the end of my life; and of this I give you my faith." The said Marjory replied to him, "Here I take you John as my husband, to have and to hold until the end of my life, and of this I give you my faith." And then the said John kissed the said Marjory through a wreath of flowers, in English "Garland".'

What the witness describes here is essentially a private contract. It was made clandestinely, without 'benefit of clergy', and with no apparent thought of resorting to the parish church. Elsewhere we hear of marriages contracted under an ash tree, in a bed, in a garden, in a small storehouse, in a field. There were marriages contracted in a blacksmith's shop, near a hedge, in a kitchen, by an oak tree, at a tavern. Even the King's Highway was the scene of one alleged marriage.[7]

It does not follow that a majority of marriages were contracted away from the parish church. First of all, very little evidence has so far been collected for other parts of Europe than England. Secondly, it is evident that some of these marriages had been lightly entered into: that the deep confusion (as we should see it) between betrothal and marriage meant that a number of those involved in these cases probably imagined they had stated a mere intention, possibly a frivolous intention. More important, it is abundantly clear that these betrothals were often followed by a church wedding—and we have no means of knowing how many of these cases would have come to church had the marriage not foundered.[8] Yet the fact

---

[7] Helmholz 1978, pp. 28–9. The quotation is from York, Borthwick Institute, C.P. E121 (cause papers: the Latin text is in Helmholz 1978, p. 29 n. 15). There was a witness, but it was none the less clandestine, for it was a private contract, without any kind of public ceremony or publication of banns (cf. Helmholz 1978, p. 27). Cf. Schabacher 1972, pp. 395–6.

[8] See Helmholz 1978, chaps. 2 and 3, esp. pp. 28–9; Sheehan 1971.

remains: it is evident that many marriages were not made in church, and that this was partly because, in the view of some—perhaps of very many—the church was not the place for a marriage. An extreme example has been discovered in Toulouse. There the marriage contracts were made in the presence of a notary: if some marriages were made in heaven, all had to be made on earth if they were to take legal effect, and a notary's register was better evidence than the memory of priest and witnesses. Out of 551 cases counted by G. Laribière from fourteenth- and fifteenth-century Toulouse, 541 were by *verba de praesenti*:[9] how many of these married folk went on to church we cannot tell; but it is evident that a church ceremony was not an essential feature of match-making.

It is sometimes alleged that marriage in the home was a special custom of this or that part of Europe—of some regions of Germany, for instance, or the Low Countries. But for this I have seen no evidence cited. It would be a very valuable exercise to collect more testimony, and I am sure that some exists and that one day a fuller picture can be drawn. But I very much doubt if there is satisfactory evidence covering the whole of Europe: we must be content to be ignorant.

One notable reflection of the practice of solemnizing marriages at church door must be the sumptuous provision of porches in the late Middle Ages. It would be wrong to deduce from their absence in some early churches that marriages were not held in them; it would be quite consistent with the mores of tenth and eleventh century Europe to suppose that married couples and their witnesses might brave the elements to win through to their union. But late medieval porches are often strikingly large and handsome, and we may reasonably suppose that one of their main functions was to provide an

---

[9] Laribière 1967, p. 344, cited Helmholz 1978, p. 28 n. 14.

appropriate setting for weddings. It was not their only function: other liturgical functions could be performed there, other contracts entered; they were used for funerals as well as weddings and sometimes as burial places.[10] But they must have been especially associated, in the minds of many of the clergy, of many patrons of such buildings, and of countless married folk, with the ceremonies of marriage at church door.

The history of porches is peculiarly difficult to trace, anyway in the present state of knowledge. The early Christian basilicas had large atria, forecourts with covered walks, and where they survived or were later rebuilt—as at Sant'Ambrogio at Milan—these would have rendered any mere porch superfluous.[11] Most churches of the early Middle Ages have been so altered that all trace of a porch (if ever there was one) has departed. Harold Taylor's very full analysis of Anglo-Saxon churches has shown that the porches were an occasional, not a normal feature of early churches in England;[12] but the matter is complicated by the use of the word *'porticus'* in the texts, which can mean a separate room or transept as often as, or more often than, a porch. Such rooms—and porches—were used for all manner of purposes—for meeting rooms, lawcourts, baptisteries; perhaps also for weddings, but we have no reason to suppose that they were regularly provided for any such purpose. Major Continental churches of the Carolingian period commonly had elaborate westworks, and it is quite possible that weddings were among the many different functions which have been discerned for these strange buildings. In the eleventh and twelfth centuries large Continental churches commonly had atria

---

[10] On porches see Clapham 1934, p. 69 (for the eleventh century in England): 'a very unusual adjunct, if indeed they existed at all, . . . and even in the twelfth century they were by no means common'; Walls 1912; cf. Brooke 1981, p. 29.

[11] Brooke and Swaan 1974, pp. 219–23, and esp. pl. 356 and fig. 27.

[12] Taylor 1978, chap. 2.

or narthexes.[13] But their use is (in the present state of knowledge) highly conjectural. We should probably learn more from a close study of smaller churches, which are more likely to have been, or to have become, the normal scene of weddings at church door.

It is none the less worth dwelling for a moment on some English examples. At Tewkesbury the magnificent twelfth-century nave of the abbey church is adorned with an exceptionally ample porch for its period (Pl. 3). Although its precise date is not known, the eastern part of the church was probably complete by 1102, and we may assign the nave, at latest, to the age of its greatest twelfth-century patron, Robert earl of Gloucester, that is between 1122 and 1147.[14] It is thus possible, likely indeed, that the porch was contemporary with the Bury missal. In that epoch the great naves attached to abbeys and cathedrals were evidently meeting-places of the church and the world: they provided space and shelter in which large throngs of laymen could gather, and we may well suppose that weddings were among the celebrations which took place there, especially in buildings like Tewkesbury which enshrined ancient parochial rights. But there were moves afoot, perhaps already in the twelfth century, to limit the secular noise and confusion in these great naves, and to turn out the tables of the money-changers and others. This may have encouraged the building of porches to provide for the laity outside the main fabric. Thus at Ely we find, in the course of the early thirteenth century, a

[13] There are numerous plans in Conant 1959 and Clapham 1934; but the relevant details are often conjectural for such early periods.
[14] Comparison of Tewkesbury annals etc. (Dugdale 1817–30, ii. 60 and Luard 1864–9, i. 44) with Orderic, iii. 226–9, seems to make clear that sufficient of Tewkesbury abbey church was built by Robert Fitzhamon by 1102 for the monks to be moved there from Cranborne—i.e. presumably the east end. His son-in-law and heir, Earl Robert, was a great patron and may be presumed to have completed the church. Cf. also Clapham 1934, p. 34. The architectural evidence has been partly obscured by substantial restoration, esp. in the seventeenth century.

substantial porch incongruously added to the great westwork.[15] At Peterborough a similar porch of even larger dimensions is none the less absurdly dwarfed:[16] it can hardly have been, in any ordinary sense, an entry to the abbey; but it is very likely that it was provided as compensation to lay worshippers only occasionally allowed within: a space for weddings and other events they had been accustomed to perform at the abbey church's door or within it.

However this may be there can be little doubt that the ample, often magnificent, porches added to parish churches in the late Middle Ages were partly intended as wedding marquees (Pl. 4). Some had chambers over them for school rooms, guild halls, and the like; and they received the dead as well as the living. But we need not doubt that when, in the fifteenth century, St Mary Redcliffe at Bristol received a porch almost as large as, and much more ornate than the Norman porch at Tewkesbury less than forty miles up the Severn, matrimony was a part of its purpose.

Porches can be suggestive evidence, no more; and the same goes for most of the painting and sculpture which survives. Numerous representations of husbands and wives greet us in painting and sculpture; illustrated copies of Gratian's *Decretum* have intriguing representations of his unlikely marriage cases, and some more normal portrayals of husband and wife such as we meet representing Christ and the Church in the initials of the Song of Songs.[17] The marriage of Adam and Eve in Paradise inspired a number of medieval pictures.[18] Many a charming romance is illustrated in late medieval manuscripts; and time and again the Holy Family gave

[15] Swaan 1969, pl. 244.   [16] Swaan 1969, pl. 225.
[17] For all this see Frugoni 1977. Gratian is magnificently illustrated in Melnikos 1975, iii, especially the illustrations to *Causa* 36.
[18] Heimann 1975.

the opportunity to portray the incidents of domestic life, including midwives, babies' baths, attendants carrying soap and hot water, distaffs, and what-have-you. Satirical scenes will show husband and wife linked in the sin of avarice, or grown old in dull dyspepsia. Misericords show wives vigorously beating their husbands, and so forth.[19] Some of these may stir the imagination, but they have little perhaps to contribute to a serious enquiry into medieval marriage. To this there is a unique exception, the *Arnolfini Marriage* of Jan van Eyck, which shall form our epilogue.[20]

[19] E.g.: Marinus, *The Banker and his Wife*, 1538 (Madrid, Prado, Murray 1965, pl. 377); for misericords, Bond 1910, pp. 88–90; Remnant 1969, pp. 164, 176. For other examples of marriage scenes, Schabacher 1972, p. 396 n. 53a.

[20] See pp. 280–6, but see also pl. 9.

TOWARDS A THEOLOGY OF
MARRIAGE[1]

We cannot study the history of marriage without imagination and insight—without infusing into our scholarship
our knowledge of ourselves and of human nature. Our
presuppositions will enter our history—and if our history
is worth anything it will affect our reflections on marriage
itself. This should inspire us to caution: history inspired
by dogma loses its meaning and value and becomes
tedious. But it would be absurd to study an area of human
experience so vital and so controversial in our world
without considering if our enquiry lends anything to the
debate—and if we fail to do so, we may be suspected or
convicted of indifference or cynicism. So the attempt shall
be made, and I shall call back a few of our witnesses—
asking them to repeat a little of their message—with the
intent of pondering their evidence rather more deeply,
and considering what they may contribute to our understanding of marriage and its place in human affairs and
Christian theology.

I do not suppose that the limited evidence of human
history can or should dictate to us a theology of marriage;
but it can help to put our thoughts and the history of such
thoughts into perspective, and to test some of our views

---

[1] For those for whom theology, and the personal views of the author, have
small interest, pp. 258–80 may be best omitted; but pp. 280–6 form the true
conclusion to the book. In this chapter I resume arguments and illustrations
drawn from every part of the book, which involves a certain measure of
repetition. The literature is vast; most helpful is Schillebeeckx 1965.

and assumptions by experience. The difficulty of studying medieval marriage is much enhanced by the silence of our chief witnesses. It is often supposed, indeed, that almost all our evidence comes from clergy, who were celibate, none from laymen or women. The clergy are not to be underestimated—the outsider may sometimes see most of the game, and of such an intimate relationship one may perhaps learn more from the confessional than from the social survey. In any case the statement is not wholly true, as is very clear if we reflect on some of the most notable of our witnesses, who will include a woman and two laymen.

Heloise

In 1116 or 1117, the reader will recall, the great scholar and teacher Peter Abelard married his mistress Heloise, niece of a canon of the cathedral of Notre-Dame in Paris.[2] It was the briefest of unions. Her uncle had Abelard castrated, which Abelard took for a divine judgement: he insisted on their marriage being dissolved by the only legal means—by both entering religious orders. She was the product of a world in which the clerical concubine was still respectable—she and her like enjoyed an Indian summer at the turn of the eleventh and twelfth centuries, in a few cathedral chapters especially (so far as the sparse documentation goes) in northern France and England, strangely little touched by the immensely powerful propaganda of the age for clerical celibacy.[3] Heloise and Abelard met at a turning-point in this world of opinion. She strenuously objected to marriage because it would ruin his career; her arguments evidently sharpened the

[2] See chap. 5.
[3] See chap. 4.

edge of his views on the sacrament, as his devotion to her enhanced his sense of the sacredness of the union.

The whole correspondence reveals two exceedingly vigorous, articulate, and intelligent minds very much accustomed to argue and debate between themselves; and the discussion of love and marriage very evidently echoed many discussions they had held in earlier days. We can indeed deduce pretty much the tenor of these. The argument of Heloise's first letter echoes her own resistance to their marriage: 'You have passed over in silence [she tells him, referring to his summary of her arguments in the *Historia Calamitatum*] many of the grounds which led me to set love before marriage and liberty before the chain.'[4] Abelard had set forth a brilliant display of debating points—just the kind of thing he and she would have bandied between them in discussion and argument: that it would cause a scandal harmful to both if he bound himself to one woman, though he was meant to be teacher of all men; that the Apostle and the Fathers had warned of the difficulties of marriage; that the life of a philosopher and a nursery were incompatible—with a great deal of merry quotation from Jerome against Jovinian, and much more learning of the kind, including the rules attaching to a clerk and a canon. But he had passed delicately over her deepest ground—'She added, finally, both how dangerous it would be to me to take her back and how much dearer to her it would be, and better for me, for her to be called mistress [*amicam*] than wife—so that affection [*gratia*] alone should keep me for her, and no force of a nuptial chain constrain me. If we were separated for a time the joys of meeting would be all the keener for being more rare.'[5] Heloise carries this argument in her letter a great deal further. She puts it

---

[4] Muckle 1953, p. 71 (Radice 1974, p. 114).
[5] Monfrin 1962, p. 78 (Radice 1974, p. 74). An abbreviated version of pp. 260–3 was published in Brooke 1987, pp. 463–5.

indeed in the form of a debating point—she would rather be Abelard's mistress than the emperor's wife—an argument which she thought must be irresistible to him. Yet a deeper argument lies beyond: their relationship was the deepest thing in her life; it could be described in many ways—in the protocol to her first letter she uses the words lord, father, husband, brother, slave-girl, daughter, wife, sister:[6] in her second simply *'unico . . . unica'*[7]—but its essence lay in a love which was eternal, not broken by the *divortium* which had ended their marriage; and a love which was wholly unselfish, which consisted entirely in giving—without any thought of or corruption by reward.

We do not have to believe that Heloise took a low view of marriage, least of all her own. It is implicit in the whole story, and in many parts of the letters, that this was not at all the case. Her argument had been—not that love was always selfless and marriage a mere legal contract for mutual, and possibly corrupting, benefits—but that this *could* be so. She is very aware of stating a paradox, and the logic of the paradox is clear enough. Marriage itself is a sacrament—and like any sacrament capable of leading its devotees to hell as well as to heaven. But at its highest and best and most blessed it is based on selfless love, on mutual self-giving. 'God knows I looked for nothing in you at any time except yourself.'[8] I have little doubt that the letter sincerely expresses her previous attitudes or prejudices. For she was brought up in a cathedral close where relationships of love were known and accepted, where marriage in the strict sense was alien and forbidden; and marriage was something of the outside

---

[6] Muckle 1953, p. 68 (Radice 1974, p. 109).

[7] Muckle 1953, p. 77 (Radice 1974, p. 127). Her final letter opens *'Domino specialiter sua singulariter'*, whatever that meant. On the whole, Betty Radice's 'God's own in species, his own as individual'—allowing that *specialiter* and *singulariter* both have overtones to which we should listen—may well be right (Radice 1974, p. 159 and n. 1). It echoes Heloise's own argument against marriage.

[8] Muckle 1953, p. 70 (Radice 1974, p. 113). For what follows see above, pp. 89–92.

world, a contract of convenience among worldly, landed folk, to sustain and enhance the fortunes of their families. Heloise viewed the strange alliance of church and secular nobility in the institution of marriage with a cool eye: she would hardly have seen divine providence in the union of the Christian sacrament and family ambition. But the drama of her story and her devotion to Abelard compelled her to unite in her own person selfless love and the sacrament of marriage; and we are shown in this human situation—as the actors must surely have realized—a crucial step in the development of thought and doctrine about marriage: that it is a sacrament between the partners, a sacrament of mutual giving. Heloise would have sympathized with, and recognized the expression Wolfram was to give the same doctrine a century later.[9]

As her first letter very plainly shows, this deep insight leaves many problems behind it. For marriage itself carries many social and legal consequences and simply must be a public act; it cannot be wholly a private compact between husband and wife. It is also very clear that Heloise's intuitive, idealistic, romantic view of Christian love makes it eternal—gives it a quality quite apart from the accidents of human life, of marriage ceremonies and death. Marriage vows in the Middle Ages 'till death us do part' meant in practice for about ten or twelve years if you were lucky—or, as it might be, very unlucky; it could last much, much longer—but there was no reasonable expectation of it; second and third marriages were common; what happened to these in heaven? This is very much more than a rhetorical question, though it certainly cannot be answered. When Jesus himself was asked (if correctly reported) the question he did not answer it.[10] Because expectation of life was so

---

[9] See pp. 194–6.
[10] Mark 12: 18–25. See p. 48. Dr Sherwin Bailey is one of the few writers to

brief marriage was almost as unstable an institution in the Middle Ages as now. We are in deep waters; but however we view it—whatever our personal beliefs may be—there is no doubt of the power and force of the doctrine of human love which Heloise laid bare in her two letters. How it was communicated we do not know; for the correspondence itself may not have been known to any but themselves till near the end of the thirteenth century.[11] But many knew something of their story, and Heloise herself commanded in later life a deep respect as a person, which sanctified both her life and her marriage.

The history of marriage must be viewed at two levels, or it will cease to bear any relation to our experience of how human affairs are conducted. It is a piece of social history, related to the whole pattern of customs, laws, relations, aspirations, what-have-you—which lie at the centre of the history of family life. But it is at every point deeply affected by its inner life, full of variety, tragic and comic, romantic and very unromantic, a tale of joy and suffering and humdrum, most of it hidden from the historian's eye. The twelfth century marks an important phase in the formation of marriage custom and marriage law: for the Church had gained formal control of marriage and so imposed its rule of monogamy; and the European upper classes came to centre many of their aspirations more firmly than before on rules of inheritance which also presupposed monogamy. At the same time a tradition of the Christian experience of marriage and the romantic attitude to love—also very often in conflict, and equally often in alliance, also doubtless with a long history behind them—found expression of a marked and lasting

face squarely the issue of what happens to marriage after death: Bailey 1952, pp. 96–8, 120–4.

[11] For the latest appraisal of the textual history—allowing for larger gaps in the evidence than used to be thought—see Luscombe 1980, pp. 28–31. But David Luscombe has pointed out to me the argument in Laurie 1986 that the letters were known to Chrétien of Troyes: see above, chap. 4 n. 32.

quality. It is indeed a piquant and remarkable fact that at a critical moment in the history we have been exploring we should have preserved in the letters of Heloise and Abelard so vivid and revealing a vision of the world in which these qualities met, as seen through the eyes of a woman. Much of the history of theology is abstract and intellectual; here for a moment we may see a major step in theology urged and prompted by a personal experience of great profundity.

Three Popes: Adrian IV, Alexander III, and Innocent III

By the twelfth century the law of marriage and jurisdiction over marriage had fallen into the hands of the Church, the Church's courts, and above all the pope and papal Curia. Opinions greatly differ whether their interventions were beneficent or not; my own view is that they frequently were—that they brought humanity and good sense into this very difficult arena. Such general statements cannot apply to a whole range of cases, and we need not doubt that they had many failures, and that even from their successes some deserted wives or bewildered families suffered. But there were some substantial gains. I take three notable popes to illustrate the theme.

In the mid 1150s Pope Adrian IV was posed the question whether a slave could marry. Here was a region of human experience in which the law and custom of the Roman Empire took an unconscionable time in dying. Slavery was still legal in the eyes of the Church; a lord's rights were not to be lightly set aside—and in any case in a hierarchical society which really believed in hierarchy, at least in one part of its mind, the idea of unfree persons having free will in choosing marriage partners and such like important decisions was almost unthinkable. Pope Adrian's answer was simple: he turned to the Epistle to the Galatians. 'Just as in Christ Jesus there is neither a free man nor a slave—who may be kept apart from the sacraments of the Church—so too ought not marriages between slaves to be in any way prevented.'[12] Contemporaries and modern historians have vied with one another in incredulity; but the authenticity of the decretal is not now in doubt. What is more surprising is that—after an infinite number of hiccoughs—it took effect. It was a major turning point in the history of slavery, and of marriage.

The papal doctrine in this case was biblical—securely based on a reading of a basic biblical text. Many modern commentaries have concentrated on the ascetic tradition in medieval teaching on sex and marriage—on such excrescences as the notion that sex even in marriage was only wholly free from sin if there was no pleasure in it—a doctrine severely trounced by Abelard.[13] But there was another tradition too. Dr Sherwin Bailey, in his moving book on *The Mystery of Love and Marriage*, asserts that the medieval Church—theological tradition indeed—made little of the biblical doctrine that husband and wife are 'one flesh', 'comparatively little' of the analogy between marriage and the union of Christ and the Church in Ephesians.[14] This cannot be right. They are essential presuppositions of the whole structure of medieval thought on the subject: the first helps to explain why medieval marriage doctrine is so sex-ridden; the second why an ascetic, celibate community of theologians paid marriage the high honour of making it a sacrament.

Adrian's successor, Alexander III, in his long reign from 1159 to 1181, did more than any other medieval pope to clarify the law of marriage. It was in his time that the greatest efforts were made—before the Council of Trent, that is, and the Reformation—to find a universal

[12] See pp. 51–2.   [13] Abelard in Luscombe 1971, pp. 20–1.
[14] Bailey 1952, esp. pp. 45, 109.

definition of marriage. Christian marriage grew up in the Roman Empire, and however much it owed (and it owed much) to Jewish inspiration, however much it developed its own Christian ethos, it lived for many centuries under the umbrella of Roman law. 'It is not consummation but consent which makes marriages' said the great jurisconsul Ulpian, and no canon lawyer wholeheartedly disagreed with him.[15] Alexander III handled a number of cases in which this was precisely the issue. His own views are not always clear to us because he did not utter general principles or issue legislation, but settled cases; the statements of the law which he made are always in some measure moulded to the peculiar circumstances of each case; and he was a man who had thought deeply on the matter—or taken a lot of good advice—and greatly valued consent, consummation, and the marriage service as elements in the making of marriage.[16] But he deliberately accepted, and shrewdly modified the legacy he had inherited. Perhaps the nicest example of all is the treatment the popes meted out to a favourite phrase of the Roman jurists: *'Maritalis affectio'*. This originally simply meant the intent to get married—a very important element in the very informal marriage procedures of the Roman Empire. But Pope Alexander III (who knew what it had originally meant) deliberately read into it another meaning of *affectio*—our affection—as an essential part of a serious intent to enter marriage.[17]

Another book could be written on the shifting attitudes to human love, and their relation to marriage, in the Middle Ages. One tradition stemming from the ancient world saw human affection issuing in real comradeship as chiefly to be found in the relation of man to man. In a famous passage Augustine firmly stated that comradeship could not be the reason for the creation of Eve: a man

[15] See chap. 6, n. 29.
[16] See chap. 6, nn. 37, 54, and references cited.   [17] Noonan 1967.

would have done the job better.[18] In the literature of the twelfth century there is much greater variety of view. St Bernard stoutly proclaimed that human and divine love were part of a single ladder, not in contradiction to one another—though clearly for him human love was infinitely less than the love of God, married love less than the love between male friends.[19] So clear was this to him that he could use a language of affection which might be supposed homosexual—but one has only to contemplate the use he makes of erotic imagery in his *Sermons on the Song of Songs* to realize that metaphor was to him a wholly abstract thing—as to many other writers of the eleventh and twelfth centuries, a fact which renders their full meaning peculiarly difficult for us to grasp. But there is no doubt of the warmth of friendship in Bernard; even clearer is the same emotion expounded humanely and in depth by St Aelred of Rievaulx.[20] But Bernard did not exclude women from his friendships, still less refuse to allow that the love of husband and wife could partake of the quality of true human friendship. This view was made even more specific by Hugh of St Victor, though both he and Bernard evidently thought spiritual friendship a higher form of love. The passage in Paul's Epistle to the Galatians which made the free man and the slave equal in Christ performed the same service for male and female; and so Hugh was compelled to say that woman was 'given to man as a comrade, not a servant or a mistress' even though she was also (in his view) in some way inferior.[21] This contradiction runs through much later literature and has been justly pilloried; but in fairness one may say that

---

[18] See p. 55.

[18] See p. 55.

[19] See Leclercq 1979, pp. 16–26, 99–108, 121–9; Leclercq 1982, pp. 73–86; cf. Kooper 1985, pp. 37 ff.

[20] Text in Hoste 1971, trans. in Laker 1974; cf. commentary and references in Kooper 1985, pp. 46–56, 245–6.

[21] Hugh of St Victor, *De sacramentis*, ii. 11. 4, *PL* clxxvi. 485; cf. Kooper 1985, pp. 42–3.

it preserved through all the vicissitudes of time and social change the basic proposition that husband and wife could be equal partners—must be so in Christ; and that view, and a simple humanity, lay at the root of Alexander III's decretals—though often overlaid with the harsh facts of life and the prejudices which so frequently obscured the purity of Paul's vision.[22]

The two cases which we studied in detail—those of Richard of Anstey and the Countess Agnes—show Alexander firmly supporting marriage by consent, and upholding the binding force of consent here and now, *de praesenti*. But his handling of impotence, and his references to *una caro*, one flesh, show a different tradition at work.[23] A man who had pondered the meaning of Jesus' insistence that man and wife were 'one flesh' might well feel bound to accord an essential place to consummation in his theology of marriage; Roman law had already for many centuries united in its ample grasp the assertion that consent not consummation makes a marriage with permission to those who cannot consummate their marriages to part. The contradiction was evidently entrenched in the custom of Christendom. Here we see the elements in Alexander's theology of marriage clearly laid out. The two threads in Roman law were firmly established; each played its part in Christian doctrine; in upholding consent *de praesenti* he was confirming the rule laid down by his predecessor Innocent II in the Anstey case; in making allowances for the rather different customs of Rome and Gaul in cases of impotence he was facing squarely the need to temper his rules to established custom. Clearly he preferred the Roman custom: he had no wish to part couples who could not consummate their marriages, but were happy to enjoy

---

[22] See above, chap. 6, nn. 37, 54, and for what follows, above, pp. 148–57.
[23] See esp. Oesterlé 1953; cf. above, pp. 132–3. For what follows, see above, pp. 128–41.

the other blessings of the state of marriage. By the same token he would not change the fundamental rules of consanguinity, but forbade the marriages of third cousins to be called in question unless the facts were notorious—doing all he could to discourage tendentious genealogical enquiry by couples seeking grounds for annulment.

The bond of common interest between the pope and his world is clearly revealed in the denouement of the Countess Agnes's case. The earl accepted in the end that if he wanted to save his soul, if he wanted to pass on his earldom and his estates to a legitimate heir, if he wanted to be at peace with his neighbours, he must take Agnes to wife. The combination of worldly calculation and humanity in this case is very striking. Equally striking in Alexander's marriage doctrine is the impact of his biblical theology. Man and wife were one flesh; a husband owed his wife—a wife her husband—a debt which could only be paid in the marriage-bed. St Paul's imperative confirmed the custom of the Church and the ruling of Justinian: those who had no hope of consummating their marriages could not make complete marriages—or so it was argued. This is a question to which we shall return.

My final example of the papacy at work comes from the next generation after Alexander III; it is a charming decretal of Pope Innocent III (1198–1216), about an infidel—a Moslem, doubtless, who had been converted along with several wives. It sounds to us like an imaginary conundrum of the schools; but it was a real problem in the Crusader states in Palestine and Syria, and it came to him from the bishop of Tiberias.[24] The crucial point put to him was whether the children of these multiple wives were legitimate, a key matter in inheritance. Innocent's answer was unambiguous: the marriages were perfectly valid, the children were all

---

[24] See p. 52; *Decretals of Gregory IX*, iv. 19. 8.

legitimate; the only thing was that when the convert was baptized, he could only keep one of the wives. Here and elsewhere Innocent quotes 1 Corinthians 7, where Paul makes it abundantly clear that mixed marriages were valid but could be terminated if absolutely necessary.

Wolfram von Eschenbach

The most remarkable medieval commentary on this issue known to me comes not from a canonist or a theologian, still less from a pope, but from a layman. We are often told that we can learn nothing of medieval marriage either from women or from laymen. There are indeed not many exceptions, but they include some of the most deeply pondered commentaries of all. We have already taken evidence from the Abbess Heloise. For the mixed marriage and the consequence of conversion I call to witness one of the greatest of medieval poets, the German Wolfram von Eschenbach, who was a contemporary of Pope Innocent III. He touches these problems in both his great epics, but most fully in his *Willehalm*, based on the story of William of Orange, one of Charlemagne's peers, who late in life (in historical fact) became a monk and after his death a saint, whose shrine may still be visited in the entrancing remains of Saint-Guilhem-le-Désert near Montpellier.[25] William, so the story went, had a spell in a heathen prison, and the local queen fell in love with him and with the Christian God. Wolfram is characteristically obscure—delightfully ambiguous indeed—on which came first. Arabel was baptized and took the name of Giburc, and throughout the epic she is Willehalm's devout, devoted wife. The poem describes the invasion of Willehalm's homeland by numberless hordes of heathen led by

---

[25] Brooke and Swaan 1974, plates 65–7; on *Willehalm*, see above, pp. 202–10.

Giburc's father and her deserted husband. Two bloody battles ensue and in the end Willehalm is victorious; the heathen depart; and Giburc is left in peace. But it is a tragic peace, for she is deeply aware that she has brought fearful loss and disaster to both her own and her husband's folk. There is an overwhelming sense of disaster; and something else too—for in a celebrated outburst Giburc begs the Frankish warriors to treat the heathen fairly: 'Hear the counsel of a simple woman and spare God's handiwork.'[26] One of the major themes of the poem is a tolerance unusual in medieval literature, very unusual indeed in crusading epics. Another is the vital power of baptism. The poem opens with a formal creed, laying special emphasis on baptism. Yet the question is sharply raised—what difference does baptism make? It is central to the Christian message, it is the sole justification for Giburc flying from her first husband, a determined non-Christian. Yet the heathen are God's handiwork too, and her flight and baptism have brought irreparable disaster.

It is the quality of great poetry to pose questions not to answer them; and we do well to ponder Wolfram's probing of the issue of the mixed marriage. We do not know if he had met any Moslems—he must surely have encountered some Jews—but it may well be that he had an inkling from actual or reported experience of what unbelievers' marriages could be like. It is not at all improbable that the marriage customs of the Jewish communities of Europe sometimes inspired their Christian neighbours. But in any case the question is still with us. To the Christian, marriage is a sacrament, inseparable from the heart of his faith. But both the inner and the outer faces of marriage can be met in their most impressive character among non-Christians. What difference does it make?

[26] Above, p. 207.

11. *Towards a Theology of Marriage*

The Capetian Kings

The most notorious difference between medieval marriage and marriage under most of the legal systems of Europe and America today is that it is now freely terminable. Jesus' saying—'What therefore God hath joined together, let not man put asunder'—is immensely impressive and inspiring to married Christian folk. But it has proved very difficult to interpret in law courts. Idealists, including many influential theologians, have longed to say that it means that marriage can never be terminated. But from an early date it was accepted that they were terminated by death; at least in the sense that widows and widowers could remarry. To us this is a vital and essential element in Christian marriage: if human experience means anything we have witnessed the divine blessing on innumerable such marriages. Yet there was a certain hesitation which took centuries to eradicate: a priestly blessing on a second marriage was still being denied on occasions in the twelfth century. To deny it seems to us logic run mad or custom ossified. Death apart, it was generally held or hoped that there were no other exceptions. But what about adultery, which Jesus seems to make an exception?[27] What if the partners were not free to marry, because too closely related—a likely circumstance in the late eleventh or early twelfth century when you were not supposed to marry any relative, not even your sixth cousin? What if you got married by mistake, under a misapprehension?—not at all an impossible event in a world in which arranged marriages were common, and not unknown today. When the Church became responsible for marriage jurisdiction it had to admit that there were marriages or what appeared

[27] For the problem of interpreting his sayings, see chap. 2, n. 13. For the French kings below, see pp. 120–4.

272

to be marriages which could not survive scrutiny. One can look at this in two ways. The French kings of the eleventh and twelfth centuries with one exception all had at least one annulment—commonly (though not always) after a reasonable period of marriage and child-bearing. There was even one, Robert II in the early eleventh century, who in effect alternated between two wives—partly because each represented a powerful faction in the kingdom, and sometimes one was in the ascendant, sometimes another—partly because popes and bishops differed on which was more truly his wife, but mainly (so far as we can see) because one wife was better company, while the other bore the children he needed. In the end he seems to have repented of both his wives and died in the odour of sanctity. Such marriages were easily broken by working out the partners' family trees and declaring them too closely related. These stories make us sceptical of the word 'annulment': clearly the partners and those around them viewed them as divorce—not quite identically with, but not far differently from, modern divorce. There is another side, however. Richard Helmholz, in his brilliant study of the English court books (a rare kind of source for ordinary marriage problems not grand enough to reach Rome) has shown that annulment on the ground of consanguinity was very rare indeed among ordinary mortals in late medieval England.[28] The Church's rules no doubt led to much hardship; but they provided a stable anchor too, for which on the whole the children at least must have had reason to be grateful.

Marriage as Sacrament: Hugh of St Victor

I have spoken of marriage as a sacrament. But what do I mean by this? In the twelfth century the sacraments were

---

[28] Helmholz 1978, pp. 74–87.

defined and listed and the many and various meanings of the word *sacramentum* sorted out and clarified.[29] From then on there were seven sacraments, including marriage. But the reformers dismantled this list and the Protestant tradition has tended to deny the title sacrament to the marriage bond. There is a certain irony in the story. The word *sacramentum* was canonized in the Vulgate version of Ephesians 5: 32, for the hidden truth which likened the union of husband and wife to the union of Christ and the Church. *Sacramentum* also meant an oath and that too fitted marriage, since the exchange of promises, the *consensus*, lay at its heart. By such means one could argue that marriage entered the lists of sacraments by a sort of verbal accident; and that Luther's marriage was sanctified in a truer sense than that of many medieval couples even if he refused to solemnize it in church. Let me cut this knot by a personal statement. Marriage can never be a sacrament in the same degree as baptism or eucharist since it cannot be enjoyed by all Christians alike. I note for example the definition in the report of the Anglican–Roman Catholic commission: 'In the eucharist the human person encounters in the faith the person of Christ in his sacramental body and blood.'[30] That sets in clear perspective some of the differences and similarities. In marriage we could say that two human persons encounter each other in the faith and presence of God. For many of us married folk God's blessing on our marriage is central to our faith, indistinguishable from the graces and blessings we receive in these other ways. If it has not received God's special blessing, my faith is void; and for that reason to deny the word sacrament to marriage seems to me wrong, misleading, a play on words. But I fully respect those who see it differently, and acknowledge that the view I have stated carries many difficulties with it.

---

[29] *DTC* xiv. 546–9 sv. Sacrements (A. Michel); Le Bras 1926, cols. 2202–6.
[30] ARCIC, *The Final Report* (London, 1982), p. 22.

Let us reflect a while on one or two of these. How does Christian marriage differ from secular marriage? One traditional view has been that it is baptism that makes the difference. While I could not deny that baptism does make some difference, it does not answer my problem, any more than Wolfram's. We all know Jews and agnostics—to shorten what could be a much longer list—whose marriages are a wonderful example to us. It is evident that one may achieve the quality of Christian marriage without the faith. And that to me is the point: it is precisely because my faith in God's blessing on human marriage is deeply united to my faith in God that I believe Christian marriage to be sacramental—God's grace can be showered on man in innumerable hidden ways; but faith in Christ and in Christian marriage can only be united in a Christian.

There was naturally much discussion among medieval theologians about the nature of the sacrament; and it would be surprising if it had not been deeply influenced by contemporary study of the eucharist. Modern theologians of almost every persuasion have been more interested in the dynamic of eucharistic theology—in the place of the sacrament in the life of the Church, in the Body of Christ in the largest sense of the term—than in precise definitions of the nature of the consecrated bread and wine. It used to be said that medieval theologians had an opposite interest, and concentrated solely or primarily on the nature of the elements. Gary Macy's recent book on *The Theologies of the Eucharist in the Early Scholastic Period* (1984) is the most substantial of many studies which have shown this to be false. There was a consistent tradition of sacramental theology profoundly interested in the eucharist as part of the Church's life. There was also a deep interest in the host as a relic—like the bones of a saint—which issued in the other tradition, of precise attempts to define the elements, and, from the thirteenth century on, of the meaning of 'transubstantiation'.[31] The two traditions also subsisted in marriage doctrine. Marriage is palpably a way of life, not a moment; and that was clear to all the innumerable theologians who read and commented on Augustine's celebrated definition of the good of marriage as *fides, proles, sacramentum*—fidelity, children, and the binding union which *can* only be broken by death.[32] But there was also a tradition which naturally found favour with lawyers seeking simple answers to complex questions which looked for a moment, an event, which marked the entry to marriage and could be defined as the 'sign' of the sacrament. In the thirteenth century a fashion arose for defining the form and matter of the sacraments, and there was a remarkable variety of different definitions of where the form and matter of marriage might lie.[33] For some the matter lay in the formula of promise and consent, in the words; for others in some physical act of obedience or in the consummation of the marriage. For Albertus Magnus the form lay in the inner consent, a private thing; for St Thomas in the words; Duns Scotus wished to find it in the words, but was puzzled by the wide variety of local customs which meant that different words were used. Others again tried to see in the priestly blessing the form of the sacrament, and the *Glossa Ordinaria* on the Decretals of Pope Gregory IX even went so far as to assert that the reason why a priestly blessing on a second marriage was prohibited was that the form of the sacrament could not be repeated. I have never understood how any particular moment or event could make or create so deep and lasting a union, and I shall presently return to the medieval theological tradition which saw it as process rather than event.

[31] Macy 1984, esp. chaps. 3–5; *DTC* v. 1209–1302, esp. 1302–26 (E. Mangenot), s.v. Eucharistie.
[32] See above, chap. 2, n. 30.
[33] For what follows, see Le Bras 1926, cols. 2202–4.

Marriage as Sacrament

One essential reason why Abelard dissolved his marriage with Heloise was because sexual union was no longer possible. This touched an issue which was deeply controversial in the twelfth century. It would be universally assumed that sexual union was a normal and inherent part of marriage; but that is a very different thing from saying it is essential to marriage—that a couple who cannot, or do not wish to, engage in sexual union may not, cannot, or should not marry. That is a notion which seems to me quite unacceptable, and it is here that the medieval Church faced an inconsistency it never resolved. This is all the more striking—and I dwell on it—because it illustrates in a remarkable way the kind of sense in which Christian marriage as we know and value it was created in the medieval Church, sometimes by deliberate act, sometimes by inadvertence.

Medieval celibate clergymen accepted that marriage was of divine institution, but many of them thought it pretty rum—on the most optimistic view a second best; and this prompted the enquiry in ingenious ascetic minds whether it might not be possible to combine marriage and virginity. Thus in the seventh century St Etheldreda, foundress of Ely, was married to King Ecgfrith of Northumbria (her second husband) for twelve years, and 'preserved the glory of perfect virginity' in Bede's words.[34] Ecgfrith thought ill of the arrangement, and eventually allowed her to depart. This story and many like it—some of them of much more dubious veracity—greatly edified the ascetic writers of the early and mid Middle Ages. But such a marriage was clearly at variance with Augustine's definition of the good of marriage—and, as many thought, with Paul's insistence on the payment of the marriage debt—and there was much debate on the point.

[34] Bede, *Hist. Eccl.* iv. 19, ed. and trans. B. Colgrave and R. A. B. Mynors (OMT, 1969), pp. 390–3. Cf. Ridyard 1988, p. 53.

11. Towards a Theology of Marriage

The centre of the argument turned on the marriage of Mary and Joseph. It was universally supposed in the Middle Ages that Mary remained always a virgin. This is a matter of dogma, not history; I do not have to believe it as a historian, but I acknowledge that the idea did much to humanize medieval notions of marriage. For it put a firm check on the notion of marriage as simply a baby machine. The Holy Family and the marriage of Mary and Joseph must be perfect—or so many argued.[35] And this was the cue for admirable statements by Hugh of St Victor, the most genial and profound of the early twelfth-century commentators on the sacraments, of all the other elements which go to make a happy, sacred marriage, apart from the marriage-bed—of mutual help and comfort and the like.[36]

Can you find anything else in marriage except conjugal society which makes it sacred and by which you can assert that it is holy? And if this is true when the two become one flesh, is it not even more so when they become one mind? If they make each other partner of their flesh and are holy, is it possible for them to be partners in the soul and not be holy? Far be it! 'The two shall become one flesh. This mystery is a profound one, it refers to Christ and the Church' (Eph. 5: 31–32). The two shall become one soul [in corde uno]. This is a great mystery, it refers to God and the soul [in Deo et anima]. See now the nature of the contract by which they bind themselves in consented marriage. Henceforth and forever, each shall be to the other as a same self in all sincere love, all careful solicitude, every kindness of affection, in constant compassion, unflagging consolation, and faithful devotedness. And this in such a way

---

[35] DTC ix, esp. 2386–7 (E. Dublanchy), s.v. Marie.

[36] This quotation is from De uirginitate B. Mariae, PL clxxvi. 860, as translated in Leclercq 1982, p. 26, slightly adapted.

that each shall assist the other as being one's own self in every good or evil tiding, the companion and partner of consolation, thus proving that they are united in trial and tribulation. Finally, each one shall attend outwardly to the needs of the other's body, taking it as being his and her own flesh to cherish, and so shall they also attend inwardly to love for the heart, as though it were his and her own soul to keep in peace and quiet (as far as lies within them) without worry. In this way they shall dwell in the peace of a holy society and the communion of a sweet repose so that each no longer lives for self, but for the other. Thus each shall live for self even more happily and blessedly. Such are the good things of marriage and the happiness of those who love chaste companionship.

But it was very difficult for some theologians, and especially for the canon lawyers, to accept that a marriage could be perfect without consummation. So it was argued that Mary's was a rather special kind of marriage, not in all respects to be imitated by ordinary mortals. The power of tradition and the use of the phrase 'one flesh', *una caro*, for husband and wife both in Genesis and in the Gospels, made medieval lawyers and theologians extremely reluctant to accept a marriage that had not been consummated as complete and binding; and Alexander III—whose praises I was singing a while ago—unleashed much mischief by consecrating the doctrine that an unconsummated marriage could under certain circumstances be annulled.[37] Alexander III correctly perceived that witnesses to a binding promise can in favourable circumstances be summoned to court. But in retaining a space for argument about consummation in his decretals he encouraged the *reductio ad absurdum* (as many a married man could have

[37] See above, pp. 132–4, 268. Dr P. Lyndon Reynolds is writing a full study of marriage as a sacrament in the twelfth and thirteenth centuries.

told him) of allowing the issue of consummation to be discussed in court. In the early sixteenth century the lawyers argued for five and a half years whether Catherine of Aragon had really consummated her first marriage, and if so what bearing that might have on her marriage to Henry VIII; and we can understand, even if we condemn, the conclusion he drew once Catherine was dead that the best way to dispose of any of her successors who proved unsatisfactory was to remove her head.[38]

I hasten on to my last witness.

Jan Van Eyck

The *Arnolfini Marriage* by Jan van Eyck is one of the greatest treasures of the National Gallery in London (Pls. 5, 6).[39] It is a portrait of a man and a woman, each drawn in marvellous detail, solemn in expression, dressed in the height of fashion. They are standing in a bedroom, beside the bed, on the bare boards of the floor; the room is sumptuously furnished—there is a carpet, and a wooden chest by the window; and the visible woodwork of the chairs by the bed is richly carved; over their heads hangs an elaborate candelabra. At their feet is a small terrier, alert, tail erect. The man has his right hand raised as if for an oath or solemn adjuration; with his left he holds the lady's right hand—and her left hand lifts the folds of a stately train so as, in effect, to cover her body below her belt. The colours are rich, but not startling—the man's brown robe, the lady's green velvet mantle; a low key red in bed and chair covers—and so forth; the colours

---

[38] See above, pp. 162–9.

[39] The foundation of modern study is Panofsky 1934; see also Panofsky 1953, pp. 201–3. Out of the numerous modern studies I have been particularly helped by Smith 1977. There are convenient details of the mirror in Lassaigne and Argan n.d., p. 21, and of the mirror, the roundels and the inscription in Murray 1965, colour plate 22. This includes, e.g. the beads, the brush, and St Margaret.

glow with the magical skills of the newly fashioned techniques of oil painting of which Jan van Eyck was so great a master; but the picture remains still and dignified, unemphatic.

Yet there is much more to describe. For it is also a puzzle picture. The man has his hat on, but both he and his wife have cast their shoes aside. The candelabra has only one candle in it, and that is lit, though it is broad daylight. There is a mirror on the further wall, reflecting every item in the room—save, rather pointedly, the dog—but it also shows two figures not revealed in the main painting, witnesses of the scene. One of them was evidently the painter, who has emphasized his presence and his witness by setting an inscription above the mirror: '*Johannes de Eyck fuit hic.* 1434'—'Jan van Eyck was here in 1434'. Round the mirror are set eight roundels with scenes so minute they can only just be made out with the naked eye—and not at all from a distance. They represent the Passion from the agony in the Garden to the resurrection of Christ. The back of the chair next the bed is surmounted by a carving of a lady—a lady at prayer emerging from a dragon, which identifies her as St Margaret. To the left of the mirror hang some beads, presumably prayer beads (twenty-nine on a chain with tassles); to the right, hanging on a hook beside St Margaret, is a dusting brush. On the window-sill is an apple, on the chest more fruit—three peaches or oranges.

It is commonplace that these elaborate late medieval— or renaissance—paintings were meant to be read; that we must absorb them in minute detail before we can begin to understand them. In a celebrated article the great American art historian Erwin Panofsky set out to explain every detail in the picture, and to show that it represented (as many had long supposed) the Lucchese Giovanni Arnolfini and his wife Giovanna or Jeanne Cenami, and that it was also—as had scarcely been considered

11. Towards a Theology of Marriage

before—a formal certificate of their marriage and a celebration of the sacrament.[40] He explained everything, and has charmed most scholars into acceptance; and though there have been voices raised in protest at his solution, or at some of his answers, his inspired success has largely hidden one crucial element in the picture: that it is meant to puzzle as well as to enlighten us. The single candle, the shoes, the almost invisible roundels, the second figure in the mirror—all these enforce this fundamental point.

First of all, let us agree that it is overwhelmingly probable that the picture portrays the marriage of Giovanni Arnolfini and Giovanna Cenami, rich expatriates from Lucca living in Bruges in the 1430s.[41] The date fits what is known of their marriage; and the picture answers to descriptions of a painting—said to be of folk who can evidently be identified as the Arnolfini—in the Habsburg collections in the Netherlands and Spain in the sixteenth and eighteenth centuries. If it is not correctly identified, a series of extraordinary coincidences has to be assumed. The objections so far raised are not substantial. It has been alleged that if two Lucchesi married in the early fifteenth century, the man must have held the woman's right hand with his own right hand, not with his left.[42] What do we know of the matter?—and even if this is probable in real life, we have nothing but the extraordinary illusion of exactitude—what used to be called 'realism'[43]—to make us believe that this is a slice of ordinary life. We have much to tell us that it is not.

Why are their clogs and slippers ostentatiously pushed aside? Quite natural, one may say, in a bedroom. But it could also be a sign that they are in a holy place—'put off

[40] Panofsky 1934.
[41] See Mirot 1930, esp. p. 114 and nn. The following details are conveniently summarized in Smith 1977.
[42] See Schabacker 1972.
[43] And, no doubt, still is, to our confusion.

the shoes from thy feet', said the Lord to Moses, 'for the place whereon thou standest is holy ground'.[44] The roundels of the Passion, the prayer beads, the saint, point the same way: so does the candelabra, with crosses interspersed among the candlesticks, and the mysterious single candle, set amid empty sockets. What does it signify?[45] The candle given to a married person when he went into church?—if so, why not two? The candle has been given many significances, most plausibly that of the one who is all in all, symbol of the presence of Christ himself. It is at least a guarantee that there are symbols here, and that we are meant to be left with a mystery.

The couple seem most naturally to be exchanging wedding vows. If we take it so, much falls into place. The two witnesses in the mirror make it a valid betrothal; the artist's signature makes it (as Panofsky perceived) a kind of marriage certificate; St Margaret was the patron saint of childbirth, the dog of fidelity. Above all, if the couple are making their promises, the bed signifies the other chief element in marriage, its consummation. Panofsky called the room a 'Nuptial Chamber' . . . 'hallowed by sacramental associations'. It could be thought that in the Low Countries marriages frequently took place in bedrooms, or anyway in houses. But no evidence has ever been discovered for this assertion—though it is not at all improbable. Panofsky's own deployment of the symbols, however, strongly suggested that it is much more than a certificate: that it represents not only their wedding-day, but their marriage as a whole—stretching from exchange of vows through consummation to its fruit—and marriage itself. If it were a certificate, why is it unique? Is that solely owing to the accident of survival? It seems most improbable: the

[44] Exodus 3: 5 (Douai version).
[45] See Panofsky 1934, p. 126, for various suggestions. For a criticism of Panofsky's somewhat cavalier approach to symbols and historical detail, see Kelly (H.A.) 1975, p. 174 n. 40. For candles in marriage liturgy, see Molin and Mutembe 1974, p. 285; but the candles do not figure in later liturgies.

more it is studied, the more its unique quality stands out. It is true that the sacrament of marriage was and is made by the partners; that wherever they make their vows is thus holy ground; that consent and mutual promises lead to consummation and all the blessings of a happy marriage. All this is represented. It may be too that we can discern two elements which specifically suggest it was not intended to represent a day or a moment of time. When Van Eyck dated a picture, he commonly noted the month and the day; here is a year only, and it has been suggested that this was a deliberate attempt to spread the time. It may be so; we cannot be sure. Since the eighteenth century most viewers not accustomed to fifteenth-century conventions have assumed that Giovanna was pregnant; and there is no doubt that she holds her train at a discreet distance and that it falls away from her left hand at an angle, in a manner extremely suggestive. But it was the fashion in the fifteenth and early sixteenth centuries for Netherlandish painters to portray attractive women with swelling stomachs: there are virgin saints, sufficiently naked, undergoing torture and martyrdom, to put the matter beyond doubt (Pl. 7);[46] and the splendid portrayal of St Mary Magdalene by Hugo van der Goes in the Uffizi in Florence (Pl. 8) is an excellent example of how this convention looks on ladies amply draped. Among art historians it is now dogma that she is *not* pregnant. And yet, even in the fifteenth century, pregnant women looked

[46] See e.g. *Belles Heures*, fo. 17[r–v]; Murray 1965 pl. 356 (pls. 7–8). It is striking in this second case that the lady donor at the saints' feet is shown with a relatively narrow waist. The doctrine is expounded in special relation to van Eyck's and van der Goes's portrayals of Eve in Clark 1960, pp. 309–13. The matter is complicated by Eve, for she seems in both cases, especially in the van Eyck, to be clearly pregnant. It is just conceivable that the naked virgins (see esp. St Catherine in the *Belles Heures*, fo. 17[r–v]) were supposed to be carrying the child Jesus in their wombs, like the Blessed Virgin herself; but in any case it is clear that folk in the Low Countries reckoned a pregnant woman the height of female beauty. Such speculations underline the *ambiguity* of Giovanna's shape and stance. On the date, see Smith 1977.

like that. We have seen enough of this picture to know that nothing in it is there by accident. The lady stands close to the bed, with her head encompassed, as it were, by St Margaret and the bed-curtains; the artist must either have been in very innocent mood or he must have realized that his audience, any audience, would ask themselves if she was expecting a child. We cannot know precisely what was in the painter's mind; but this seems to me most likely to be another of his deliberate acts of mystification.

The husband died in 1470, the wife in 1480; and their fortune passed to a nephew.[47] It may be that they had no children; it may be that she never was pregnant. But the picture was anyway a prophecy, painted in the year of their marriage.

It is a picture of great beauty. We cannot contemplate it without intense admiration, without deep emotion. For the sitters, for whose benefit it was presumably painted, it must have been a joy beyond price. For in the hands of Jan van Eyck marriage itself becomes a thing of beauty, a sacrament in which the divine light—from the sun and the candle—shines brilliantly upon the young couple. But it also signified that marriage is solemn and serious; that every aspect of it is under the eye and the providence of God; that God's blessing is on the bed as well on the couple in their devotions; that it is compounded of ordinary things—shoes and dusting brushes and boards and apples—as well as crosses and candlesticks. Panofsky in his enthusiasm saw symbols of purity in the beads and the 'spotless mirror', of innocence in the apple.[48] It may be so, though he had perhaps forgotten Eve. Let us hope that the scenes of the Passion did not symbolize that the artist thought suffering and torment a part of marriage

---

[47] Mirot 1930, p. 114 and nn., corrected by Schabacher 1972, p. 394 n. 38, cf. p. 381.
[48] Panofsky 1934, pp. 125–6.

too. We can only be sure that he meant to puzzle us—meant us to enquire, to search, to *think*; and that there is laughter as well as prayer in the room.

The heart and core of it is mutual giving, sure enough—but also marriage as a way of life, a process, not just an event. It is a life in which consent and consummation and childbirth play their roles—and, may I add, husband and wife may grow old hand in hand together. Such is the way of Christian marriage.

BIBLIOGRAPHICAL REFERENCES

Abélard 1975: *Pierre Abélard, Pierre le Vénérable*, Colloques internationaux du Centre national de la recherche scientifique, no. 546, Abbaye de Cluny, 1972, publ. Paris, 1975.

Abélard 1981: *Abélard en son temps: Actes du Colloque international organisé à l'occasion du 9e centénaire de la naissance de Pierre Abélard (14–19 mai 1979)*, Paris, 1981; *and see* McLaughlin, Muckle, Radice.

Anderson, H., 1976, *The Gospel of Mark*, New Century Bible Commentaries, Grand Rapids, 1976.

Anderson, M. O., ed., 1938, *A Scottish Chronicle known as the Chronicle of Holyrood*, Scottish History Society, 3rd Series, xxx, 1938.

Anderson, O., 1975, 'The incidence of civil marriage in Victorian England and Wales', *Past and Present*, lxix (Nov. 1975), 50–87.

ARCIC, 1982, *The Final Report*, London, 1982.

Bachrach, B., 1978, 'Robert of Blois abbot of Saint-Florent de Saumur and Saint-Mesmin de Micy (985–1011). A study of small power politics', *Revue bénédictine*, lxxxviii (1978), 123–46.

Bacon, S. A., 1910, *The Source of Wolfram's Willehalm*, Sprache und Dichtung 4, Tübingen, 1910.

Bailey, D. Sherwin, 1952, *The Mystery of Love and Marriage: a Study in the Theology of Sexual Relations*, London, 1952.

Bargellini 1936: *Le prediche volgari di S. Bernardino da Siena dette nella Piazza del Campo l'anno 1427*, ed. L. Banchi (Siena, 1880–8), rev. ed. P. Bargellini, Milan and Rome, 1936.

Barlow, F., 1986, *Thomas Becket*, London, 1986.

Barnes, P. M., 1962, ed., 'The Anstey Case', in *A Medieval Miscellany for Doris Mary Stenton*, ed. P. M. Barnes and C. F. Slade, Pipe Roll Society, lxxvi, London, 1962, pp. 1–24.

Barrow, J., 1986, 'Cathedrals, provosts and prebends: a comparison of twelfth-century German and English practice', *JEH*, xxxvii (1986), 536–64.

—— 1987, 'A twelfth-century bishop and literary patron: William de Vere', *Viator*, xviii (1987), 175–89.

Bates, D., 1982, *Normandy before 1066*, London, 1982.

Bauer, J. B., 1970, 'Marriage', in Bauer, *Encyclopaedia of Biblical Theology*, iv, London, 1970, pp. 551–6.

Bautier, R.-H., 1981, 'Paris au temps d'Abélard', in *Abélard 1981*, pp. 21–77.

—— and Gilles, M., eds., 1979, *Chronique de Saint-Pierre-le-Vif de Sens dite de Clarins*, Paris, 1979.

—— and Labory, G., eds., 1965, Helgaud de Fleury, *Vie de Robert le Pieux*, Paris, 1965.

Beare, F. W., 1964, *The Earliest Records of Jesus*, Oxford, 1964.

Becker, G. W., 1956, *Das Recht in 'Parzival'*, Diss., Bonn, 1956.

Becquet, J., 1975, 'La Réforme des chapitres cathédraux en France aux xie et xiie siècles', *Bulletin philologique et historique*, 1975, pp. 31–41.

Behrman, S. N., 1960, *Conversations with Max*, London, 1960.

Belles Heures: Meiss, M., and Beatson, E. H., eds., *Les Belles Heures de Jean duc de Berry*, London, 1974.

Benson, R. L., and Constable, G. (with C. D. Lanham), 1982, *Renaissance and Renewal in the Twelfth Century*, Cambridge, Mass., and Oxford, 1982.

Benton, J. F., 1961, 'The court of Champagne as a literary center', *Speculum*, xxxvi (1961), 551–91.

—— 1962, 'The evidence for Andreas Capellanus re-examined again', *Studies in Philology*, lix (1962), 471–8.

—— 1975, 'Fraud, fiction and borrowing in the correspondence of Abelard and Heloise', in *Abélard 1975*, pp. 469–506 (discussion 507–11).

—— 1980, 'A reconsideration of the authenticity of the correspondence of Abelard and Heloise', in Thomas 1980, pp. 41–52.

Bernardino 1945: S. *Bernardino da Siena: Saggi e ricerche pubblicate nel quinto centenario della morte*, Milan, 1945.

Bernardino 1976: *Bernardino predicatore nella società del suo tempo*, Atti del Convegno del Centro di studi sulla spiritualità medievale, Todi, 9–12 ottobre 1975, publ. Todi, 1976.

Best, G., 1985, 'Owen Chadwick and his work' in *History, Society and the Churches: Essays in Honour of Owen Chadwick*, ed. D. Beales and G. Best, Cambridge, 1985, pp. 1–8.

Biddle, M., 1983, 'The study of Winchester: Archaeology and history in a British town', *Proceedings of the British Academy*, lxix (1983), 93–135.

Blakemore Evans, G., 1984, ed., *Romeo and Juliet*, New Cambridge Shakespeare, Cambridge, 1984.

Boase, R., 1977, *The Origin and Meaning of Courtly Love*, Manchester, 1977.

Bolton, B., 1973, 'Mulieres sanctae', *SCH*, x (1973), 77–95.

Bond, F., 1910, *Wood Carvings in English Churches*, i. *Misericords*, London, 1910.

Bowdler, T., 1818, *The Family Shakespeare*, London, 1818.

Boyle, L., 1981, 'Montaillou revisited: *Mentalité* and Methodology', in *Pathways to Medieval Peasants*, ed. J. A. Raftis, Toronto, 1981, pp. 119–40.

Bradshaw, B., and Duffy, E., eds., 1989, *Humanism, Reform and the Reformation: the Career of Bishop John Fisher*, Cambridge, 1989.

Brandl, L., 1955, *Die Sexualethik des hl. Albertus*, Regensburg, 1955.

Brewer, D. S., 1954, 'Love and marriage in Chaucer's Poetry', *Modern Language Review*, xlix (1954), 461–4.

—— 1977, review of Kelly 1975, *Review of English Studies*, xxviii (1977), 194–7.

Brooke, C. N. L., 1951, 'The composition of the Chapter of St Paul's, 1086–1163', *Cambridge Historical Journal*, x, no. 2 (1951), 111–32.

—— 1956, 'Gregorian reform in action: clerical marriage in England, 1050–1200', *Cambridge Historical Journal*, xii, no. 1 (1956), 1–21, appendix in no. 2 (1956), 187–8 (also repr. in *Change in Medieval Society*, ed. S. Thrupp, New York, 1964, pp. 49–71; Brooke 1971, pp. 69–99).

—— 1957, 'The earliest times to 1485', in *A History of St Paul's Cathedral*, ed. W. R. Matthews and W. M. Atkins, London, 1957, pp. 1–99, 361–5.

—— 1961, *From Alfred to Henry III, 871–1272* (Nelson's History of England, ii), Edinburgh, 1961.

—— 1964, 'Problems of the Church historian' in *SCH* i (1964), 1–19 = Brooke 1971, pp. 39–56.

—— 1967a, 'Religious sentiment and church design in the later Middle Ages', *Bulletin of the John Rylands Library*, l (1967), 13–33, here cited from repr. in Brooke 1971, pp. 162–82.

—— 1967b, 'Archbishop Lanfranc, the English bishops, and the Council of London of 1075', *Studia Gratiana*, xii = *Collectanea Stephan Kuttner*, ii (1967), 39–59.

—— 1968, 'Heresy and religious sentiment: 1000–1250', *Bulletin of the Institute of Historical Research*, xli (1968), 115–31, here cited from repr. in Brooke 1971, pp. 139–61.

—— 1969, *The Twelfth Century Renaissance*, London, 1969.

—— 1978, *Marriage in Christian History* (Inaugural Lecture), Cambridge, 1978.

—— 1980, 'Aspects of marriage law in the eleventh and twelfth centuries', *Proceedings of the 5th International Congress of Medieval Canon Law*, Salamanca, 1976, publ. Vatican City, 1980, pp. 333–44.

—— 1981, 'Marriage and society in the central middle ages', in *Marriage and Society*, ed. R. B. Outhwaite, London, 1981, pp. 17–34.

—— 1982, 'Aspetti del matrimonio e della famiglia nel mondo di Santa Caterina e di San Bernardino', in Maffei and Nardi 1982, pp. 877–89.

—— 1983, 'Homage to the Lady Margaret', *Cambridge Review*, civ (1983), 14–17.

—— 1987, *Europe in the Central Middle Ages*, 2nd edn., London, 1987.

—— and Highfield, J. R. L., 1988, with photos by W. Swaan, *Oxford and Cambridge*, Cambridge, 1988.

—— and Keir, G., 1975, *London 800–1216: the Shaping of a City*, London, 1975.

—— and Ortenberg, 1988, 'The birth of Margaret of Anjou', *Historical Research*, lxi (1988), 357–8.

—— and Postan, M. M., eds., 1960, *Carte Nativorum: a Peterborough Abbey Cartulary of the Fourteenth Century*, Northamptonshire Record Society, xx, 1960.

—— and Swaan, W., 1974, *The Monastic World*, London, 1974.

Brooke, N. [S.], 1968, *Shakespeare's Early Tragedies*, London, 1968.

—— 1987, 'What kind of play is *Macbeth*?', in *Mirroirs de l'être: Macbeth, the Man of Mode*, ed. J.-P. Debax and Y. Peyré, Toulouse, 1987, pp. 11–22.

Brooke, R. B., 1970, ed. and trans., *Scripta Leonis, Rufini et Angeli*, OMT, 1970.

Brooke, R. and C., 1974–7, 'I vescovi di Inghilterra e Normandia nel secolo XI: contrasti', in Mendola 1974–7, pp. 536–45.

—— and —— 1984, *Popular Religion in the Middle Ages: Western Europe 1000–1300*, London, 1984.

Brooke, Z. N., 1931, *The English Church and the Papacy from the Conquest to the Reign of John*, Cambridge, 1931.

Brown, J. R., ed., 1955, W. Shakespeare, *The Merchant of Venice*, London, 1955.

Brown, P., 1967, *Augustine of Hippo*, London, 1967.

Brühl, C., 1974–7, 'Die Sozialstruktur des deutschen Episkopats im 11. und 12. Jahrhundert', in Mendola 1974–7, pp. 42–56.

Brundage, J. A., 1967*a*, 'The crusader's wife: a canonistic quandary', *Studia Gratiana*, xii = *Collectanea Stephan Kuttner*, ii (1967), 425–41.

—— 1967*b*, 'The crusader's wife revisited', *Studia Gratiana*, xiv (1967), 241–51.

—— 1969, *Medieval Canon Law and the Crusader*, Madison, 1969.

—— 1975, 'Concubinage and marriage in medieval canon law', *Journal of Medieval History*, i (1975), 1–17.

—— 1980, 'Carnal Delight: canonistic theories of sexuality', in *Proceedings of the 5th International Congress of Medieval Canon Law*, Salamanca, 1976, publ. Vatican City, 1980, pp. 361–85.

—— 1982, 'Marriage law in the Latin kingdom of Jerusalem', in *Outremer: Studies in the History of the Crusading Kingdom of Jerusalem Presented to Joshua Prawer*, ed. B. Z. Kedar, H. E. Mayer, and R. C. Smail, Jerusalem, 1982, pp. 258–71.

—— 1986, 'Marriage and sexuality in the decretals of Pope Alexander III', in *Miscellanea Rolando Bandinelli, Papa Alessandro III*, ed. F. Liotta, Siena, 1986, pp. 57–83.

—— 1987, *Law, Sex, and Christian Society in Medieval Europe*, Chicago, 1987.

Bultot, R., 1963, *Christianisme et valeurs humaines*, A. *La Doctrine du mépris du monde, en Occident, de S. Ambroise à Innocent III*, iv. *Le XIe siècle*, i. *Pierre Damien*, Louvain and Paris, 1963.

Burton, J., 1979, *The Yorkshire Nunneries in the Twelfth and Thirteenth Centuries*, Borthwick Papers, no. 56, York, 1979.

Cartellieri, A., 1899–1922, *Philipp II. August, König von Frankreich*, 4 vols. in 5, Leipzig, 1899–1922.

Chadwick, H., 1986, *Augustine*, Oxford, 1986.

Chadwick, O., 1987, 'Acton and Butterfield', *JEH*, xxxviii (1987), 386–405.

Charrier, C., 1933, *Héloïse dans l'histoire et dans la légende*, Paris, 1933.

Chaucer, G., ed. F. N. Robinson, *The Works of Geoffrey Chaucer*, 2nd edn., London, 1957. *Troilus and Criseyde* is quoted from Windeatt 1984.

Cheney, C. R., 1967, *Hubert Walter*, London, 1967.

—— 1973, *Medieval Texts and Studies*, Oxford, 1973.

—— 1976, *Pope Innocent III and England*, Stuttgart, 1976.

Cheney, M. G., 1980, *Roger, Bishop of Worcester, 1164–1179*, Oxford, 1980.

Chrétien: Christian von Troyes, *Sämtliche erhaltene Werke*, ed. W. Foerster and A. Hilka, 5 vols., Halle, 1884–1932. For translations see Comfort 1914; Linker 1952.

Clapham, A. W., 1934, *English Romanesque Architecture after the Conquest*, Oxford, 1934.

Clark, K., 1960, *The Nude*, Harmondsworth, 1960.

—— 1966, *Rembrandt and the Italian Renaissance*, London, 1966.

Clerval, A., 1895, *Les Écoles de Chartres au moyen âge*, Paris, 1895.

Comfort, W. W., 1914: Chrétien de Troyes, *Arthurian Romances*, trans. W. W. Comfort, Everyman edition, London, 1914.

Conant, K. J., 1959, *Carolingian and Romanesque Architecture, 800–1200* (Pelican History of Art), Harmondsworth, 1959.

Constable, G., ed., 1967, *The Letters of Peter the Venerable*, 2 vols., Cambridge, Mass., 1967.

Cooper, C. H., 1874, *Memoir of Margaret, Countess of Richmond and Derby*, Cambridge, 1874.

Corbett, P. E., 1930, *The Roman Law of Marriage*, Oxford, 1930.

Councils: *Councils and Synods with other Documents relating to the English Church*, i, *AD 871–1204*, ed. D. Whitelock, M. Brett and

C. N. L. Brooke, 2 parts, Oxford, 1981; ii, AD *1205–1313*, ed. F. M. Powicke and C. R. Cheney, 2 parts, Oxford, 1964.

Coxe, H. O., ed., 1852, *Catalogus Codicum MSS qui in collegiis aulisque Oxoniensibus hodie adservantur*, 2 vols., Oxford, 1852.

CP: *The Complete Peerage* by G. E. C., revised edn. by Vicary Gibbs *et al.*, 12 vols., London, 1910–59.

Crouzel, H., 1971, *L'Église primitive face au divorce du premier au cinquième siècle*, Paris, 1971.

Crow, M. M., and Olson, C. C., eds., 1966, *Chaucer Life Records*, Oxford, 1966.

Damian, *see* Peter.

Daudet, P., 1941, *L'Établissement de la compétence de l'église en matière de divorce et de consanguinité*, Paris, 1941.

Dauvillier, J., 1933, *Le Mariage dans le droit classique de l'Église*, Paris, 1933.

Davies, R. R., 1980, 'The status of women and the practice of marriage in late-medieval Wales', in Jenkins and Owen 1980, pp. 93–114.

D'Avray, D. L., and Tausche, M., 1980, 'Marriage sermons in *ad status* collections of the central Middle Ages', *Archives d'histoire doctrinale et littéraire du moyen âge*, xlvii (1980), 71–119.

DDC: *Dictionnaire de droit canonique*, ed. R. Naz, 7 vols., Paris, 1935–65.

Decretals of Gregory IX, ed. E. Friedberg, *Corpus Iuris Canonici*, ii, Leipzig, 1881.

Decretum: *Decretum Gratiani*, ed. E. Friedberg, *Corpus Iuris Canonici*, i, Leipzig, 1879.

Delcorno, C., 1976, 'L'exemplum nella predicazione di Bernardino da Siena', in *Bernardino predicatore nella società del suo tempo*, Atti del Convegno del Centro di studi sulla spiritualità medievale, Todi, 9–12 ottobre 1975, publ. Todi, 1976, pp. 71–107.

Delhaye, P., 1951, 'Le Dossier anti-matrimonial de l'*Adversus Iovinianum* et son influence sur quelques écrits latins du xiie siècle', *Mediaeval Studies*, xiii (1951), 65–86.

—— 1970, 'The development of the medieval Church's teaching on marriage', *Concilium*, v, no. 6 (1970), 83–8.

Denzler, G., 1973, *Das Papsttum und der Amtzölibat*, i (Päpste und Papsttum, v, i), Stuttgart, 1973.

De Smedt, E.-J., 1964, *Married Love*, Eng. trans. by J. Nicholson, London, 1964.

Dhondt, J., 1964–5, 'Sept femmes et un trio de rois', *Contributions à l'histoire économique et sociale*, iii (1964–5), 35–70.

Dickinson, J. C., 1950, *The Origins of the Austin Canons and their Introduction into England*, London, 1950.

DNB: Dictionary of National Biography, ed. L. Stephen and S. Lee, 66 vols., London, 1885–1901, repr. Oxford, 1921–2.

Dobson, R. B., and Donaghey, S., 1984, *The History of Clementhorpe Nunnery*, York, 1984.

Donahue, C., 1976, 'The policy of Alexander the Third's consent theory of marriage', *Proceedings of the Fourth International Congress of Medieval Canon Law*, Toronto, 1972, ed. S. Kuttner, Rome, 1976, pp. 251–81.

—— 1982, 'The dating of Alexander the Third's marriage decretals: Dauvillier revisited after fifty years', *Zeitschrift der Savigny-Stiftung für Rechtsgeschichte*, xcix, Kanonistische Abteilung lxviii (1982), 70–124.

Dronke, P., 1968, *Medieval Latin and the Rise of European Love Lyric*, 2 vols., Oxford, 1968.

—— 1976, *Abelard and Heloise in Medieval Testimonies*, Glasgow, 1976.

—— 1980, 'Heloise's *Problemata and Letters*: some questions of form and content', in Thomas 1980, pp. 53–73.

—— 1984, *Women Writers of the Middle Ages*, Cambridge, 1984.

DTC: Dictionnaire de théologie catholique, ed. A. Vacant *et al.*, 15 vols., Paris, 1923–50.

Duby, G., 1977, *The Chivalrous Society*, trans. C. Postan, London, 1977.

—— 1978, *Medieval Marriage*, trans. E. Forster, Baltimore, 1978.

—— 1983–4, *The Knight, the Lady and the Priest*, trans. B. Bray, New York and Harmondsworth, 1983–4.

Dugdale, W., 1817–30, *Monasticon Anglicanum*, ed. J. Caley, H. Ellis, and B. Bandinel, 6 vols. in 8, London, 1817–30.

Duggan, C., 1981, 'Equity and compassion in papal marriage decretals to England', in Van Hoecke and Welkenhuysen 1981, pp. 59–87.

Dusinberre, J., 1975, *Shakespeare and the Nature of Women*, 1975.

Duvernoy, J., ed., 1965, *Le Registre d'Inquisition de Jacques Fournier, évêque de Pamiers (1318–1325)*, 3 vols., Toulouse, 1965.

Eadmer 1884: Eadmer, *Historia Novorum in Anglia*, ed. M. Rule, RS, 1884.

Edwards, K., 1967, *The English Secular Cathedral in the Middle Ages*, 2nd edn., Manchester, 1967.

Edwards, P., ed., 1985, *Hamlet, Prince of Denmark*, New Cambridge Shakespeare, Cambridge, 1985.

Esmein, A., 1919–35, *Le Mariage en droit canonique*, 2nd edn., ed. R. Génestal, 2 vols., Paris, 1929–35.

Evans, *see* Blakemore Evans.

Farmer, D. H., 1978, *The Oxford Dictionary of Saints*, Oxford, 1978.

Fawtier, R., 1981, *Sainte Catherine de Sienne: Essai de critique de sources*, i, *Sources hagiographiques*, Paris, 1921.

Fedrick, A. S., 1970, *The Romance of Tristan by Béroul*, Harmondsworth, 1970.

Fliche, A., 1912, *Le Règne de Philippe Ier, roi de France (1060–1108)*, Paris, 1912.

Foakes, R. A., ed., 1984, *A Midsummer Night's Dream*, New Cambridge Shakespeare, Cambridge, 1984.

Foerster 1884–99: Christian von Troyes, *Werke*, i–iv, ed. W. Foerster, Halle, 1884–99. For vol. v, see Hilka. And see Chrétien.

Fransen, G., 1977, 'La Rupture du mariage', in Spoleto 1977, ii. 603–30.

Frugoni, C., 1977, 'L'iconografia del matrimonio e della coppia nel medioevo', in Spoleto 1977, ii. 901–63.

Gaudemet, J., 1980, *Sociétés et mariage*, Strasbourg, 1980.

Gerson, H., 1968, *Rembrandt Paintings*, London, 1968.

GF: A. Morey and C. N. L. Brooke, *Gilbert Foliot and his Letters*, Cambridge, 1965.

GFL: *The Letters and Charters of Gilbert Foliot*, ed. A. Morey and C. N. L. Brooke, Cambridge, 1967.

Gibbs and Johnson, 1984: Wolfram von Eschenbach, *Willehalm*, trans. M. E. Gibbs and S. M. Johnson, Harmondsworth, 1984.

Gibson, M., 1978, *Lanfranc of Bec*, Oxford, 1978.

Gilchrist, J., 1965, ' "*Simoniaca Haeresis*" and the problem of orders from Leo IX to Gratian', *Proceedings of the Second International Congress of Medieval Canon Law, Boston College, 12–16 August 1963*, ed. S. Kuttner and J. J. Ryan, Vatican City, 1965.

Gilson, E., 1960, *Heloïse and Abélard*, Eng. trans., Ann Arbor, 1960.

Giraldus, *Opera: Giraldi Cambrensis Opera*, ed. J. S. Brewer, J. F. Dimock, and G. F. Warner, 8 vols., RS, 1861–91.

Gold, P. S., 1985, *The Lady and the Virgin*, Chicago, 1985.

Goody, J., 1983, *The Development of the Family and Marriage in Europe*, Cambridge, 1983.

Göszmann, W., 1954, 'Die Bedeutung der Liebe in der Eheauffassung Hugos von St Viktor und Wolframs von Eschenbach', *Münchener Theologische Zeitschrift*, v (1954), 205–13.

Gottfried: Gottfried von Strassburg, *Tristan*: for edition, see Weber 1967; for translation, see Hatto, 1960.

Goy, R., 1976, *Die Überlieferung der Werke Hugos von St Viktor: Ein Beitrag zur Kommunikationsgeschichte des Mittelalters*, Monographien zur Geschichte des Mittelalters, 14, Stuttgart, 1976.

Gratian, *see Decretum*.

Green, D. H., 1979, *Irony in the Medieval Romance*, Cambridge, 1979.

—— and Johnson, L. P., 1978, *Approaches to Wolfram von Eschenbach*, Mikrokosmos, v, Bern, 1978.

Green, H. B., 1975, *The Gospel according to St Matthew*, Oxford, 1975.

Greenway, D. E., ed., 1968, 1971, 1977: Le Neve, J., *Fasti Ecclesiae Anglicanae, 1066–1300*, i, *St Paul's*, London; ii, *Monastic Cathedrals*; iii, *Lincoln*, London, 1968–77.

—— 1985, 'The false *Institutio* of St Osmund', in Greenway, Holdsworth, and Sayers 1985, pp. 77–101.

Greenway, D., Holdsworth, C., and Sayers, J., eds., 1985, *Tradition and Change: Essays in Honour of Marjorie Chibnall*, Cambridge, 1985.

Grundmann, H., 1961, *Religiöse Bewegungen im Mittelalter*, 2nd edn., Hildesheim, 1961.

Guillemain, B., 1971–4, 'Les origines des évêques en France aux xie et xiie siècles', in Mendola 1971–4, pp. 374–407.

Hajnal, J., 1965, 'European marriage patterns in perspective', in *Population and History*, ed. D. V. Glass and D. E. C. Eversley, London, 1965, pp. 101–43.

Hallam, E., 1980, *France under the Capetians*, London, 1980.

Handbook, 3rd edn.: *Handbook of British Chronology*, 3rd edn., ed. E. B. Fryde, D. E. Greenway, S. Porter, and I. Roy, Royal Historical Society Guides and Handbooks, 2, London, 1986.

Hatto 1960: Gottfried von Strassburg, *Tristan*, trans. A. T. Hatto, with the *Tristran* of Thomas, Harmondsworth, 1960.

—— 1980: Wolfram von Eschenbach, *Parzival*, trans. A. Hatto, Harmondsworth, 1980.

Heads 1972: *The Heads of Religious Houses, England and Wales, 940–1216*, ed. D. Knowles, C. N. L. Brooke, and V. C. M. London, Cambridge, 1972.

Heaton, E. W., 1956, *Everyday Life in Old Testament Times*, London, 1956.

Heimann, A., 1975, 'Die Hochzeit von Adam und Eva in Paradies nebst einigen andern Hochzeitbildern', *Wallraf-Richartz-Jahrbuch*, xxxvii (1975), 11–40.

Helmholz, R. H., 1978, *Marriage Litigation in Medieval England*, Cambridge, 1978.

Henry of Huntingdon, 1879, *Historia Anglorum*, ed. T. Arnold, RS, 1879.

Herlihy, D., 1985, *Medieval Households*, Cambridge, Mass., 1985.

—— and Klapisch-Zuber, C., 1978, *Les Toscans et leurs familles: Une étude du catasto Florentin de 1427*, Paris, 1978.

HF: M. Bouquet *et al.*, eds., *Recueil des historiens des Gaules et de la France*, nouv. édn., ed. L. Delisle, 24 vols., Paris, 1869–1904.

Hilka 1932: Christian von Troyes, *Werke*, v (cf. Foerster 1884–99), ed. A. Hilka, *Li Contes del Graal*, Halle, 1932.

Hill, G. B., and Powell, L. E., eds., 1934–50, *Boswell's Life of Johnson*, 5 vols., Oxford, 1934–50.

Hill, R. M. T., and Brooke, C. N. L., 1977, 'From 627 until the early thirteenth century', in *A History of York Minster*, ed. G. E. Aylmer and R. Cant, Oxford, 1977, pp. 1–43.

Hodgett, G. A. J., ed., 1971, *The Cartulary of Holy Trinity Aldgate*, London Record Society, 7, 1971.

Hoffmann, P., 1970, 'Jesus' saying about divorce and its interpretation', *Concilium*, v, no. 6 (1970), 51–66.

Holdsworth, C., 1978, 'Christina of Markyate', in *Medieval Women, Dedicated and Presented to Professor Rosalind M. T. Hill, SCH Subsidia*, i, Oxford, 1978, pp. 185–204.

Holt, J. C., 1982–5, 'Feudal society and the family in early medieval England, I–IV' (Presidential Addresses), *TRHS*, 5th Series, xxxii (1982), 193–212; xxxiii (1983), 193–220; xxxiv (1984), 1–25; xxxv (1985), 1–28.

Homans, G. C., 1942, *English Villagers of the Thirteenth Century*, Cambridge, Mass., 1942.

Hope, W. H. St John, 1913–14, 'Report on the excavation of the cathedral church of Old Sarum in 1913', *Proceedings of the Society of Antiquaries*, xxvi (1913–14), 100–19.

Hoste, A., and Talbot, C. H., eds., 1971, *Aelredi Rievallensis Opera Omnia*, i, Corpus Christianorum Continuatio Mediaeualis, Turnhout, 1971 (incl. *'De spiritali amicitia'*, ed. A. Hoste, pp. 279–350).

Hugh the Chanter: *The History of the Church of York (1066–1127)*, ed. and trans. C. Johnson, NMT, Edinburgh, 1961; 2nd edn. by M. Brett, C. N. L. Brooke, and M. Winterbottom, OMT, 1990.

Hunt, N., 1967, *Cluny under St Hugh*, London, 1967.

Ives, E. W., 1986, *Anne Boleyn*, Oxford, 1986.

Ivo of Chartres, Epistolae, in *PL* clxii; nos. 1–70 also in Yves de Chartres, *Correspondance*, ed. J. Leclercq, i, Paris, 1949.

James, M. R., Brooke, C. N. L., and Mynors, R. A. B., eds. and trans., 1983, Walter Map, *De nugis curialium: Courtiers' Trifles*, OMT, Oxford, 1983.

JEH: Journal of Ecclesiastical History.

Jenkins, D., and Owen, M. E., eds., 1980, *The Welsh Law of Women: Studies Presented to Professor Daniel A. Binchy on his 80th Birthday*, Cardiff, 1980.

Jeremias, J., 1954, 'Die missionarische Aufgabe in der Mischehe', *Neutestamentliche Studien für Rudolf Bultmann*, Beiheft zur Zeitschrift für die neutestamentliche Wissenschaft, xxi (1954), 255–60.

JL: P. Jaffé, *Regesta Pontificum Romanorum ad annum 1198*,

ed. W. Wattenbach, S. Loewenfeld, F. Kaltenbrunner, and P. Ewald, 2 vols., Leipzig, 1885–8.

John of Salisbury, *Historia Pontificalis*, ed. and trans. M. Chibnall, NMT, Edinburgh, 1956, repr. OMT, Oxford, 1986.

—— *Letters*, ed. and trans. W. J. Millor, H. E. Butler, and C. N. L. Brooke, 2 vols., i, NMT, Edinburgh, 1955 (repr. OMT, 1986), ii, OMT, Oxford, 1979.

Jolivet, J., 1977, 'Abélard entre chien et loup', *Cahiers de civilisation médiévale*, xx (1977), 307–22.

Karnein, A., 1981, 'La Réception du "De amore" d'André le Chapelain au xiiie siècle', *Romania*, cii (1981), 324–51, 501–42.

Kartschoke, D., ed., 1971, *Das Rolandslied des Pfaffen Konrad*, i, Munich, 1971.

Kealey, E. J., 1972, *Roger of Salisbury, Viceroy of England*, Berkeley, 1972.

Kelly, H. A., 1975, *Love and Marriage in the Age of Chaucer*, Ithaca, 1975.

—— 1976, *The Matrimonial Trials of Henry VIII*, Stanford, 1976.

Kelly, J. N. D., 1975, *Jerome: his Life, Writings and Controversies*, London, 1975.

Ker, N. R., 1964, *Medieval Libraries of Great Britain*, 2nd edn., Royal Historical Society Guides and Handbooks, 3, London, 1964 (supplement by A. G. Watson, 1987).

Kirshner, J., 1978, 'Pursuing honour while avoiding sin. The *Monte delle Doti* of Florence', *Studi Senesi*, lxxxix (1978), 177–258.

—— and Molho, A., 1978, 'The dowry fund and the marriage market in early Quattrocento Florence', *Journal of Modern History*, i (1978), 403–38.

Kittredge, G. L., 1911–12, 'Chaucer's discussion of marriage', *Modern Philology*, ix (1911–12), 435–67.

Klapisch, C., 1973, 'L'enfance en Toscane au début du xve siècle', *Annales de démographie historique*, 1973, 99–122.

Knowles, (M.) D., 1963, *The Historian and Character and other Essays*, Cambridge, 1963.

—— 1967, *Decreta Lanfranci*, 2nd edn. in *Corpus Consuetudinum Monasticarum*, ed. K. Hallinger, iii, Siegburg, 1967.

—— and Hadcock, R. N., 1971, *Medieval Religious Houses: England and Wales*, 2nd edn., London, 1971.

Kooper, E. S., 1985, *Love, Marriage and Salvation in Chaucer's Book of the Duchess and Parlement of Foules*, doctoral thesis, Utrecht, 1985.

Labonté, Y., 1965, *Le Mariage selon Yves de Chartres*, Rome etc., 1965.

Ladurie, E. Le Roy, 1978, *Montaillou*, Paris, 1975; Eng. trans. by B. Bray, London, 1978.

Laker, M. E., trans., 1974, Aelred of Rievaulx, *Spiritual Friendship*, Kalamazoo, 1974.

Landau, P., 1967, 'Hadrians IV. Dekretale "Dignum est" (X. 4. 9. 1) und die Eheschliessung Unfreier in der Diskussion von Kanonisten und Theologen des 12. und 13. Jahrhunderts', *Studia Gratiana*, xii (1967) = *Collectanea S. Kuttner*, ii, 511–53.

Laribière, G., 1967, 'Le Mariage à Toulouse aux xive et xve siècles', *Annales du Midi*, lxxix (1967), 335–61.

Laslett, P., 1976, 'The wrong way through the telescope: a note on literary evidence in sociology and in historical sociology', *British Journal of Sociology*, xxvii (1976), 319–42.

—— 1983, *The World We Have Lost Further Explored*, 3rd edn., London, 1983.

Lassaigne, J., and Argan, G. C., n.d., *The Great Centuries of Painting: the Fifteenth Century, from Van yck to Botticelli*, Skira, New York, n.d.

Latham, A. ed., 1975, Shakespeare, *As You Like It*, The Arden Shakespeare, London, 1975.

Latouche, R., ed. and trans., 1930–7, Richer, *Histoire de France*, 2 vols., Paris, 1930–7.

Laurie, H., 1986, 'The "letters" of Abelard and Heloise: a source for Chrétien de Troyes?', *Studi Medievali*, xxvii (1986), 123–46.

Le Bras, G., *et al.*, 1926, 'Mariage', in *DTC* ix (Paris, 1926), coll. 2044–317.

Leclercq, J., 1979, *Monks and Love in Twelfth-Century France*, Oxford, 1979.

—— 1982, *Monks on Marriage: a Twelfth-Century View*, New York, 1982.

Leeming, B., 1956, *Principles of Sacramental Theology*, London, 1956.

Levy, J.-P., 1965, 'L'Officialité de Paris, et les questions familiales à la fin du xive siècle', in *Études d'histoire du droit canonique dédiées à Gabriel Le Bras* (2 vols., Paris, 1965), ii. 1265–94.

Lewis, C. S., 1936, *The Allegory of Love*, London, 1936.

Leyser, K., 1960, 'England and the empire in the early twelfth century', *TRHS*, 5th Series, x (1960), 61–83; repr. in *Medieval Germany and its Neighbours* (London, 1982), pp. 191–213.

Liebertz-Grün, U., 1977, *Zur Soziologie des 'amour courtois'*, Beihefte zum Euphorion, x, Heidelberg, 1977.

Lightfoot, R. H., 1950, *The Gospel Message of St Mark*, Oxford, 1950.

Linker, R. W., 1960, *Chrestien de Troyes, The Story of the Grail*, trans. R. W. Linker, 2nd edn., Chapel Hill, 1960.

Loomis, R. S., ed., 1959, *Arthurian Literature in the Middle Ages*, Oxford, 1959.

Lot, F., 1891, *Les Derniers Carolingiens*, Paris, 1891.

—— 1903, *Études sur le règne de Hugues Capet et la fin du Xe siècle*, Paris, 1903.

Lovatt, R., 1968, 'The *Imitation of Christ* in late medieval England', *TRHS*, 5th Series, xviii (1968), 97–121.

Luard, H. R., ed., 1864–9, *Annales Monastici*, 5 vols., RS, 1864–9.

Lucchesi, J., ed., 1983, *Sancti Petri Damiani Sermones*, Corpus Christianorum Continuatio Mediaeualis, 57, Turnhout, 1983.

Luchaire, A., 1890, *Louis VI le Gros: annales de sa vie et de son règne*, Paris, 1890.

Luscombe, D. E., ed. and trans., 1971, *Peter Abelard's Ethics*, OMT, Oxford, 1971.

—— 1979, *Peter Abelard*, Historical Association pamphlet, General Series, G. 95, London, 1979.

—— 1980, 'The Letters of Heloise and Abelard since "Cluny 1972"', in Thomas 1980, pp. 19–39.

McKendrick, N., 1977, 'In search of a secular ideal', in C. Trebilcock, *The Vickers Brothers* (London, 1977), pp. ix–xxxiv.

—— 1978, 'Literary Luddism and the businessman', in P. N. Davis, *Sir Alfred Jones*, London, 1978, pp. ix–lvi.

McLachlan, E. P., 1978, 'The Bury Missal in Laon and its Crucifixion Miniature', *Gesta*, xvii (1978), 27–35.

McLaughlin, M. M., 1975, 'Peter Abelard and the dignity of women: twelfth century "feminism" in theory and practice', in *Abélard* 1975, pp. 287–333.

McLaughlin, T. R., 1956, 'Abelard's Rule for religious women', *Mediaeval Studies*, xviii (1956), 241–92.

McLeod, E., 1971, *Héloïse*, 2nd edn., London, 1971.

McNeill, J. T., and Gamer, H. M., 1938, *Medieval Handbooks of Penance*, Columbia Records of Civilisation, 29, New York, 1938.

Macy, G., 1984, *The Theologies of the Eucharist in the early Scholastic Period*, Oxford, 1984.

Maffei, D., and Nardi, P., ed., 1982, *Atti del Simposio internazionale cateriniano—bernardiniano* (1980), Siena, 1982.

Maitland, F. W., 1897, 'Magistri Vacarii Summa de Matrimonio', *Law Quarterly Review*, xiii (1897), 133–43, and text, pp. 270–87 (introduction repr. in Maitland, *Collected Papers*, iii, Cambridge, 1911, pp. 87–105).

Mâle, E., 1908, *L'Art religieux de la fin du moyen âge en France*, Paris, 1908.

Martindale, C., ed., 1988, *Ovid Renewed*, Cambridge, 1988.

Mas Latrie, M. le Comte de, 1889, *Trésor de chronologie*, Paris, 1889.

Mayor, J. E. B., ed., 1876, *The English Works of John Fisher*, Early English Text Society, Extra Series, xxvii, London, 1876.

Melnikos, A., 1975, *The Corpus of the Miniatures in the Manuscripts of Decretum Gratiani*, 3 vols., *Studia Gratiana*, xvi–xviii, Rome, 1975.

Mendola 1959–62: *La vita comune del clero nei secoli XI e XII*, Atti della settimana di studio Mendola, settembre 1959, *Miscellanea del Centro di Studi Medioevali*, iii, 2 vols., Milan, 1962.

Mendola 1971–4: *Le istituzioni ecclesiastiche della 'Societas Christiana' dei secoli XI–XII, papato, cardinalato ed episcopato*, Atti della quinta settimana di studio Mendola, 26–31 agosto 1971, *Miscellanea*, vii, Milan, 1974.

Mendola 1974–7: *Le istituzioni ecclesiastiche della 'Societas Christiana' dei secoli XI–XII, diocesi, pievi e parrochie*, Atti della sesta settimana di studio Milano; settembre 1974, *Miscellanea viii*, Milan, 1977.

Meyer, P., ed., 1891–1901, *Histoire de Guillaume le Maréchal*, 3 vols., Société de l'histoire de France, Paris, 1891–1901.

MGH Monumenta Germaniae Historica (LL = Legum; SS = Scriptores).

Miccoli, G., 1959–62, 'Pier Damiani e la vita comune del clero', in Mendola 1959–62, i. 186–219.

Minnis, A. J., 1982, *Chaucer and Pagan Antiquity*, Cambridge, 1982.

—— 1986, 'From medieval to renaissance? Chaucer's position on past gentility', *Proceedings of the British Academy*, lxxii (1986), 205–46.

Mirot, L., 1930, 'Études Lucquoises, chapitre iv, les Cenami', *Bibliothèque de l'École des Chartes*, xci (1930), 100–68.

Misch, G., 1959, *Geschichte der Autobiographie*, iii. 1, Frankfurt, 1959.

Mitton, C. L., 1951, *The Epistle to the Ephesians: its Authorship, Origin and Purpose*, Oxford, 1951.

Molin, J.-B., and Mutembe, P., 1974, *Le Rituel du mariage en France du XIIᵉ au XVIᵉ siècle*, Théologie historique 26, Paris, 1974.

Molinier, A., and Longnon, A., eds., 1906, *Obituaires de la province de Sens*, ii, Paris, 1906.

Molk, V., 1981, 'Saint Alexis et son épouse dans la légende latine et la première Chanson française', in Van Hoecke and Welkenhuysen 1981, pp. 162–70.

Monfrin, J., ed., 1962, *Abélard, Historia Calamitatum*, 2nd edn., Paris, 1962.

—— 1975, 'Le Problème de l'authenticité de la correspondance d'Abélard et d'Héloïse', in *Abélard* 1975, pp. 409–24.

Monson, D. A., 1988, 'Andreas Capellanus and the problem of irony', *Speculum*, lxiii (1988), 539–72.

Moore, R. I., 1975, *The Birth of Popular Heresy*, London, 1975.

—— 1977, *The Origins of European Dissent*, London, 1977.

Moorhouse, G., 1972, *Against all Reason* (1969), Harmondsworth, 1972.

Morey and Brooke 1965, 1967, see *GF, GFL.*

Moule, C. F. D., 1965, *The Gospel according to St Mark*, Cambridge, 1965.

Moule, C., 1983, 'Entry into marriage in the late eleventh and twelfth centuries, c.1090–1181', University of Cambridge Ph.D., 1983.

Muckle, J. T., ed., 1950, 'Abelard's letter of consolation to a friend (*Historia Calamitatum*)', *Mediaeval Studies*, xii (1950), 163–213.

—— ed., 1953, 'The personal letters between Abelard and Heloise', *Mediaeval Studies*, xv (1953), 47–94.

—— ed., 1955, 'The letter of Heloise on the religious life and Abelard's first reply', *Mediaeval Studies*, xvii (1955), 240–81.

Murphy, V. M., 1984, 'The debate over Henry VIII's first divorce: an analysis of the contemporary treatises', University of Cambridge Ph.D., 1984.

Murray, A., 1978, *Reason and Society in the Middle Ages*, Oxford, 1978.

Murray, P. and L., 1965, *Dictionary of Art and Artists*, London, 1965.

Newman, F. X., ed., 1968, *The Meaning of Courtly Love*, Albany, 1968.

Nicholl, D., 1964, *Thurstan Archbishop of York (1114–1140)*, York, 1964.

Nineham, D. E., 1963, *St Mark*, Pelican Gospel Commentaries, Harmondsworth, 1963.

NMT: Nelson's Medieval Texts (formerly Classics: now Oxford Medieval Texts).

Noble, P. S., 1982, *Love and Marriage in Chrétien de Troyes*, Cardiff, 1982.

Noonan, J. T., 1965, *Contraception: a History of its Treatment by the Catholic Theologians and Canonists*, Cambridge, Mass., 1965.

—— 1967, 'Marital affection in the canonists', *Studia Gratiana*, xii = *Collectanea Stephan Kuttner*, ii (1967), 479–509.

—— 1973, 'Power to choose', *Viator*, iv (1973), 419–34.

OCD 1970: *Oxford Classical Dictionary*, 2nd edn., ed. N. G. L. Hammond and H. H. Scullard, Oxford, 1970.

Oesterlé, G., 1953, 'Impuissance', in *DDC*, v (Paris, 1953), cols. 1262–92.

Offler, H. S., ed., 1968, *Durham Episcopal Charters, 1071–1152*, Surtees Society, clxxix, 1968.

—— 1971, *Ranulf Flambard as Bishop of Durham, 1099–1128*, Durham Cathedral Lecture, 1971.

Olson, P., 1957, '*A Midsummer Night's Dream* and the meaning of court marriage', *ELH: A Journal of Literary History*, xxiv (1957), 95–119.

Bibliographical References

OMT: Oxford Medieval Texts (formerly NMT).

Orderic: *Orderic Vitalis, Ecclesiastical History*, ed. and trans. M. Chibnall, 6 vols., OMT, Oxford, 1968–80.

Origo, I., 1963a, *The World of San Bernardino*, London, 1963.

—— 1963b, *The Merchant of Prato*, edn. of Harmondsworth, 1963.

Otto of Freising, *see* Waitz and Von Simson 1912.

Owen, D., 1984, 'The Norman cathedral at Lincoln', *Anglo-Norman Studies*, vi (Woodbridge, 1984), 188–99.

Painter, S., 1933, *William Marshal*, Baltimore, 1933.

—— 1940, *French Chivalry*, Baltimore, 1940.

Panofsky, E., 1934, 'Jan van Eyck's *Arnolfini Portrait*', *Burlington Magazine*, lxiv (1934), 117–27.

—— 1953, *Early Netherlandish Painting*, Cambridge, Mass., 1953.

Parry, J. J., trans., 1969, Andreas Capellanus, *The Art of Courtly Love*, edn. of New York, 1969.

Passage, C. E., trans., 1977, *The Middle High German Poem of Willehalm by Wolfram von Eschenbach*, New York, 1977.

Pellens, K., ed., 1966, *Die Texte des Normannischen Anonymus*, Wiesbaden, 1966.

—— ed., 1977, *Der Codex 415 des Corpus Christi College, Cambridge, Facsimile-Ausgabe . . .*, Wiesbaden, 1977.

Peter Damian, *Letters: Die Briefe des Petrus Damiani*, ed. K. Reindel, MGH, *Die Briefe der deutschen Kaiserzeit*, iv. 1, 2, Munich, 1983–8.

—— *Liber Gratissimus*, ed. L. von Heinemann, MGH, *Libelli de Lite*, i (Hanover, 1891), pp. 15–75.

—— *Opera*, in *PL* cxliv–cxlv.

—— *Sermones*, *see* Lucchesi.

Peter the Lombard, *Sentences: Sententiae in IV Libris Distinctae*, 2 vols., Spicilegium Bonaventurianum, iv–v, Grottaferrata, 1971–81.

Pfister, C., 1885, *Études sur le règne de Robert le Pieux (996–1031)*, Bibliothèque de l'École des hautes études, sciences philologiques et historiques, lxiii, Paris, 1885.

Phillips, D., 1985, *Excavations at York Minster*, ii, Royal Commission on the Historical Monuments of England, London, 1985.

PL: *Patrologiae cursus completus, series Latina*, ed. J. P. Migne, 221 vols., Paris, 1844–64.

Pollock, F., and Maitland, F. W., 1898, *A History of English Law before the Time of Edward I*, 2 vols., 2nd edn., Cambridge, 1898.

Poole, R. L., 1934, *Studies in Chronology and History*, ed. A. L. Poole, Oxford, 1934.

Powicke, F. M., 1947, *King Henry III and the Lord Edward*, 2 vols., Oxford, 1947.

Previté-Orton, C. W., 1912, *The Early History of the House of Savoy (1000–1233)*, Cambridge, 1912.

Radice, B., trans., 1974, *The Letters of Abelard and Heloise*, Harmondsworth, 1974.

Raftis, J. A., 1964, *Tenure and Mobility: Studies in the Social History of a Medieval English Village*, Toronto, 1964.

Rahner, K., 1963, *The Church and the Sacraments*, English trans. by W. J. O'Hara, London, 1963.

Raisin, S., 1943, 'L'Efflorescence cistercienne et le courant féminin de piété au treizième siècle', *Revue d'histoire ecclésiastique*, xxxix (1943), 342–78.

Raymond of Capua: *Legenda Maior b. Catharinae Senensis*, in *Acta Sanctorum Bollandiana*, April, iii. 853–959.

Razi, Z., 1980, *Life, Marriage and Death in a Medieval Parish: Economy, Society and Demography in Halesowen, 1270–1400*, Cambridge, 1980.

Remnant, G. L., 1969, *A Catalogue of Misericords in Great Britain*, Oxford, 1969.

Resnick, I. M., 1988, 'Peter Damian on the restoration of virginity: a problem for medieval theology', *Journal of Theological Studies*, New Series, xxxix (1988), 125–34.

Reuter, T., ed., 1978, *The Medieval Nobility*, Amsterdam, 1978.

Richards, M., trans., 1954, *The Laws of Hywel Dda (The Book of Blegywryd)*, Liverpool, 1954.

Richey, M. F., 1935, *The Story of Parzival and the Graal*, Oxford, 1935.

Rickert, M., 1962, 'The so-called Beaufort Hours and York Psalter', *Burlington Magazine*, civ (1962), 238–46.

Ridyard, S. J., 1988, *The Royal Saints of Anglo-Saxon England*, Cambridge, 1988.

Rigord: *Œuvres de Rigord et de Guillaume le Breton*, ed. H. F. Delaborde, Société de l'histoire de France, Paris, 1882–5, i.

Robin, G., 1970, 'Le problème de la vie commune au chapitre de la cathédrale Saint-Maurice d'Angers du ixe au xiie siècles', *Cahiers de civilisation médiévale*, xiii (1970), 305–22.

Roy, B., 1985, 'A la recherche des lecteurs médiévaux du "De amore" d'André le Chapelain', *Revue de l'Université d'Ottawa*, lv (1985), 45–73.

RS: Rolls Series (London).

Rubingh-Bosscher, J., ed., 1987, *Peter Abelard, Carmen ad Astralabium. A Critical Edition*, Groningen, 1987.

Rumen de Armas, A., ed., 1974, *Itinerario de los Reyes Católicos*, Madrid, 1974.

Ryan, J. J., 1956, *Saint Peter Damiani and his Canonical Sources*, Toronto, 1956.

Sacker, H., 1963, *An Introduction to Wolfram's Parzival*, Cambridge, 1963.

Salter, E., 1962, *Chaucer: The Knight's Tale and The Clerk's Tale*, London, 1962.

Scammell, G. V., 1956, *Hugh du Puiset, Bishop of Durham*, Cambridge, 1956.

Scarisbrick, J. J., 1968, *Henry VIII*, London, 1968.

SCH: *Studies in Church History*, Edinburgh, London, Cambridge and Oxford.

Schabacher, P. H., 1972, 'De Matrimonio ad Morganaticum contracto: Jan van Eyck's "Arnolfini" portrait reconsidered', *Art Quarterly*, xxxv (1972), 375–98.

Schanzer, E., 1960, 'The marriage contracts in *Measure for Measure*', *Shakespeare Survey*, xiii (1960), 81–9.

Schillebeeckx, E., 1965, *Marriage: Secular Reality and Saving Mystery*, 2 vols., trans. N. D. Smith, London, 1965. ·

Schmeidler, B., 1914, 'Die Briefwechsel zwischen Abälard und Heloïse eine Fälschung?', *Archiv für Kulturgeschichte*, xi (1913–14), 1–30.

Schnur, H. C., 1981, 'Jüdische Ehe und Familie im Mittelalter', in Van Hoecke and Welkenhuysen 1981, pp. 88–101.

Schröder, W., ed., 1982, *Die Namen im 'Parzival' und im 'Titurel' Wolframs von Eschenbach*, New York, 1982.

Schumacher, M., 1967, *Die Auffassung der Ehe in den Dichtungen Wolframs von Eschenbach*, Heidelberg, 1967.

Schweizer, E., 1971, *The Good News according to Mark*, trans. D. H. Madwig, London, 1971.

Shahar, S., n.d., *The Fourth Estate: a History of Women in the Middle Ages*, trans. C. Galain, London, n.d.

Sheehan, M. M., 1971, 'The formation and stability of marriage in fourteenth-century England: evidence of an Ely register', *Mediaeval Studies*, xxxiii (1971), 228–63.

—— 1978, 'Marriage theory and practice in the conciliar legislation and diocesan statutes of medieval England', *Mediaeval Studies*, xl (1978), 408–60.

—— and Scardellato, K. D., 1979, *Family and Marriage in Medieval Europe: a Working Bibliography*, Vancouver, 1976.

Silvestre, H., 1985, 'L'idylle d'Abélard et Héloïse: la part du roman', in *Académie royale de Belgique: bulletin de la classe des lettres et des sciences morales et politiques*, 5ᵉ série, lxxi (1985), 157–200.

Smith, A., 1977, *The Arnolfini Marriage by Jan van Eyck* (Painting in Focus no. 8), National Gallery, London, 1977.

Smith, R. M., 1979, 'Some reflections on the evidence for the origins of the "European marriage pattern" in England', in *The Sociology of the Family*, ed. C. Harris, *Sociological Review Monograph*, no. 28 (Keele, 1979), pp. 74–112.

—— 1981, 'The people of Tuscany and their families in the fifteenth century; medieval or mediterranean?', *Journal of Family History*, vi (1981), 107–28.

—— 1983, 'Hypothèses sur la nuptialité en Angleterre aux xiii– xivᵉ siècles', *Annales*, xxxviii (1983), 107–36.

—— 1986, 'Women's property rights under customary law: some developments in the thirteenth and fourteenth centuries', *TRHS*, 5th Series, xxxvi (1986), 165–94.

Southern, R. W., 1953, *The Making of the Middle Ages*, London, 1953.

—— ed. and trans., 1962, Eadmer, *The Life of St Anselm*, NMT, 1962, repr. OMT 1972.

—— 1963, *St Anselm and his Biographer*, Cambridge, 1963.

—— 1970a, *Medieval Humanism and Other Studies*, Oxford, 1970.

—— 1970b, *Western Society and the Church in the Middle Ages*, Harmondsworth, 1970.

—— 1982, 'The schools of Paris and the school of Chartres', in Benson and Constable 1982, pp. 113–37.

Spoleto 1977: *Il matrimonio nella società altomedievale*, 2 vols.,

Settimane di studio del Centro italiano di studi sull'alto medioevo, xxiv, Spoleto, 1977.

Stevenson, K. W., 1982, *Nuptial Blessings: A Study of Christian Marriage Rituals*, London, 1982.

Stone, L., 1977, *The Family, Sex and Marriage in England 1500–1800*, London, 1977.

Stones, E. L. G., and Simpson, G. G., 1978, *Edward I and the Throne of Scotland*, 2 vols., Oxford, 1978.

Stubbs, W., ed., 1876, *Radulfi de Diceto opera historica*, 2 vols., RS, 1876.

Suger, *see* Waquet 1929.

Surtz, E., and Murphy, V., eds., 1988, *The Divorce Tracts of Henry VIII*, Angers, 1988.

Swaan, W., 1969, *The Gothic Cathedral*, London, 1969.

Swete, H. B., 1898, *The Gospel according to St Mark*, London, 1898.

Talbot, C. H., ed. and trans., 1987, *The Life of Christina of Markyate*, Oxford, 1959, here cited from repr. with corrigenda, OMT, 1987.

Taylor, H. M. (and J.), 1978, *Anglo-Saxon Architecture*, iii, Cambridge, 1978.

Taylor, V., 1953, *The Gospel according to St Mark*, London, 1953.

Thomas 1980: *Petrus Abaelardus (1079–1142). Person, Werk und Wirkung*, ed. P. Thomas, with J. Jolivet, D. E. Luscombe and M. de Rijk, *Trierer Theologische Studien*, 38, Trier, 1980.

Thomas of Chobham: *Thomae de Chobham, Summa Confessorum*, ed. F. Broomfield, Louvain, 1968.

Thompson, A. Hamilton, ed., 1923, *Liber Vitae Ecclesiae Dunelmensis*, i, Facsimile and general introduction, Surtees Society, cxxxvi, 1923.

Thouzellier, C., 1969, *Catharisme et valdéisme en Languedoc*, 2nd edn., Louvain and Paris, 1969.

Tillmann, H., 1926, *Die päpstlichen Legaten in England bis zur Beendigung der Legation Gualas (1218)*, Bonn, 1926.

Topsfield, L. T., 1981, 'Fin'Amors in Marcabru, Bernart de Ventadorm and the *Lancelot* of Chrétien de Troyes' in Van Hoecke and Welkenhuysen 1981, pp. 236–49.

Toubert, P., 1973, *Les Structures du Latium médiéval*, 2 vols., Rome, 1973.

Bibliographical References

TRHS: *Transactions of the Royal Historical Society.*

Trojel, E., ed., 1892, *Andreae Capellani . . . De amore libri tres*, Copenhagen, 1892.

Underwood, M., 1982, 'The Lady Margaret and her Cambridge connection', *Sixteenth Century Journal*, xiii (1982), 67–82.

—— 1987, 'Politics and piety in the household of Lady Margaret Beaufort', *JEH*, xxxviii (1987), 39–52.

Urbanek, F., 1971, 'The Rolandslied by Pfaffe Conrad: some chronological aspects as to its historical and literary background', *Euphorion*, lxv (1971), 219–44.

Vacandard, E., 1890, 'Le divorce de Louis le Jeune', *Revue des questions historiques*, xlvii (1890), 408–32.

Van den Eynde, D., 1962, 'En marge des écrits d'Abélard: les "Excerpta ex regulis Paracletensis monasterii"', *Analecta Praemonstratensia*, xxxviii (1962), 70–84.

—— 1963, 'Détails biographiques sur Pierre Abélard', *Antonianum*, xxxviii (1963), 217–23.

Van der Meer, F., 1965, *Atlas de l'ordre cistercien*, Amsterdam and Brussels, 1965.

Van Hoecke, W., and Welkenhuysen, A., eds., 1981, *Love and Marriage in the Twelfth Century*, Mediaevalia Lovaniensia, Series i, Studia viii, Leuven, 1981.

Vollebregt, G. N., 1965, *The Bible on Marriage*, Eng. trans. by R. A. Downie, London, 1965.

Von Ertzdorff, X., 1981, 'Ehe und höfische Liebe im Tristan Gottfrieds von Strassburg', in Van Hoecke and Welkenhuysen 1981, pp. 197–218.

Vongrey, F., and Hervay, F., 1967, 'Kritische Bemerkungen zum Atlas de l'Ordre cistercien von Frédéric Van der Meer', *Analecta Cisterciensia*, xxiii (1967), 115–52.

Von Moos, P., 1971–2, *Consolatio, Studien zur mittellateinischen Trostliteratur über den Tod und zum Problem der christliche Trauer*, 4 vols., Munich, 1971–2.

—— 1975a, 'Cornelia und Heloise', *Latomus*, xxxiv (1975), 1024–59.

—— 1975b, 'Le Silence d'Héloïse et les idéologies modernes', in *Abélard* 1975, pp. 425–68.

—— 1980, '*Post festum*—Was kommt nach der Authentizitätsdebatte über die Briefe Abaelards und Heloises?', in Thomas 1980, pp. 75–100.

Voss, L., 1932, *Heinrich von Blois, Bischoff von Winchester* (1129–72), Historische Studien, ccx, Berlin, 1932.

Waitz, G., and Von Simson, B., ed., 1912, *Ottonis et Rahewini Gesta Friderici I. Imperatoris, MGH Scriptores Rerum Germanicarum*, Hanover and Leipzig, 1912.

Wall, J. C., 1912, *Porches and Fonts*, London, 1912.

Wallace-Hadrill, J. M., 1983, *The Frankish Church*, Oxford, 1983.

Waquet, H., ed. 1929, Suger, *Vie de Louis VI le Gros*, Paris, 1929.

Warner, G. F., and Gilson, J. P., eds., 1921, *Catalogue of the Western Manuscripts in the Old Royal and King's Collections in the British Museum*, 4 vols., London, 1921.

Warren, W. L., 1973, *Henry II*, London, 1973.

Weber 1967: Gottfried von Strassburg, *Tristan*, ed. G. Weber, with G. Utzmann and W. Hoffman, Darmstadt, 1967.

Weigand, R., 1963, *Die bedingte Eheschliessung im kanonischen Rechts*, i, Munich, 1963.

—— 1981, 'Liebe und Ehe bei den Dekretisten des 12. Jahrhunderts' in Van Hoecke und Welkenhuysen 1981, pp. 41–58.

Wells, S., and Taylor, G., eds., 1986, W. Shakespeare, *The Complete Works*, Oxford, 1986.

Westermarck, E. A., 1921, *The History of Human Marriage*, 3 vols., 5th edn., London, 1921.

WH refers to Walther Holtzmann's numbering of papal decretals, especially e.g. in Chodorow and Duggan 1982, pp. viii, xi, and *passim*.

Wiegand, H. E., 1972, *Studien zur Minne und Ehe im Wolframs Parzival und Hartmanns Artusepik*, Berlin, 1972.

Wimsatt, J. I., 1967, 'The apotheosis of Blanche in *The Book of the Duchess*', *Journal of English and Germanic Philology*, lxvi (1967), 26–44.

Windeatt, B. A., ed., 1984, Geoffrey Chaucer, *Troilus and Criseyde*, London, 1984.

Winnett, A. R., 1958, *Divorce and Remarriage in Anglicanism*, London, 1958.

Wolfram, *Parzival, Willehalm*: Wolfram von Eschenbach, *Parzival, Willehalm*, ed. K. Lachmann, 6th edn., by E. Hartl, Berlin and

Leipzig, 1926; trans. (*Parzival*) A. T. Hatto, Harmondsworth, 1980; (*Willehalm*) M. E. Gibbs and S. M. Johnson, Harmondsworth, 1984.

Wollasch, J., 1971, 'A Cluniac necrology from the time of Abbot Hugh', in *Cluniac Monasticism in the Central Middle Ages*, ed. N. Hunt, London, 1971, pp. 143–90.

Wrigley, E. A., and Schofield, R. S., 1981, *The Population History of England, 1541–1871: A Reconstruction*, London, 1981.

Wynn, M., 1980, 'Book I of Wolfram von Eschenbach's "Willehalm" and its Conclusion', *Medium Aevum*, xlix (1980), 57–65.

—— 1984, *Wolfram's Parzival: On the Genesis of its Poetry*, Frankfurt, 1984.

Zerbi, P., 1981, 'Abelardo ed Eloisa: il problema di un amore e di una corrispondenza', in Van Hoecke and Welkenhuysen 1981, pp. 130–61.

Zerwick, M., 1960, 'De matrimonio et divortio in Evangelio', *Verbum Domini*, xxxviii (1960), 193–212.

Ziegler, J. G., 1956, *Die Ehelehre der Pönitentialsummen von 1200–1350*, Regensburg, 1956.

Addenda

Brand, P. A., 1983, 'New light on the Anstey case', *Essex Archaeology and History*, xv (1983), 68–83.

Brundage, J. A., 1988, 'Impotence, frigidity and marital nullity in the decretists and early decretalists', in *Proceedings of the Seventh International Congress of Medieval Canon Law, Cambridge, . . . 1984*, ed. P. Linehan, Vatican City 1988, pp. 407–23.

Jones, M. K., and Underwood, M. G., 1992, *The King's Mother: Lady Margaret Beaufort, Countess of Richmond and Derby*, Cambridge, 1992.

Luscombe, D. E., 1988, 'From Paris to the Paraclete: the correspondence of Abelard and Heloise,' *Proceedings of the British Academy*, lxxiv (1988), 247–83.

Noonan, J. T., 1977, 'Who was Rolandus?', in *Law, Church and Society: essays in Honor of Stephan Kuttner*, ed. K. Pennington and R. Somerville, Philadelphia, 1977, pp. 21–48.

INDEX

Numbers in italics refer to plates. Medieval men and women are usually indexed under their Christian names, with cross references under surnames where necessary; a few, such as Abelard, are indexed under surnames, where these are much more familiar.

Index

Catherine, St, of Alexandria 284 n.; 7

Catherine (Caterina), St, of Siena 23–7, 31, 145; her *Life* 23–7; her mother *see* Lapa

Catherine (Swynford), duchess of Lancaster 211

Catherine (of Aragon), queen of England 35, 163–8, 280

Catherine (Howard), queen of England 165

Catherine (Parr), queen of England 165

celibacy, celibate ideal, virginity 21, 61–77; in Matthew 46–7; in 11th cent. 41; of canons 105–7; of Christina of Markyate 148; of St Catherine of Siena 27

Cenami *see* Arnolfini

Cerberus 221

Chadwick, Owen 10 n.

Châlons, bishop of *see* William de Champeaux

Champagne, count of *see* Henry; countess *see* Marie

Chapman's Homer 204–5

Charlemagne 202, 204, 206, 270

Charles V, Emperor 166

Chartres, bishop of *see* Ivo; cathedral chapter 79, 89

Chaucer, Geoffrey 176, 211–27; his life and marriage 211; his wife Philippa 211; and Shakespeare 228 n.

   his works: *Book of the Duchess* 213–15, 218, 226; *Canterbury Tales, Prologue* 212, 226; *Clerk's Tale* 217–19; *Franklin's Tale* 213, 219–20; *Knight's Tale* 215; *Parson's Tale* 219; *Wife of Bath's Tale* 212–13, 226; *Troilus and Criseyde* 215, 217, 220–7

Cheney, C. R. 18

childhood 11, 24–7; children 56–7, 126, 130, 273, 283–6

Chiswick, prebend of St Paul's 84

chivalry 177, 190, 199

Chrétien of Troyes 102 n., 177, 180–3, 187, 195, 263 n.; *Chevalier de la charette* 182–3; *Cligès* 180–1; *Contes del Graal* (Grail) 177, 184, 188–90; *Erec et Enide* 180

Christina, princess 77

Christina, prioress of Markyate 144–8

Christus, Petrus 9

Chrodegang, bishop of Metz 70

Circe 216

Cîteaux, Cistercians 157

cities, history of 13

Clairvaux, abbot of *see* Bernard

Clamide 192–3

Clarendon, Constitutions of (1164), 140, 155

Clergue, Pierre 159, 161

Cluny 96; abbot of *see* Peter; Abelard at 103, 109

Colchester, abbot of *see* Gilbert; archdeacon of 87; *see also* Cyprian; Geoffrey; Quintilian

Colly Weston (Northamptonshire) 35

Cologne 212

Compostela 212

concubines 224; in early church 64–6; in 11th–12th cent. cathedrals 83, 91, 105; Heloise as 91, 92 n., 107; in St Paul's 84, 88–9; *see also* Alveva

Condwiramurs 188 n., 189–201

consanguinity, and prohibited degrees 46 n., 59, 125, 134–6, 171, 273

consent, consummation *see* marriage

Constance (of Arles), queen of France 121–2

contraception 8

Corinth, Corinthian church 7

Cornelia 107

court(s), church 21, 39, 127–72

court rolls 14–15

courtly love 57, 177–83, 186, 196, 263

Coutances, bishop of *see* Geoffrey; cathedral chapter 79

Coventry cathedral priory 83

Cranborne abbey, later at Tewkesbury 255 n.

Cranmer, Thomas, archbishop of Canterbury 125, 165, 168

Cressida 241

Criseyde 221–7

Cromwell, Thomas 163

crusades 207; and Wolfram 202–3

Cundrie 189, 198

Cupid 226

Cyprian, archdeacon of Colchester 87

Index

Index

Index

Jesus, as a baby 53; Christina's visions of 144; sayings on marriage ix, 43–8, 209, 262, 275; and Wife of Bath 212–13

Jews, Jewish marriage customs ix, 39, 41–3, 266, 271; synagogues, 58

John (of Gaunt), duke of Lancaster 211, 213–14

John, duke of Somerset 35

John, king of England 127, 141

John of Salisbury, on marriage of Louis VII and Eleanor 124; letters 175; letter 131 (Anstey case) 128 n., 149–52, 171; works 175

Johnson, Samuel 161

Jonson, Ben 228–9

Joseph, St, and his marriage 53–4, 71, 131, 278–9

Jovinian 61, 260

Judaism see Jews

Juliet 3, 173–4, 243–6

Juno 213

Jupiter 197, 217

Justinian 40 n., 132; and impotence 269

Kardeiz 200–1

Kelly, H. A. 224–5

Kent, Chaucer as knight of the shire in 211

Kirshner, J. 15, 18

Klapisch-Zuber, C. 15

Knowles, D. 74

Kooper, E. 213 n., 214

Kyot, Duke 200–1

Kyot, the Provençal 183, 190

Ladurie, E. le Roy 2, 157–62, 247

Lancaster, duke of see John; duchess see Blanche, Catherine

Lancelot 176, 182–3

Lanfranc, archbishop of Canterbury 82–3; his monastic customs 75

Lapa, mother of St Catherine of Siena 23–7, 31

Laribière, G. 253

Laslett, P. 7, 173–4

Laurence, Friar 243, 245–6

Laurie, H. 102 n.

Lear, King 229, 234

Leclercq, J. 93

Leo I, St, the Great, Pope 68

Leo IX, St, Pope 69–70

letters see Abelard, Datini, Heloise, John of Salisbury

Lewis, C. S. 225

Liaze 189, 192

Lincoln, bishops of 147–8; see also Remigius; see of 148; cathedral chapter 80–1

Lire abbey (Normandy), pontifical of 248–50

liturgy, ritual of marriage 56, 248–50; see also marriage

Livre Griseldis, Le 218

Loherangrin 190, 200–1

London, archdeacons of 87; see also Hugh, William; bishops of see Gilbert, Richard; as dean of the province 81; his court 154–5; see of 85; vicar of see 150

St Paul's cathedral, chapter and canons 2, 80–1, 83–9, 91, 148; canons see Ailward, Algar, Anger, Audoen, Dereman, Edmund, Ralph, Ranulf, Thurstan, Walter, William; deans 87; see also Hugh, Ralph, William; married canons 84–9; prebendal catalogue 84–5, 88; prebends see Chiswick, Islington, Newington, Rugmere and Chaucer 211; National Gallery 280; 5–6; Tower Green 163

Lorenzo 241

Lothar II, Emperor 40 n.

Louis the Pious, Emperor 206

Louis VI, king of France, and his wives 122–3; see also Adelaide

Louis VII, king of France, and his wives 123–4, 182; see also Eleanor

Louis VIII 124

Low Countries, female religious in 17–18, 69; marriage customs in 253, 283

Lucan 107–8

Lucca 281–2

Luscombe D. E. 94, 97, 100, 102 n.

Luther, M. 274

Mabel de Francheville 133 n., 148–52

Macbeth 234; Lady Macbeth 229, 234

McKendrick, N. 174

Macy, G. 275

Mahald 84

320

Index

Maitland, F. W. 171–2

Manichees 72; on marriage 62

Map, Walter 63

Marcigny priory (of nuns) 97, 117, 148

Margaret, St 280 n., 281, 283–5; 9

Margaret, Lady *see* Beaufort

Margaret (of Anjou), queen of England 12

Margaret, queen of Scotland 35

Margherita, wife of Francesco di Marco Datini 32–4

Marie, countess of Champagne 182

Mark, St 208

Mark, King 185

Markyate priory 144; prioress *see* Christina

Marriage: history, scheme for 5–6; in Roman Empire and under Roman law 39–41; in Bible and early Church 39–56, 61–3; *see also* Bible; in 11th and 12th cents. 56–60, 103–57, 169–72; in 12th–13th cent. literature 173–210; in 14th cent. 157–62, 211–27; in 15th and 16th cents. 27–38, 162–9, 228–47; 'European marriage pattern' 15–17

entry to marriage, by consent 55, 57, 128–33, 137–40, 274; in van Eyck 281–3, 286; and Christina 146–8; consent *de praesenti* 138–9, 151–3, 165, 169–72, 268; consummation 28–9, 55, 57, 128–33, 138, 150, 169–72, 196, 266, 276; in contrast with abstinence 277–9; in *Parzival* 192, 196; consummation and van Eyck 283–6; and Catherine of Aragon 166–7; of Romeo and Juliet 246; *in facie ecclesiae* 133 n., 139, 147, 170–1, 250; at church door 146–7, 248–51, 253–6; in other places 251–3; *maritalis affectio* 40, 128–9, 266; putative marriage 152; marriage as a process 286

evidence from art and architecture 253–7, 280–6; law and legal sources 56, 119–72, 251–2; decretals, *see esp.* 169–72; Council of Trent 169, 250; in Church of England 250; literature 173–247;

marriage of Parzival and Condwiramurs 189–96; liturgy 150, 248–52; nuptial mass 248–9; statistics 11–19

marriage of heathens 49, 52, 210 and n.

theology of marriage, *esp.* 39–60, 103–18, 258–86; marriage as sacrament 47, 51, 57, 104, 107, 111, 115, 132, 138, 147, 201, 260–2, 265, 271, 273–80, 284; form of sacrament 276

Mars 215–17

Martène, Dom E. 249

Martext, Sir Oliver 237

Mary, St, Blessed Virgin Mary, Our Lady, marriage of 53–4, 71, 131, 278–9; in Chaucer 214, 218; image of 180

Mary (of Blois), abbess of Romsey and countess of Flanders 76

Mary I, queen of England 164

Mary Magdalene St 9

mass 192, 194 n.; nuptial 248–9

Matilda, Empress, and countess of Anjou 104, 142

Matilda (Edith), queen of England 75–6

Matilda of Ramsbury 89

Maury, Pierre 158

Mazzei, Ser Lapo 32–4

Medea 216, 241

Melun 90

Mercutio 243–4

Metz, bishop of *see* Chrodegang

Middlesex, archdeacon of 87; *see also* Richard

Milan, Sant'Ambrogio 254

misericords 257

Molho, A. 15, 18

Molin, J.-B. 248

Monfrin, J. 94

Montaillou 143, 157–62

Montpellier 204

Moos, P. von 94

Morpheus 213

Moses 43, 46, 283

Moslems, and marriage 269; and Wolfram 271

Moule, C. 170

Muckle, J.T. 100

Mutembe, P. 248

Index

Portia 239–42, 245 n.
Postan, Sir Michael 9
Prato 32–4; Fondazione Datini 32–3; merchant of see Datini
prebends 78
Priam 221; Priam's 'parliament' 222
Price, Fanny 175
Provençal lyric 178
Pyramus 232, 241
Pyrenees 157, 160

Quince 232
Quintilian, archdeacon of Colchester 87

Rainald, monk (of Saint-Evroult) 75
Ralph (of Langford), dean of St Paul's 86
Ralph (son of Algod or Algot), canon of St Paul's 84
Ranulf (Flambard), canon of St Paul's and bishop of Durham, and his family 85, 87, 148; and Christina 144–5
Raymond of Capua, OP 23–7, 31
Raymond of Peñaforte, St, OP 52
Reformation, the 265
Rembrandt ix–xi; 1
Remigius, bishop of Lincoln 80
Rennes, missal of 249–50
Rennewart (Renouart) 206–8
Repanse de Schoye 187 n., 197–8
Rheims, archbishop of see William; Council of (1049) 69–70
Richard (de Belmeis or Beaumais, I), bishop of London 85–7
Richard (de Belmeis or Beaumais, II), bishop of London, previously archdeacon of Middlesex 85–7
Richard (Ruffus, I), archdeacon of Essex 86
Richard (Junior), canon of St Paul's 86
Richard (Ruffus, II), canon of St Paul's 86
Richard of Anstey 148–52, 171, 268
Robert, earl of Gloucester 255
Robert II, king of France 120–1, 273; his queens see Bertha, Constance, Rozala
Robert de Belmeis 86
Robert Fitzhamon 255 n.
Roger, bishop of Salisbury 82 n., 83, 89

Roland see Alexander III
Roland, Song of, and *Rolandslied* 202
Rolandus, canonist 169
Roman de la Rose 91, 211
romances, French courtly 177–83; *see also* Wolfram; late medieval 256
romantic love 177 and n.; *see also* courtly love
Rome 212; Roman empire, concubines under 66–7; marriage under 58, 66–7, 128, 266; emperors 39; pagan Rome 40–1; Roman law of marriage 39–41, 54, 104, 128–30, 132, 133 n., 136–7
  Church of, Papacy, cardinals *see* Alberic, Peter Damian, Wolsey; legates *see* Alberic, Henry; popes 293; *see also* Adrian, Alexander, Benedict, Calixtus, Eugenius, Gregory, Innocent, Leo, Paschal; papal chancellor 70; papal curia, and appeals 140, 151–2, 155–6, 166, 264, 273; and the Anstey case 149–52; the papal reform 68–70; the pope and marriage law and litigation 51–2, 119–72 *passim*, 264–70; *see also* Alexander III; 'Roman' tradition on impotence 132, 268
  Council of (1059) 82 n.; First Lateran (1123) 67 n.
  Santa Sabina ix
Romeo 236, 243–6
Romsey abbey, abbess of see Mary
Rosalind 237–9, 245 n.
Rouen, Anonymous of Rouen or York 77; cathedral chapter 79
Rozala, or Susanna, countess of Flanders and queen of France 121
Rugmere, prebend of St Paul's 84

sacraments 12, 47, 273–80; lists of 56; *sacramentum* 45 n., 274; *see also* baptism, eucharist, marriage
St Albans 144–5; abbot of *see* Geoffrey; Psalter 145
Saint-Denis, abbey 90, 108–9; abbot of *see* Suger; monk *see* Abelard
Saint-Guilhem-le-Désert 204
St Osyth, canon of *see* William (de Vere)

323

Index